MID- CONNACHT

The Ancient Territory of Sliabh Lugha

Máire McDonnell-Garvey

DRUMLIN PUBLICATIONS

First published in Ireland in 1995 by
Drumlin Publications

© Máire McDonnell-Garvey

*This book has been published with the assistance of Moate Dairies and
North Connacht Farmers, Ballaghaderreen & District Dev Committee*

ISBN   1 873437 12 9

Cover Painting & inside Line Drawing: *The Four Altars (Edmondstown)*
      by Ann Dundon
Cover Design: Declan Gray, Sylvia Parke
Maps: Paul Walsh, Ordnance Survey of Ireland.
Prints: by kind permission of The Architectural Archives &
      The National Library of Ireland

All rights reserved. No part of this publication may be reproduced or transmitted in any form or by any means, without the prior permission of the publisher.

**Published by Drumlin Publications, Nure,
Manorhamilton, Co. Leitrim, Ireland. (072) 55237**
Printed by Colour Books Ltd. Dublin

MID-CONNACHT
The Ancient Territory of Sliabh Lugha

Castlemore, Mayo

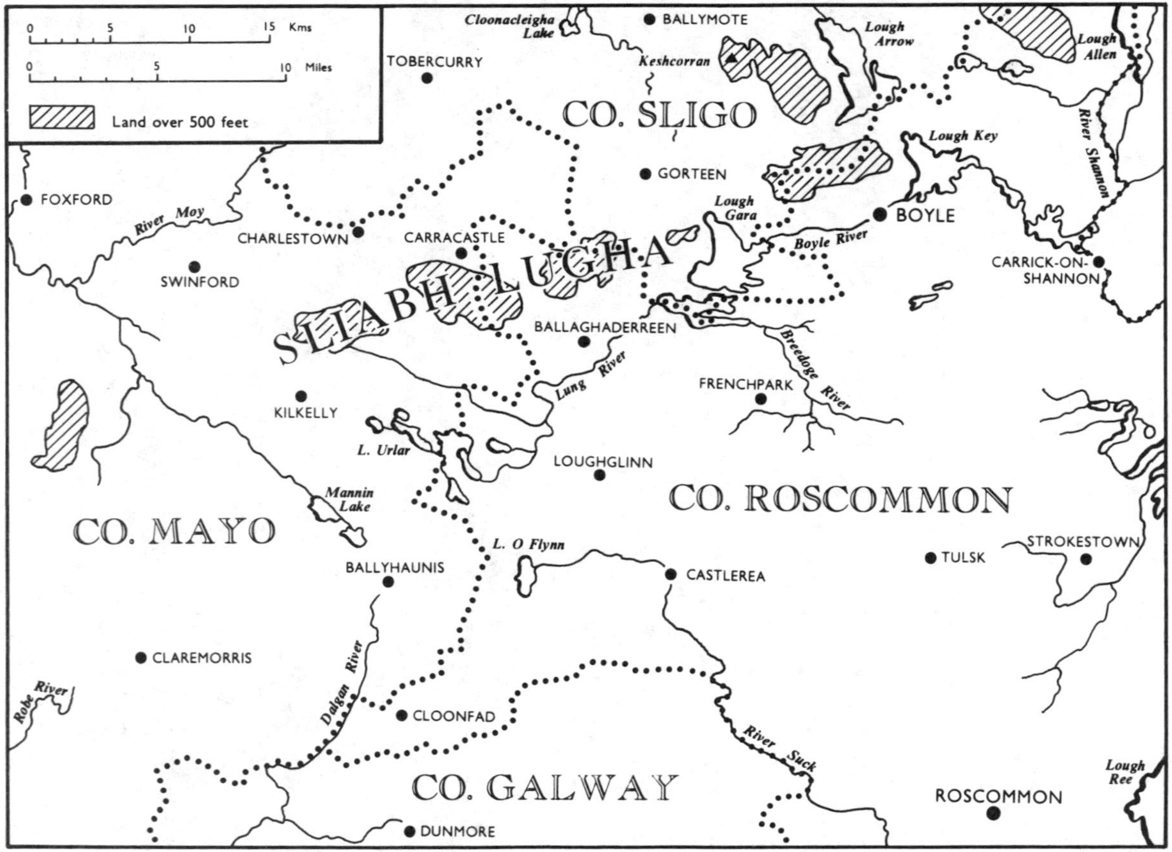
0 5 10 15 Kms
0 5 10 Miles
Land over 500 feet
CO. SLIGO
CO. MAYO
CO. ROSCOMMON
CO. GALWAY
SLIABH LUGHA
FOXFORD
TOBERCURRY
BALLYMOTE
Cloonacleigha Lake
Keshcorran
GORTEEN
Lough Arrow
Lough Allen
Lough Key
River Shannon
Lough Gara
BOYLE
Boyle River
CARRICK-ON-SHANNON
River Moy
CHARLESTOWN
CARRACASTLE
SWINFORD
BALLAGHADERREEN
Breedoge River
FRENCHPARK
Lung River
KILKELLY
L. Urlar
LOUGHGLINN
Mannin Lake
L. O Flynn
BALLYHAUNIS
CASTLEREA
TULSK
STROKESTOWN
CLAREMORRIS
Robe River
Dalgan River
CLOONFAD
River Suck
Lough Ree
ROSCOMMON
DUNMORE

FOREWORD

The growing interest in local history has been a welcome feature of recent years. It reflects a natural desire to know more about one's 'own place', to give a historical dimension to an attachment formed by birth and upbringing. The study of any district demands not just a training in history but also an intimate knowledge of the area and its place names and traditions. In choosing to write a history of Sliabh Lugha from the earliest times to the end of the nineteenth century, Máire Garvey brings to the task the essential element of a love of the locality, which has inspired the dedication to span the centuries. The vicissitudes of this area, now the northern half of the barony of Costello in Co. Mayo, have been charted with care and diligence. While the work will be of interest primarily to those living in or familiar with the area, it also makes a contribution to the general history of Ireland. Local issues are often more important than national ones and in a country where the variety of accents is but one illustration of continuing particularism national history can be simply the aggregate of the histories of different districts. Such works as this are a reflection and a reinforcement of local patriotism, of pride in one's own 'country' in the older sense of that term. I congratulate Máire Garvey on her achievement and wish the book every success.

ART COSGROVE, President, UCD.

ACKNOWLEDGEMENTS

I wish to express my sincere gratitude to all who encouraged and assisted me to carry out the research necessary to write this history. Many of them did not live to see the end result – the late Dr James Fergus, Bishop of Achonry, Charles the late Prince of Coolavin, the late Sr Mary Martin McLoughlin and Sr Brigid of the Sisters of Charity, the late R.W. Edwards and his wife Sheila O' Sullivan (who was my very dear friend).

My special thanks to Roscommon County Council, Canon Costello of Ballyhaunis, E.S.B. Sligo and Dr Thomas Flynn, Bishop of Achonry for financial asistance during my research. My thanks to all my family who had infinite patience with me. I thank Sr Vincent Fahy, Sisters of Mercy, Castlebar, Fr Martin Jennings, St. Nathy's College, Ballaghaderreen, Madam Felicity Mc Dermot who never lost hope in me, Dónal O'hÉalaidhe, Anne Dundon from Wakefield, an artist and good friend. It was Anne who did the Four Altars and who worked on the Costello Flag with such minute patience. My sincere thanks to Nollaig O'Muraile of Queens University, Belfast, who edited my original MS. and who allowed me to use his material on the leaseholders on the Dillon Estate, Loughglynn, and helped me with references. Go raibh mile maith agat Nollaig. My thanks to Paul Walsh of the Ordnance Survey Department who drew the maps. Thanks also to Luke Dodd, curator of Strokestown House, County Roscommon, who gave me the sketches of the famine in Roscommon,. A special word of thanks to the publishers Proinnsias and Betty O' Duigneain, who have been more than helpful.

Thanks sincerely to the organisations who were so helpful in every way –The National Library of Ireland, including those in the Prints and Drawing section, the National Architectural Archives, Merrion Square, Dublin, for the copies of old prints, the Central Library in Pearse Street, including the Gilbert Section, the P.R.O. the S.P.O, the Genealogical Office and the National Archives in Bishop St., the Land Commission, the Registry of Deeds, Henrietta St. the Land Registry, Setanta House, the Dublin Diocesan Library, Clonliffe Road, the Mayo County Library, the County Roscommon Library and the County Sligo Library, the Sligo county librarian John C. Mc Ternan, and any others I may have left out. I dedicate this study to the generations who lived in the area and are now gone. It has been a labour of love.

CONTENTS

Foreword   5

Acknowledgements   6

Chapter 1:
    SLIABH LUGHA IN ANCIENT TIMES   9

Chapter 2:
    LANDLORDS, RAPAREES AND WILD GEESE   25

Chapter 3:
    PENAL DAYS AND THE YEAR OF THE FRENCH   37

Chapter 4:
    EAST MAYO IN THE EARLY 19th CENTURY   45

Chapter 5:
    SECRET SOCIETIES   59

Chapter 6:
    THE BAD TIMES 1830s & 40s   69

Chapter 7:
    EDUCATIONAL DEVELOPMENT OVER TWO CENTURIES   87

Chapter 8:
    THE FENIAN MOVEMENT AT BALLAGHADERREEN   109

Chapter 9:
    LAND WAR IN THE VICINITY OF SLIABH LUGHA   125

Chapter 10:
    1881-1903 LAND TRANSFER IN CO. MAYO   141

Chapter 11:
    THE END OF THE DILLON AND COSTELLO LINE   151

Appendix 1: Leaseholders on the Dillon Estate   161

Appendix 2: Tenants on Costello Estate   175

Appendix 3: Names of Parishes   187

Appendix 4: Poems of P.J. Coleman   189

Appendix 5: Castlerea Famine Sermon   193

Appendix 6: Report of Land Conference   195

Abbreviations   196

References   197

Index   202

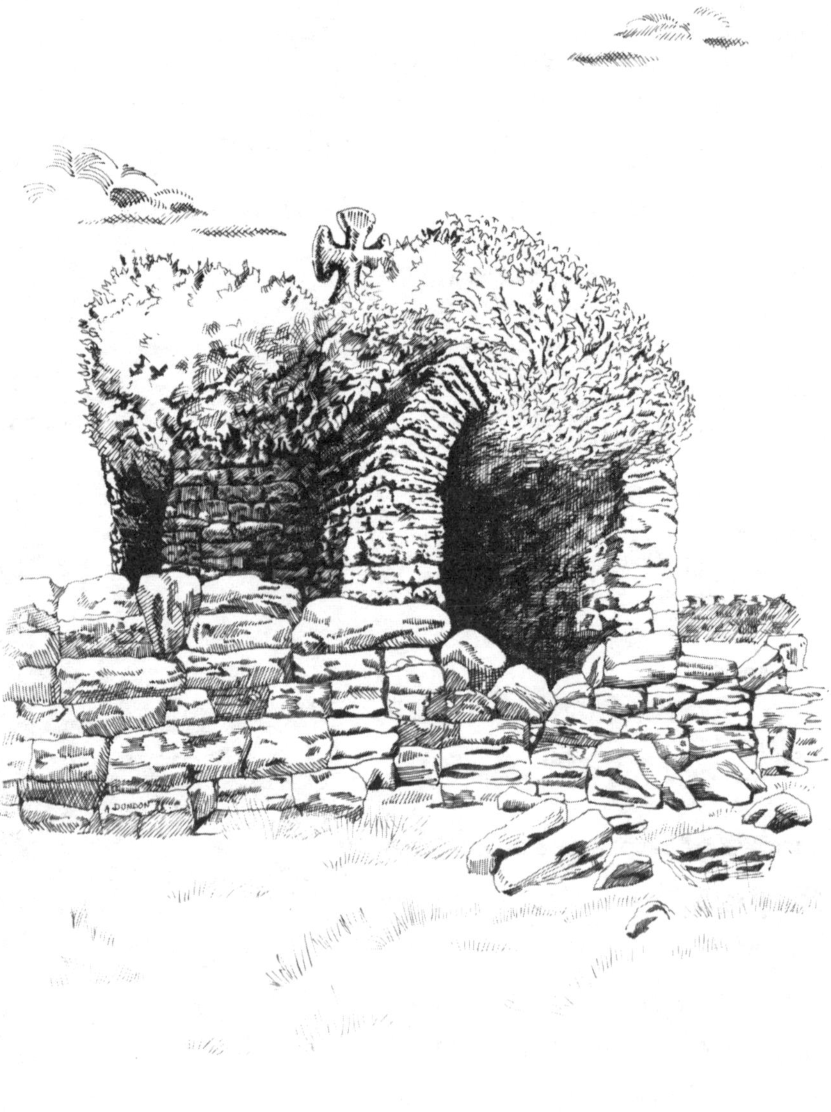
A DUNDON

CHAPTER I

SLIABH LUGHA

IN ANCIENT TIMES

Few people are now aware that the northern half of the barony of Costello, on the borders of Cos. Mayo and Roscommon, was anciently known as Sliabh Lugha - the mountain land of Lugh.[1] The area comprises the civil parishes of Kilbeagh, Kilmovee, Kilcolman and Castlemore (as well as part of Kilturra) which belong to the diocese of Achonry. The southern part of the barony - comprising the parishes of Aghamore, Annagh, Bekan and Knock – belong to the archdiocese of Tuam. The latter area was in ancient times known as the Ciarraighe – a branch of whom in west Munster gave their name to Co. Kerry (Contae Chiarraighe or, in modern spelling, Contae Chiarraí).[2] The Ciarraighe of mid-Connaught were divided into three groups: (a) those of Magh Aoi, the great plain stretching between the present towns of Roscommon and Castlerea, (b) those of Loch na nAirne or Loch Nairne, the old name of Lough Mannin which lies between Kilkelly and Ballyhaunis,[3] and (c) those of Airteach, the name of an ancient territory around Loughglynn.

Little is known of the ancient rulers of Sliabh Lugha, but the area's name may give us a clue. The second part of the name is that of the most famous of the Celtic Gods – known to the Irish as Lug Lámfata (in modern Irish, Lugh Lámhfhada – 'Lugh the Longarmed'); he was also held in high regard among the continental Celts, as placenames such as Lyons (from Lugdunum) in France, Léon in Spain and Leyden in Holland testify. Immediately adjacent to Sliabh Lugha was the territory of an ancient people called the Luigne. Their name, which means 'people of Lug', survives as that of the barony of Leyney, Co. Sligo. According to early Irish genealogical tracts, which are thought to date from shortly after the year 600 – almost 1400 years ago – the Luigne were closely related to a people called the Gailenga; these latter have given name to the barony of Gallen Co. Mayo, which borders Sliabh Lugha on the west. The same two peoples were also settled close to one another in ancient Meath where they gave name to the baronies of Lune and Morgalion/Machaire Gaileang. Support is lent to this view by the fact that the ruling family of

Luigne in the later medieval period was that of O hEaghra (O'Hara) while the ruling family of Sliabh Lugha – surnamed ó Gadhra (O'Gara) was said to be an offshoot of the O'Haras.

Irish history proper – the recording of contemporary, or at least remembered events – is generally considered to begin in or about the 6th century. Very early in the historical period we find mention of divisions called cóiceda or 'fifths' (in modern Irish cúigí, a term now generally translated 'province'). But at no time in the period for which we have contemporary written records do we actually find five 'fifths' in place. The cóiced, therefore, is either a prehistoric division of which some vague memory survived into the historical era or an idealised division of the island which never existed in practice. The western province, in which we are principally interested, bore the name of a population group called the Connachta. This name it has recently been suggested, may mean the 'chief or leading people'. It later came to be linked with the name of a legendary prehistoric king, Conn Cétchathach, Conn the hundred-battler. The area appears to have had another, more ancient name, Ólnécmacht, whose meaning is a matter for debate.

At the beginning of the historical period Connacht was a patchwork of ancient peoples and small kingdoms. We have already come across the Ciarraighe, the Luigne and the Galenga. In north west Mayo were the Domnainn; these have been equated with the Dumnonii who gave name to Devon in the south of England. In south Mayo, in the vicinity of Lough Mask, were the Partraige whose name, it has been suggested, may be related to that of a resort-town called Garmisch-Partenkirchen in southern Bavaria not far from Innsbruck – but a long way indeed from the shores of Lough Mask! In the very south of County Mayo, in the present barony of Kilmaine, were the Conmaicne Cúile Talad. These were but one branch of the Conmaicne, a widely scattered people. A branch in northwest Co. Galway, the Conmaicne Mara, gave name to Connamara, while more of the Conmaicne were settled around Dunmore Co. Galway. Two branches of a people called the Delbna were to be found in west Galway and in south Roscommon respectively. In various parts of Connacht were branches of a people called the Calraige: one near Lough Gill Co. Sligo, has given name to the parish Calry, but they were also to be found in southeast Co. Sligo, in Co. Leitrim and in several parts of Co. Mayo – in the vicinity of Bunnyconnellan, around Crossmolina and to judge by the evidence afforded by placenames, near Ballycastle (in the townland of Glencalry – Gleann Chalraí) in the north of the county and in the parish of Knock (anciently known as Cnoc Droma Calraí) in the southeast. On the shores of Lough Gara, in south Sligo, were a people called the Gregraige whom we will meet again presently. There were several other population-groups throughout Connacht whose details need not concern us here.

Very early in the Christian era (by about the 6th century) we find a dynasty called Uí Fhiachrach (descendants of Fiachra) claiming the kingship of Connacht.[4] Soon afterwards they were being challenged by a rival dynasty called the Uí Briúin, descendants of Brión. Somewhat later, the professional Gaelic learned class appear to have concocted a genealogical scheme in which Fiachra and Brión were brothers; they were also made brothers to another famous figure, Niall Noígiallach ('Niall of the Nine Hostages'). Niall was the eponymous ancestor of the dynasty known as the Uí Néill which came to dominate the northern half of Ireland for much of the period between the time of St. Patrick and the coming of the Normans in the 12th century. It is impossible to tell just how much of a kernel of truth the many legends about Niall may contain: we just cannot know if he was an actual historical personage. Whether or not Niall himself really existed, recent studies suggest that the roots of the Uí Néill may lie among the Gregraige ('the horse-people') around Lough Gara, in the present barony of Coolavin. From this area just east of Sliabh Lugha, this new and very dynamic force burst on the Irish political scene in or about the fifth century. It was probably only later, as the Uí Néill grew in power and influence that the genealogists decided to link to them the already existing Connacht dynasties of Uí Fhiachrach and Uí Briúin.

According to the early genealogical scheme, most of Co. Mayo and the barony of Tireragh in Co. Sligo were Uí Fhiachrach territory, while one of the main branches of the Uí Briúin held sway in Co. Roscommon and the adjacent areas of south Co.Sligo. The principal ruling families of the Uí Briúin were the O'Conors (Uí Chonchubhair) of Síol Muirdaedhaigh and the MacDermots (Meic Dhiarmada) of Clann Mhaoil Ruanaidh; an offshoot of the latter were the MacDonaghs (meic Dhonnchaidh) of Corran and Tirerrill. The part of Co. Sligo around Sligo town was Uí Néill territory: it bore the name Cairbre (Carbury) from a son of Niall's who was supposedly king of Ireland towards the close of the 6th century. The territory of Sliabh Lugha, and of the neighbouring Ciarraighe, lay between the lands of the Uí Briúin to the east and those of the Uí Fhiachrach to the west.

This area features also in the story of early Christian Ireland. The greatest of our saints was St. Patrick, and in the account of his missionary activities written sometime around 680 by a bishop from north Mayo called Tírechán he is said to have passed through the Sliabh Lugha area on his way to the territory of Nairne which lay on the southern borders of Sliabh Lugha.[5] The name Nairne was preserved for later ages in the name of the lake, Loch Nairne (later rationalised to Loch na nAimeadh, 'the lake of the sloe bushes'); this lake which lies between Kilkelly and Ballyhaunis, is now known as Mannin lake. According to Tírechán, Patrick came from the plain of Airteach – the area between Castlerea and Ballaghaderreen – to Drummut Cérrigi (Drumad of the Ciarraige, now the townland of Drumad in the parish of Tibohine, not far from Loughglynn). and on to northern Nairne.

He next went to Aileach Esrachta which the later (9th century) Tripartite Life of St. Patrick says was at Telach Liac or Telach na Cloch; This latter place has been identified as an early version of the name of the townland of Tullaghanrock in the parish of Kilcolman. Here the local people were said to be afraid of the stranger and the eight or nine men accompanying him, so they decided to kill them. A large crowd surrounded Patrick and his companions, but they were restrained by a brave man named named Hercait (a name later written Erccaid or Earcaid) of the race of Nath í. Having persuaded his neighbours and kinsmen not to harm the missionaries, Hercait and his son Feradach were baptised, and the son joined St. Patrick. The latter was trained by the saint for thirty years and was eventually ordained by him (in Rome, no less), and Patrick gave him a new name, Sachellus (in Irish Sachall) and wrote a copy of the Psalms for him – and Tírechán himself states categorically that he himself had seen (two centuries later) that very book in Patrick's own handwriting. (Sachall eventually became a bishop and was associated with a famous church called Basilica Sanctorum – now known as Baslick – a parish between Castlerea and Tulsk, Co. Roscommon).

There were numerous other early Christian sites in Sliabh Lugha and its vicinity– particularly those beginning with the element 'Cill' which denotes a small early church (from the Latin word cella). The most notable of these is Kilmovee, Cill Mobhí – the church of St. Mobhí. The name Mobí (or Mo-Bhí) is a pet form of various names, such as Brénainn and Berchán, but we have no indication whatever of the identity of the holy man whose name is preserved in Cill Mobhí. Another very common early Irish Christian name occurs in the placename Cill Cholmáin – the parish of Kilcolman in which Ballaghaderreen is located. Unfortunately, nothing seems to be known of the Colman who gave name to the parish. South of Kilmovee is Aghamore (Achadh Mór, the 'big field') with which Tírechán associates two other local saints, 'holy Iarnascus' (or Érnaisc) whom St. Patrick is said to have found sitting under an elm tree, and his son Lóchnarach; the latter is named —as Loarn sacart Achaid Móir (priest of Achadh Mór) – in the Martyrology of Tallaght, which was written in the south of what is now Co. Dublin, about the year 800.

Returning to the secular sphere, we may note that among the prerog-

SLIABH LUGHA IN ANCIENT TIMES

atives of the king of Connacht, according to an old Irish tract on 'The taboos of the kings of Ireland',was the right to the hunt or chase of Sliabh Lugha (selg Shlébhe Lugha).[6] Little is known of the political history of Sliabh Lugha in the centuries prior to the coming of the Normans. The area was obviously within the sphere of influence of the O'Conor kings, of whom the most powerful was the ruthless Turlogh Mór who was the dominant Irish king for much of the first half of the 12th century. He died in 1156 and was succeeded by his weaker son, Rory, who is remembered as the last Irish 'high king'. A younger brother of the latter's Cathal Crobhderg (a name rendered 'Cathal Mór of the Wine-red Hand' by James Clarence Mangan), who died in 1224, would seem to have made much more of an impact in Connacht.

The rulers of Sliabh Lugha, Muinntir Ghadhra (the O'Garas) feature occasionally in the Irish annals. The earliest mention of the family is at the year 964 (more correctly 965) when the Annals of the Four Masters report the death in battle of Toichleach ó Gadhra, 'king of south Luighne', ('South Luighne' was clearly an alternative name for Sliabh Lugha and this would tend to support the view put forward above that 'Luighne' and the latter element of 'Sliabh Lugha' were closely related.[7] Most references to the family in the annals are simply quite bare death- notices.The same Annals of the Four Masters (which were compiled under the patronage of Fergal O'Gara MP, head of the family in the early 17th century) record the slaying in 1056 of Ruaidhrí O Gara, tánaiste of Luighne, and the death three years later of another Ruaidhrí, 'heir to the lordship of Luighne'. In 1067 one Donnsléibhe O Gara was killed by a certain Brian O Hara, and in 1228 O Gara (that is 'the chief of his name') lord of Luighne was slain. In 1181 the Annals of Loch Cé announce baldly 'Donnsléibhe O Gadra mortuus est', but the Annals of Ulster tell us that he was killed. The first annalistic entry to link the O Garas explicitly with Sliabh Lugha is in the Annals of Loch Cé at the year 1207 where is record of the death of Ruaidhrí ó Gadhra, 'rí Shléibhe Lugha', and in 1218 of one Domhnall Ó Gadhra. The aforementioned Ruaidhrí's son, Donn Sléibhe is named in 1208 as one of a large force of Connachtmen who resisted the depredations of Cathal Mac Diarmada, son of the king of Magh Luirg. The Annals of Loch Cé and of Connacht both recount that in 1226 Donn Sléibhe Ó Gadra, king of Sliabh Lugha, slew Fergal ó Taidg an Teglaig, ruler of the household of Cathal Crobhderg, and his son, 'a man of great fortune and a slayer of many people'. The very next year however, Donn Sléibhe was killed by his own nephew, 'who captured the house in which he was at night'. Shortly afterwards Aed O Conor had the killer slain.[8]

The Normans came to Ireland in 1169 at the invitation of the Leinster king, Diarmaid Mac Murchadcha. In Connacht the O Conor dynasty was riven by internecine disputes, with various factions enlisting the support of Norman mercenaries.[9] Despite these early forays into Connacht, the newcomers did not undertake a concerted assault on the west until about the year 1235.[10] An English adventurer, Richard De Burgh, had fought against Cathal Crobhderg and later switched sides and fought on his behalf. Around the time of Cathal's death he had received a grant of Connacht from King John. All De Burgh lands in Connacht were thereby restored to De Burgh except the King's Five Cantreds. It was in these areas that O'Conors and other Irish rulers functioned, independent of the Burghs (see map). The King's Cantreds consisted mostly of the present Roscommon, part of Tirerrill in Co. Sligo and certain portions of Galway.[11] A cantred usually consisted of about thirty townlands.[12] De Burgh collected a group of other adventurers whose names would be indelibly imprinted on the history of Connacht.[13] They included Hugh De Lacy, Milo De Angulo, and John D'Exeter, sheriff of Connacht. They were to share in the spoils. De Lacy received most of present day Co. Sligo, as well as Sliabh Lugha, and he, in turn, granted a large tract of territory to Maurice Fitzgerald who built a monastery at Sligo and a castle at Banada. He gave another tract to Jordan D'Exeter, who formed the manor of Áth Lethan (now Ballylahan) in the barony of Gallen Co. Mayo, in 1240. His descendants were later famous as the MacJordans or Jordans of Gallen.

Sliabh Lugha was given to Milo De Angulo who had already obtained territory in Bréffni (present-day Cos. Cavan and Leitrim). About the year 1225 De Angulo introduced a large body of colonists to Sliabh Lugha. These seized a group of noblewomen from Sligo whom they carried away into captivity.[14] (Milo De Angulo's own wife was a De Burgo, a daughter of the Earl of Ulster; when she died in 1253 she was buried in the monastery of Boyle.) The newcomers quickly established firm control of the area and had expelled the O Gara lords by about the year 1260. They were no doubt assisted in this by the treacherous murder in 1256 of Ruaighrí ó Gadhra, king of Sliabh Lugha, by his own godfather, a Norman named David son of Richard Cúisín (Cushing); the latter also broke down O Gara's castle whose location is not indicated – it was probably situated at Castlemore, where the Normans later had a great stronghold. Later that same year Aed O Conor plundered Cushing's territory in revenge for the slaying of O Gara; he broke down all his castle, killing all the inmates, 'and took possession of the whole of Loch Deiched (Lough Gara). Nevertheless the rule of the O Garas over Sliabh Lugha was at an end and they were pushed eastwards into the territory of Coolavin (Cúil ó bhFinn) on the northern shores of the lake to which they gave the name,

Lough Gara. The new rulers of Sliabh Lugha were not allowed to hold territory without disturbance, however. In 1262 the Annals of Connacht tell us that Aed O Conor 'assembled a great host and plundered the English of west Connacht all the way from Mayo and Balla eastwards to Sliabh Luga, burning their towns and corn and killing many people between these points'.[15] In spite of this, the colonists held their ground. Sliabh Lugha was to remain their patrimony for another three centuries at least.

One of the De Angulos bore the name Jocelyn (or in Norman-French Gocelin); this was gaelicised at quite an early stage as Mac Goisdelbh, later mac Coistealbha and variously anglicised MacCustellagh, McGuistillo, MacCostello and, eventually, Costello. This was to be the premier surname in Sliabh Lugha for many a long year thereafter. Before the end of the thirteenth century a town had grown up around the great castle built by the De Angulos at a place which became known in consequence as Caislen Mór Mac Goisdelb.[16] (It is so called in the *Annals of Connacht* at the year 1336 – already, in 1270, the same annals refer to it as Caislen Slébi Luga, 'the castle of Sliabh Lugha'). In 1285 Pilib Mac Gosdelb routed the followers of Magnus O'Conor at the Ox Mountains, 'where many of the young levies and rabble were killed'. In the same year we can see an example of a Gaelic annalist's conservative refusal to recognise the political reality: when the Annals of Connacht tell us of Ruaidhrí O Gara being killed 'on his own lake' (Lough Gara) by MacFeorais (de Bermingham) the annalist still designates O Gara by the now anachronistic title 'king of Sliabh Lugha'. By 1330, however, Gilbert MacGoisdelbh was being styled lord of Sliabh Lugha and by this time the Norman colonists of Sliabh Lugha were behaving like denizens of any other local lordship.

In 1328 the aforementioned Gilbert met the Burkes and the MacDermots and MacDonaghs at Áth Cinn Deicet (a ford at the head of Lough Gara) and agreed to join them in an alliance against Turlogh O Conor, king of Connacht.[18] Two years later when O Conor attacked MacWilliam Burke in Moylurg (north Roscommon) MacCostello and MacDonagh both came to the latter's aid. In 1333 Gilbert was treacherously killed 'on the floor of his own house' by Cathal Mac Diarmada Gall. Three years later a party of MacDermots and O Conors raided the territory of MacCostello and Maidheag son of Baildrín MacCostello was killed while pursuing the raiders.[19] Later that same year Turlogh O Conor and his allies destroyed the great castle of MacCostello (i.e. Castlemore).[20] In 1340 Siúrtán Ruadh MacCostello was killed by Cathal Mac Diarmada Gall, and in the same year, Imag, daughter of MacCostello and wife of Eoghan Mac Finghin (whose family was an offshoot of the MacDermots), died. In 1365 the Clann Costello made an attack on their neighbours to the north, the O Haras of Leyney; according to the annalists they killed six sons of a king, along with Cormac O Hara. who was 'eligible for the kingship of Luighne'.

The incidents just recounted would seem to indicate that the Clann Costello did not coexist altogether comfortably with their various neighbours, both Gaelic and Norman. For example, there was a long-running feud between them and the family of Mac Diarmada Gall, rulers of the territory of Airteach (around present day Loughglynn). One episode in the bloody dispute occurred in 1346 when 'a great war' was fought between MacDermot and Magnus Mac Diarmada Gall; in the course of it, according to the Annals of Connacht, 'the sons of Baildrín Mac Gosdelb betrayed Magnus in their own house and he was killed there.[21] (from this Baildrín is derived the prominent east Mayo surname Waldron – Mac Bhaildrín.)

In 1366 Sean MacCostello (Mac Gillibeirt), lord of Sliabh Lugha died.[22] In another dispute with the family's Gaelic neighbours, Miles MacCostello was killed in 1383 by the sons of Fiachra O Flynn who ruled the area around Ballinlough Co. Roscommon. In 1413 one Gilbert MacCostello died; no indication is given of his rank, but he must have been of some consequence to merit an entry in the annals. Three years later Sean MacCostello went on a raid against his kinsman, Éamann an Mhachaire (Edmund of the Plain) MacCostello, and was killed by one of the pursuing party with an arrow shot.[23] (This Éamann an Mhachaire died in 1437, just a few years after he is believed to have founded the Dominican monastery on the shores of Urlar Lough – Mainistir an Urláir – in the parish of Kilmovee; another member of the family bore the same name between thirty and fifty years later, but it is unclear just how the two were related). In 1428 another Seán MacCostello accompanied MacJordan of Gallen on a raid against the Barrets of Tirawley in the course of which Seán Fionn MacCostello was killed. Clann Costello and the O'Flynns of Síol Maolruain (around present day Ballinlough) were in conflict again in 1443 when the Annals of the Four Masters report that O'Flynn (i.e. the chief of his family) and some of his kinsmen were slain in the house of Ó Cillín – this may have been in the townland of Ballykilleen which lies a few miles south east of Ballyhaunis. The next head of the family was slain six years later by the sons of Walter Boy MacCostello and, fifteen years after that again, in 1464, yet another O'Flynn chieftain fell at the hand of Clann Costello – in a skirmish at Clooncrim, near Ballinlough. O'Flynn, his brother Giolla na Naomh and five of their men were killed by the sons of Philip MacCostello.

The year 1461 witnessed conflict between the former and the current lords of Sliabh Lugha when Fergal O Gara, 'eligible prince' (rídamhna) of Coolavin, was killed by MacCostello.[25] The two families feature together in another incident three years later (1464) when, in the course of an attack by Cormac Mac Diarmada Gall on (the later) Éamann an Mhachaire MacCostello at Cluain Carthaig (Clooncartha in the parish of Kilmovee), Tomaltach Óg O Gara was killed by a javelin. Éamann an Mhachaire finally met his end four years later, in 1468, at the hands of his own brother, William MacCostello.[26] The previous year one David MacCostello had been slain by Thomas Mac Fheorais (Bermingham). In 1471 Seán Dubh MacCostello attacked some of his own kinsmen, and in the course of the affray Elec, daughter of Fergal óg O hUigínn and wife of Conor O hUiginn, was killed 'in her own house at Machaire na nAileach, most unhappily' – the place mentioned seems to have been somewhere in the vicinity of Ballaghaderreen.[27] In 1487 that same Seán Dubh MacCostello, chief of the family and lord of Sliabh Lugha, died and he was succeeded jointly by his brother, William, and by one Jordan, son of Philip MacCostello. Six years later, in 1493, one Dáibhidh MacCostello, a grandson of Éamann an Mhachaire, was slain by three members of the family of ó hEaghra Buidhe (O Hara Boy). In 1496 the chief of Clann Costello was taken prisoner by the MacDermots; the incident is mentioned only in the Annals of Ulster which give no indication of how the matter was resolved – presumably he was released after a deal was made with his captors. Forty years later, In 1536, Seán MacCostello, son of Giolla Dubh, 'a munificent, humane man and a good captain' was killed by one of his own kinsmen and by some of the family of MacDiarmada Gall of Airteach. That same year the O Conors went on a raiding expedition into the territory of Clann Costello; they encircled Kilcolman, the residence of the son of Rughraidhe MacCostello, and this individual – a grandnephew of Seán MacGiolla Dhuibh – came out of the castle and submitted to O Conor, bringing with him the mailcoat of Mac Feorais (de Bermingham).[28] O Conor took him to Sligo as a hostage for the payment of the full ransom.

Over the next half a century several other members of Clann Costello were to perish in the same kind of internecine disputes and bloody quarrels with their neighbours that we have already catalogued. Some also died at the hands of the officials of the English government as the Elizabethan regime slowly but surely extended its rule throughout Connacht. In 1545 the head of Clann Costello, Walter mac William, went on a raiding expedition against the territory of O'Conor Sligo; having reached Bunnanaddan, Co. Sligo they were attacked by the O'Conors assisted by the MacSweeneys. Walter and his son Rughraidhe, were killed and their forces routed at a place called Rúscach na Gaoithe. Two years later another skirmish occurred between the Costellos and the MacDermots when a grandson of Walter's Jordan Boy led a party of eighteen men into MacDermot territory in north Roscommon to recover stolen property and they were attacked by Brian, son of The MacDermot, with just six men. Brian and one of the Clann Costello were badly wounded in the affray, and the MacDermots were compelled to surrender to the raiders from Sliabh Lugha. No doubt in revenge for this, the MacDermots heavily raided Sliabh Lugha the next year, taking sixty cows from Clann Costello and utterly routing the latter's kinsmen, the Clann Philip (MacPhilip na Leitreach), from whom they took no fewer than 1200 cows and ten saddle horses.

Mention has already been made of Jordan Boy MacCostello who raided Moylurg (the territory of the MacDermots) in 1547 and wounded Brian MacDermot. He was to make something of a name for himself as one of the more aggressive members of Clann Costello over a period of just a decade in the middle of the 16th century. In 1551 he was involved in a bloody skirmish with the MacDermot Roes at a place called Muinchinn Uachtair in which he came off worse. With curious imprecision, the Annals of Loch Cé record that 'a score or two fell' in the battle, Jordan himself having killed two named individuals, Domhnall ó Láimhín (Lavin) and Cathal ó Mocháin (Maughan). Two years later we find Jordan Boy and the aforementioned Brian MacDermot (who had been wounded in 1547) encountering one another again: the Annals of Loch Cé having reported that a prey had been taken from Brian's people, remark 'that was not a wound without retaliation'. The retaliation came the following year, 1553, when the annals tell us that 'a great depredation was committed by the MacDermots on Jordan Boy'. In 1557 Brian MacDermot again committed 'a great depredation' on MacCostello, raiding as far as the parish of Bekan where he burned the castle of Tulrohan. The two adversaries came into conflict again in 1560 when another prey was taken by Brian from Jordan Boy and the family of Henry O'Grady — presumably an ally or lieutenant of MacCostello – were killed by MacDermot. Jordan Boy's violent career came to an end the following year when he was killed by the Burkes at Ballyloughdalla in Tirawley. The annals sum him up by saying that he was 'noble and destructive'.

Despite his prominence, this Jordan Boy was not the chief of Clann Costello. Piarais, who features only once in the annals, at the year 1555 when he was treacherously killed by some of his own kinsmen in Mannin Castle in the parish of Aghamore. There is no mention of Clann Costello in the annals for two decades after the death of Jordan Boy in 1561. The death of a certain Tomás an tSléibhe (Thomas of the Mountain), son of Richard MacCostello, is reported at the year 1581. The following year two sons of Giolla Dubh MacCostello, Giolla dubh óg and Éighneachán, were treacherously killed by MacDonagh, lord of Corran, Co. Sligo. A few years later we find the family coming into conflict with the English authorities: in 1586 the son of MacCostello, William MacPiarais, was hanged by the sheriff of Co. Roscommon at a place called Dumha na Rómhánach. At the end of the same year the annals make a statement which herald a fateful change in the fortunes of Clann Costello: 'The great castle of MacCostello (Castlemore) and half the lordship of the county were given to Theobald Dillon by MacCostello i.e. John, son of Giolla Dubh son of Hubert'. Interestingly enough, they also add that 'O Gara gave five towns in his division and the castle of Derrymore to the same man'. Thus the two families who were successfully lords of Sliabh Lugha made way for a third family, the Dillons, who would gain exclusive control of the area and retain it for three centuries.

The extensions of English rule throughout the western province was reflected in the measure known as the 'composition of Connaught' of 1585 under which both Gaelic chiefs and Hiberno-Norman lords submitted to the Crown and were believed by these chiefs to be given legal title to their estates under English law;[29] It also involved the abolition of the office and title of chieftain.[28] It appears that the composition was in the long term concerned with reducing the independent authority of the local lords and chieftains and the further anglicization of Connacht. The composition agreement comprises three separate sections. An annual rent charge was to be paid by the chiefs to the Crown of 10/- on each quarter of inhabited land. This money was not in return for a grant of title to land ; it was to be paid in place of cess or military exaction. Secondly, freeholders would answer a call to hosting within the province each year and to a general hosting if required. In accepting these two provisions the chieftains, lords, and lesser lords were accepting the President of Connacht and his council as their protectors.

The 10/- composition rent was to meet the expenses of the Connacht presidency within the province. The third section stated that all Irish titles be abolished forever. To compensate for the loss of these titles the lords were to be granted 'freedoms': A further rent was payable to the chief lord, by the lesser lords, and tenants, out of each quarter of inhabited land, and was payable over and above the composition rent payable to the English administration. No rent was charged on waste lands or uninhabited lands. So the chieftain or lord's wealth apparently lay in the tenants who lived on his property and the herds they attended.

The barony of Clancostillo (Costello) was omitted from the Composition Book in assessing the cess to be paid to the English Queen. A note to that effect by the commissioners is added in the statements of proceedings 'The Barony of Clancostilloe is not yet presented'. The commissioners claimed they could not conveniently assess this area, because of 'the hard passage and travel thither, by means of the great bogs woods, moors, and mountains, and other evil ways in and to the said barony' Only when petitioned to do so by Theobald Dillon did they undertake the survey. The survey describes the area as 'barren amongst the most barren' and 'a verie resceptacle of Scotts and a harbour for other lowse and evil people, through the strength and fastnesse thereof '. They finally came to the conclusion that only eighty three quarters could be charged with rent. This survey was taken at Athleague in Co. Roscommon. In an Inquisition letter of 10 September 1587, Sir Thomas L'Estrange said to Perrot (President of Connacht) that 10/- sterling per quarter be charged. The quantity of land in Costello comprised 255 quarters. Each quarter was 120 acres.

The annals note the death in 1588 of Éamann, son of the MacCostello. The following year Jordan, son of Tomás na gCapall ('Thomas of the Horses') MacCostello, died in the Neale while held in irons as a prisoner of the English. In 1589 the son of MacCostello, William Caoch son of Jordan son of John Dubh, and William son of John son of Meiler Ruadh – while raiding the O'Kelly territory in east Galway, – were slain on Sliabh Muire ('Mount Mary') near Ahascragh by Donnchada O'Kelly a week before Christmas. The significance of this entry is that it is the very last occasion on which the family are mentioned in the annals. For the next three centuries the newcomer, Theobald Dillon, and his descendants held almost unchallenged sway.

A good deal of mystery surrounds the circumstances in which Theobald Dillon was invited into east Mayo by MacCostello and given 'of free gift a great portion of his land', including the great Costello stronghold of Castlemore. Theobald Dillon commanded an independent troop in 1599 during the reign of Queen Elizabeth and was appointed collector and receiver of composition money for the province of Connacht.[30] His family owned extensive estates in Meath and Westmeath. He appears to have put his legal education to good use, acting as a mediator between the Connacht rebels and the Crown. In doing so he antagonized the controversial English president of Connacht, Sir Richard Bingham, who referred to Dillon as a 'great extortioner, a favouler of rebels and malefactors'. However Dillon's overriding objective appears to have been his own self-advancement and he lost no time in extending his holdings in

Costello. Within a short time Clann Costello had been virtually dispossessed of the lands for which they had fought so long and so hard over the previous three and a half centuries. Even before the end of the 1580s they had begun to realise the implications of Dillon's arrival among them but already it was too late. As early as 1587 the Lord Deputy, Sir John Perrot, in his report on the barony of Costello (alias Ballyhaunis) in connection with the composition of Connacht was able to declare that 'Theobalde Dillon inhabiteth the said barony, and hath by his industry brought the people there to obedience and subjection'.

MacCostello appears to have made one last attempt to act as an independent lord when, in 1595 he rallied, briefly, to the standard of Red Hugh O'Donnell in his war against Queen Elizabeth. When that attempt fizzled out, the majority of the MacCostelloes, Waldrons, Jordans, and other offspring of Jocelin de Angulo seem to have settled into the role of tenants of the Dillons with a fair degree of equanimity, holding land on English tenure and paying a fixed rent.[31] Not surprisingly however, some of the MacCostelloes clearly resented the manner in which they had become tenants on what had been for so long their own lands and, as we will see presently, a celebrated member of the family waged a private war on the Dillons for a time in the 1660s. In spite of this the estate established by Theobald, later created first Viscount Dillon, would weather all vicissitudes and endure down to the opening years of the 20th century.[32] The extent and value of that estate can be seen in the Appendix at the end of this book which lists Lord Dillon's leaseholders at the beginning of the 19th century).

By comparison with the Costelloes, their predecessors as lords of Sliabh Lugha, the O Garas, feature comparatively infrequently in the annals in the centuries between their loss of Sliabh Lugha and the displacement of their successors by the Dillons. We have already seen a number of references to incidents in which they came into contact with Clann Costello. The following are some other notable entries relating to Muintir Ghadhra in the annals. In 1434 Tomaltach O Gara, lord of Coolavin and his three young sons were treacherously slain by his own brothers on Inch Island (Inis Bolg) in Lough Gara. O Gara did not succumb without a struggle; he killed two of his attackers and half killed two or three others. This bloody happening had a sequel two years later when, according to the Annals of the Four Masters, the MacDonaghs of Tirerrill made an incursion into Coolavin; the MacDonaghs were worsted in the encounter, seven of them being killed, as well as Conor Cam O Gara who had some time before treacherously slain his own brother, O'Gara. In 1451 the Four Masters record that a prey was taken from the

O Garas by the O'Conors, but the O Garas in turn, took a prey from the O'Flynn of Assylin near Boyle. In the autumn of 1469 Eoghan O Gara, termed 'king of Coolavin' died and his son also named Eoghan, died of a sudden sickness; another son, Diarmaid therefore succeeded to the lordship. The Four Masters tell that Diarmaid was taken prisoner by Con O Donnell, lord of Tirconnell, in 1495 following a fierce battle near Sligo in which the north Connacht army was badly beaten and many notable Connachtmen (including a certain Cian, son of Brian O Gara) were slain. The successor to this Diarmaid as lord of Coolavin was a son named Eoghan: the record of his death in the year 1537 is the very last reference to the family in the Annals of Connacht. The very next year however, the Annals of Ulster record another attack on Sligo and north Connacht by O Donnell; having captured Sligo the Ulster army advanced against the castle of O Gara (Moygara) where O Donnell's son Niall Garbh was killed by a single gunshot. In the Annals of Lough Cé at the year 1549 there is a brief reference to the exactions imposed on neighbouring chieftains by one Ruaidhri Mac Dermot : these included the taking of sixty cows from O Gara. In 1577 the death occurred of the son of The O Gara, Cian son of Diarmaid son of Eoghan. The O Gara himself died in 1579, as did Giolla Dubh Mac Phillip, lord of the Leitir in Sliabh Lugha (in or around Cloonmore in the parish of Kilbeagh). O Gara's wife Sadhbh Mac Dermot, died five years later. In 1581 the President of Connacht, Sir Nicholas Malby, sent a great force of Scots mercenaries into north Connacht where they were opposed by a large army headed by O Conor Sligo and including members of such local families as MacDermot, MacSweeney and the O Hara Boy. Many of these notables fell in a bloody battle fought in the vicinity of Coolavin, and on the same day the castle of Moygara was burned by the Scots and Diarmaid Óg son of Cian O Gara and Tadg son Óg Ruaidhri and many others were slain. The final mention of the O Garas in the Annals of Lough Cé occurs at the year 1586 where it is reported that, as we saw above, Theobald was given five towns (or townlands) of O Gara territory, in addition to the castle of Derrymore, by Oilillín O Gara.

    The ruins of Derrymore Castle stand today at the point of Derrymore Island. Take the road to the right at Manasteraden crossroads, travel towards Killaraght Church and turn left. There is an old unused road, marked on the 1837 Ordnance Survey map, which takes you right onto the ruins of Derrymore Castle. From the top of the ruined pile Lough Gara stretches to the left where the Lung river flows into the lake. The dark blue waves lap the wooded shore of old Coolavin and high up on the summit of Mullach an tSí are the ruins of Moygara castle. To the right a

Moygara

long promontory, formerly called Inch Island, (anciently Inis Bolg) but now known as McLoughlin Island, lies parallel with Derrymore, and on it a crannóg and ring fort can be seen. To the far right where Lough Gara is joined by the Boyle river is Cuppanagh Bridge. The castle of Cuppanagh, now in ruins and covered with briars and brushwood, stands near this point. It appears that many of the stones from the old castle were used in the building of the bridge.

Derrymore is no longer an island. In 1952 the River Lung was drained by blasting the rocks near the lake and the lake waters receded. Only in exceptionally bad winter weather has Derrymore the appearance of an island. There can be little doubt that the O Garas once held the three most strategically positioned castles in this area. However, as we have seen, Malby's forces burned the great castle of Moygara in 1581 and it was never renovated, while the power of the O Garas waned considerably once Derrymore castle was given to Dillon in 1586. The ruins of Moygara Castle still stand weatherbeaten and defiant on the northern slopes of Mullach na tSí. It was 184 feet square with six square battlement towers. It is now badly in need of preservation: it may not stand the test of time much longer unless some form of restoration is undertaken.

SLIABH LUGHA IN ANCIENT TIMES

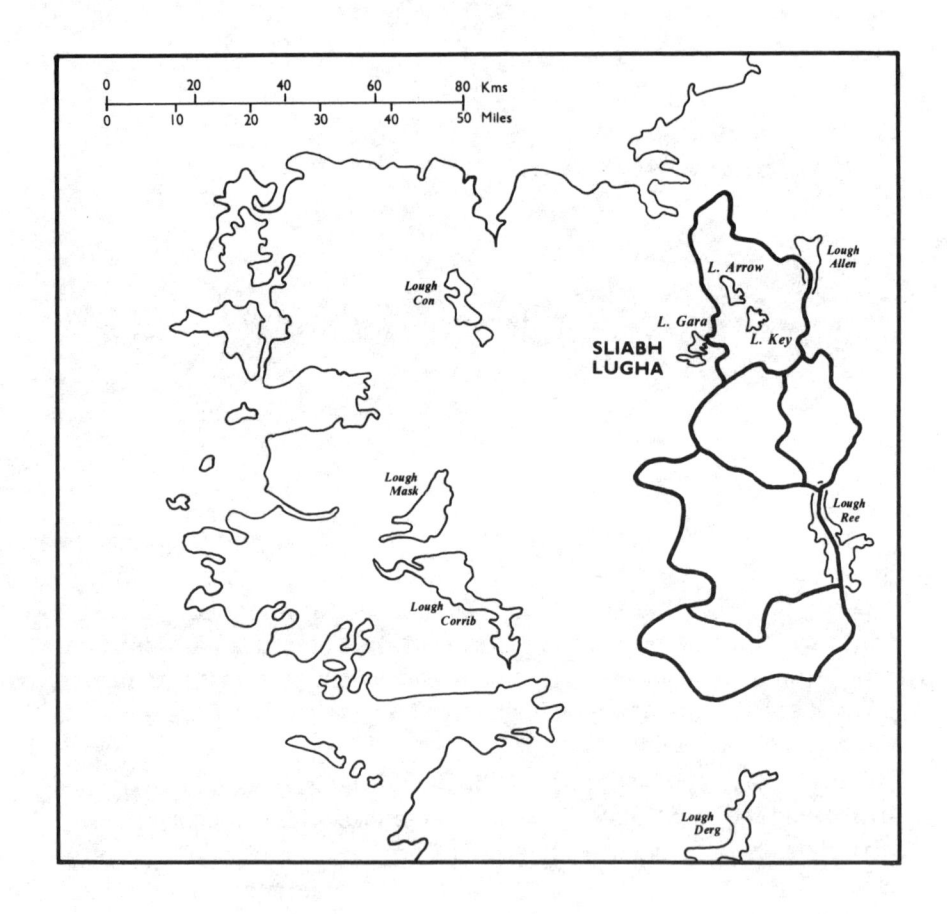

CHAPTER 2

LANDLORDS, RAPPAREES AND WILD GEESE

When the Tudor dynasty ended in 1603 Ireland had undergone a military conquest, but the majority of the people remained firmly committed to the Catholic religion. Most of the land in Connacht was in the hands of Old Irish (Gaelic) or Old English (Norman) landowners and the reign of James I witnessed persistent efforts by the Crown to ascertain the right by which these lands were held, the principal motive being to increase royal revenue from the king's Irish subjects. To this end repeated inquisitions were held and letters patent given to Irish freeholders in return for a fee.[1] One such inquisition was held at Castlemore in 'Slieve Lowe (anglicised version of Sliabh Lugha)[2] in 1607. There is a record of a grant in 1617 to Theobald Dillon of the wardship of Ferral O Gara, grandson and next heir to Uriell [Iriall] O'Gara of Moygara in Sligo County for a fine of £8.17.9.1 and an annual rent of £11. 8.0.[3] He held £9 sterling of this for his maintenance and education in the English religion and habits at Trinity College, Dublin, from the twelfth to the eighteenth year of his age. In that same year a grant was made to Ferrall O Gara of Moygara in the half barony of Coolavin of the castle and manor, town and lands of Moygara, and all rival claims (by O Conor Sligo and by two others, William Taffe and John Baxter who had previously leased land in Coolavin) were set aside.[4] The lands in question were designated the manor of Moygara. Part of the O Gara estate in Coolavin was good arable land, some of it was covered by great woods; it also had good turf, some shelter and much mountain. The woods contributed to Fergal O Gara's wealth as timber was quite an important asset in the early 17th century.[5]

The attempt to turn Fergal O Gara into a gentleman conforming to the 'English religion and habits' would seem to have been less than an unqualified success. In the early 1630s he came into contact with the scholarly Donegal Franciscan lay–brother Michael O Cleirigh who in 1627 had returned to Ireland from Louvain in order to collect material for a projected work on the lives of the Irish saints.[6] O'Cleirigh travelled the length and breadth of the country tirelessly searching out and transcribing hagiographical material in Irish from ancient manuscripts, many of which no longer survive. After a time he cast his net somewhat wider to include other historical materials. The most notable work of this kind was the great compilation popularly known as the *'Annals of the Four Masters'*. This great compendium of Irish annalistic material from the time of the Deluge ('Anno Mundi 2240') to the early 17th century was produced on the Donegal Leitrim border between the years 1632 and 1636. In point of fact there were six 'masters' in all engaged on the project at various times: Brother Michael's helpers were his brother Conaire, their cousin Cúchoigcríche Ó Duibhgeannain from Co. Leitrim and Fear Feasa and Muiris óg Maolchonaire from Roscommon. The other key figure in the production of the Annals was the project's patron, Fergal O Gara, lord of Coolavin to whom Brother Michael dedicated the great work. He it was who financed the team, allowing Brother Michael at least to travel far afield in search of manuscripts; these were then transcribed and rearranged by him and his collaborator at their 'place of refuge' at Bundrowes near Ballyshannon, Co. Donegal. During the period that the Annals were being compiled Fergal O Gara was elected M.P. for Co. Sligo in the parliament which the Lord Deputy, Thomas Wentworth, summoned to meet in Dublin in 1634.[7] (He was one of less than a dozen members of Old Irish origin in an assembly of some two hundred and forty). Later following on the outbreak of the rising of 1641, O Gara is on record as having protected a Co. Sligo family named Browne who were being persecuted on account of their religion. The only reference to him from those years tells us 'Mr.Farrel O Gara presented himself to General Neyll [the celebrated Old Irish general Owen Roe O Neill] cheerfully and prayed for his success ... and sent his son Captain John O Gara with his company to him'. After that he just disappears from history: the date of his death is unknown, but he probably died around the year 1660. We will hear more of his offspring presently.

Theobald, first Viscount Dillon of Costello Gallen, died in 1624. He left a large progeny who became linked through marriage with several other important landed families in Connacht and further afield. Sometime before his death Theobald was able to assemble over a hundred of his offspring and in-laws at his house at Killenfeagh or Killenfaghny in Co. Westmeath. One of his daughters Jane married Hugh óg O Conor Don, second son of Sir Hugh O Conor Don of Castlereagh. His eldest son, Sir Christopher, who predeceased him by just a fortnight, married Lady Jane Dillon, the eldest daughter of the Earl of Roscommon. Sir Theobald was succeeded by Sir Christopher's eldest son, Luke. Although only fourteen years of age when he became second Viscount, Luke married the following year, 1625, Lady Mary Mac Donnell, daughter of the first Earl of Antrim. However, he died just four years later, in 1629 and was succeeded, as third Viscount Dillon, by his infant son Theobald. The child lived only a short time, after which the title reverted to his uncle, Luke's younger brother Thomas.

Thomas, fourth Viscount Dillon, who was born in 1615 had a varied career. He was joint Governor of Mayo in 1641 along with Viscount Wilmot and in 1645 he was Governor of Athlone. He held the rank of lieutenant-general under the command of the Lord Lieutenant, James Butler, Earl of Ormonde. Following Cromwell's victory he and his four sons were deprived of his estates by the Commonwealth. At the Restoration, however having returned from continental exile in 1663, he was regranted these lands, 64,195 plantation acres in Cos. Mayo, Roscommon and Westmeath.

He died in 1673 and was succeeded by his only surviving son, also named Thomas, fifth Viscount, who died the following year without surviving issue.[9] The title then passed to the latter's first cousin, Luke, sixth Viscount, who was a nephew of Luke, the second Viscount, and to Thomas, the fourth Viscount. He died without issue in 1682, whereupon the title passed to a second cousin, Theobald, seventh Viscount, a great grandson of the first Viscount and a grandson of a younger brother of Sir Christopher's. Like the rest of his family, Theobald, was unwavering in his loyalty to the Stuart kings. He was a lieutenant-colonel in the guards of JamesII and he served in the war against James' royal son-in-law, William of Orange. His wife, formerly Lady Mary Talbot, was killed by a shell at the siege of Limerick and Theobald died himself at the bloody battle of Aughrim, Co. Galway, on 12th July 1691. He was succeeded by his son, Henry, who had been MP for Westmeath in James' 'Patriot Parliament' of 1688. He was also Lieutenant of Roscommon, a colonel in the Jacobite army and Governor of Galway. Although his father, the seventh Viscount, had been outlawed by the Williamites, Henry succeeded in having the outlawry reversed and he was able to retain the family's extensive estates – in 1685 Lord Dillon had been the largest single proprietor in the barony of Costello, holding 24,454 acres. The eight Viscount died in 1713 and was succeeded by his son, Richard, who married Lady Bridget Burke, daughter of the Earl of Clanricarde. It was he who built the present house at Loughglynn. The ninth Viscount died in 1737 leaving only a daughter who married her father's first cousin, Charles Dillon. The latter, who was 'Colonel Proprietor' of the famous Dillon Regiment of 'Wildgeese' in the service of France from 1730 to 1741, succeeded to the title as tenth Viscount. He died without surviving issue in 1741 and was

LOUGHLIN CASTLE.

succeeded by his brother Henry, (1705-87), who was Colonel Proprietor of the Dillon Regiment from 1741 to 1744 and from 1747 to 1772. The latter had three sons. The eldest Charles (1745-1813), who succeeded him as 12th Viscount, conformed to the Established Church in 1767. His younger brother was the tragic Arthur Dillon, a lieutenant general in the French service and last Colonel Proprietor of the Dillon Regiment 1772-1794. Following the outbreak of the French Revolution he was dismissed from the army and imprisoned in 1792. Two years later, during the Reign of Terror, he died on the guillotine, a victim of hatred and intrigue. The same year the Dillon Regiment changed sides and joined the English army under its Colonel, Major General Henry Dillon (1794-8), younger brother of Charles and Arthur.[10]

Members of other local families, notably the O Conors and the Mac Dermots, distinguished themselves in various Wild Geese regiments 'from Dunkirk to Belgrade' throughout the eighteenth century.[10] One illustrious surname which appears among them is O Gara. Colonel Oliver O Gara, a grandson of Fergal O Gara, first appears as a lieutenant in Viscount Mountjoy's Regiment of Foot in 1688.[11] We next meet him in the midst of 'the War of the Two Kings' when, in the winter of 1690-91, he was colonel of a regiment raised by himself to fight on behalf of James II. He fought at Athlone and at Aughrim and was a witness to the signing of the Treaty of Galway in 1691 with Baron De Ginkle; he was also present at the signing of the Treaty of Limerick. In the aftermath of Limerick he went to France where he was given command of the Queens Dragoons in 1696. Oliver O Gara married Lady Mary Fleming and they had four sons whom he was able to place well because of his loyal support of the Jacobite cause. Three of them entered the Spanish service. Fergal O Gara appears to have at least four sons, John, Bernard, Cian and Charles, but it is unclear which of them was the father of Colonel Oliver. The last mentioned, Charles, had two sons priests in the archdiocese of Tuam, Bernard (or Brian) and Michael. The former was parish priest of Knock about the year 1715 and in 1723 was made archbishop of Tuam. Because of the Penal Laws he was compelled to live, not in Tuam, but in the vicinity of Ballyhaunis. He died on 3 April 1740 and was probably buried in the 15th century Augustinian abbey where, the year before his own death, he had erected a fine altar-tomb in memory of his father, Charles. On the death of Archbishop O Gara he was succeeded in quite an unusual development – by his own brother, Michael, who died in 1748.

We cannot deal with any part of the story of the barony of Costello in the 17th century without referring to the dramatic and ill starred career of the famous Dubhaltach Mac Cosdealbha, the celebrated rapparee.[12]

When Captain Dudley Costello returned from exile with Charles II at the Restoration, he had high hopes of regaining the property which his ancestors almost a century previously had allowed to slip from their grasp into the hands of Theobald Dillon. Like so many of his co-religionists, however, his hopes were to be cruelly dashed. The Cromwellian settlement and previous confiscations were not to be overturned. Having failed to regain his property, Dudley turned Rapparee (a word said to derive from 'rapaire' a half sword or rapier favoured by such men – although others say the word comes from 'ropaire', a robber). He gathered a party of followers around him and carried on a vendetta of raids and burnings against Dillons in the baronies of Costello and Gallen. He sometimes ranged much further afield and caused great alarm among landowners who had benefited from the confiscation of Catholic land; their concern soon spread to government circles in Dublin. The Lords Justices issued a proclamation that any damage done by raparees to Protestant property would have to be paid for by Catholic landowners of the area. Proclaimed a tory and rebel in the summer of 1666, Dudley Costello was shot dead by soldiers of Captain Theobald Dillon near Foxford in march 1667. There is another local tradition, however, that Dudley Costello was murdered on the slopes of Sliabh Lugha, in Barnalyra (Bárr na Laidre – the top/height of the river fork), beside the new Connacht Airport.

The following story about Dudley's son was recorded in 1847. It affords an interesting insight into the rivalry between the Dillons and the Costelloes. To appreciate one of the key points in the story, it must be explained that the sixth Lord de Angulo, Philip, having spent some time in Spain, was allegedly known as 'The Castillion'; as a consequence, so the story goes, the family adopted the surname 'Mac Costillo'.

After Dudley's murder, Michael Rushe, who was foster father to Dudley's son, heard that a price had been put on Dudley's head by Dillon, who wished to exterminate all the Costello clan, so he went away by night, taking his foster son with him. After many trials they settled down near Lisnagarvey (now Lisburn) in Ulster where young Costello passed, unknown to himself, as Rushe's child.

Young Dudley attended a school in the nearby town, where Michael Rushe paid for his education out of his small earnings as a labourer – in the hope that some day that he would proclaim him as the rightful owner of the barony of Costello. Between the town and where Rushe lived ran a mountain stream over which there was no bridge. Once when the stream was swollen by recent rains the servant of a neighbouring gentleman came with a horse to take his master's children across the stream to school. Young Costello, who was fifteen years of age at this time, asked to be taken also. The servant refused, calling him 'a beggar's brat'. The blood of all his lordly Castilian forebears boiled in his veins, and with one stroke the servant was in the stream.

Next day Rushe was summoned to the big house to account for his son's misdeed. That night he decided to flit. Turning his back on the Black North, he headed westwards until he reached Carrick-on-Shannon. There he heard with a heavy heart of the strength and power of Dillon of Costello and of his influence with the English government. With Dillon all powerful there was little chance for young Dudley – the castles of his ancestors in Ballyhaunis and Artuagh (Airteach), in Kilcolman and Castlemore were in ruins and Tullaghanrock had fallen into decay; the faithful followers of his house were scattered or seeking their break from the 'Sasanaigh' Dillons. Two years passed. Still young Costello knew not his name or his origin.

Among the many pastimes in which Irishmen at that time excelled was hurling – parish against parish, barony against barony and sometimes county against county. At one of these matches young Dudley was the hero of the day. The judge of the field presented him with a yew caman or hurley with a silken tassle attached to it, the usual prize. Michael Rushe was complimented on his son. His honest heart could hold his secret no longer. There and then in the presence of thousands he tells young Costello his name and lineage and of the lands that were his and of the price Dillon had on his head.

Next day Dudley was on Tullaghanrock. His father's horse (off which he had been shot) was in Páirc an Stáil, looked after by some old follower of the house, and the Toledo blade borne by his father with honour in the service of King Charles, was there too. Young Costello confronted Dillon, declared who he was and challenged him. Dillon professed friendship but later sent a keen swordsman, Tobias Dillon after young Dudley. They fought at Toby's Ford and Tobias Dillon was killed. Some months after this young Dudley died when he fell from his horse near the pass of Bealach an Dóirín; – at that time the town of Ballaghaderren did not yet exist– a pass through the oak woods. All hope of recovering the barony of Costello from the Dillons appeared to have ended. Nevertheless, the *Proceedings of the Court of Claims* show that a Thomás Costello asserted his right to the remainder of the Mayo lands forfeited by Miles Costello. The petition was dismissed. The castle at Tullaghanrock is today a heap of rubble overgrown with briars and moss.

A beautiful Irish traditional song of the mid-17th century, 'Úna Bhan', has its origin in the barony of Costello. It was composed by Tomás Láidir Mas Coistealbha (Costello) at a time when the Irish language was the spoken language of the area. In 1937-38 the Irish Folklore Commission with the co-operation of the National schools of Ireland made a collection of all the folk stories in living memory. Among them was my grandfather's version of the story of Tomás and Úna Bhán on which he was very clear as it had been handed down from generation to generation.[13]

Tomás Costello, according to tradition, was a brother of Dudley the Rapparee who was killed on Bárr na Laidhre in the 1660s. Tullanghanrock had been their home and the borders of the Costello lands ran along Maheraboy and Tobracken, beside the present graveyard at Kilcolman. According to Douglas Hyde in his *'Love Songs of Connaught '* Tomás Láidir fought bravely against the Cromwellian foe in a fierce battle at the Curliew Mountains. Everybody looked to him in time of trouble. There are many versions of his love affair with Úna Mac Dermot. It is believed that she was the grand-daughter of Rory Mac Dermot of Dungar (Frenchpark). Rory had a castle on the Bawn of Cootehall, or Uachtar Tíre as it was known then, and he also owned Trinity Island on Lough Key (Loch Cé).

Tomás was a guest at Mac Dermot's one evening, having rescued a son of the family some time previously. A toast was proposed for the future bridegroom of Úna but she drank to Tomás whom she loved dearly. Tomás loved Úna but because there was an old enmity between the Mac Dermots and the Mac Costello families, her father forbade her to speak to him again. Úna fell ill on the Mac Dermot Island home on Lough Key where she pined away. Eventually her father gave Tomás permission to visit her. He was soon on the Island accompanied by his servant. Joy filled Úna on seeing Tomás and she fell into a pleasant sleep. He sat there for a good while beside her bed, and after a while rose and went down the stairs. There seemed to be nobody around the house and he felt ill at ease, so he rode slowly from the house. His servant gave as his opinion that the Mac Dermots were only humbugging him and that there was treachery in the air. Tomas did not believe him at first, but as the man persisted his suspicions began to grow. So he took an oath that unless he were called back before they crossed the ford of Donóige he would never speak to Úna or the Mac Dermots again. At the ford he hesitated, but the servant mocked him and eventually he drove his horse up on the bank. Just as he had crossed the ford a messenger came hurrying from Úna. But he could not break his vow, and so he did not return. Tradition has it that he struck his servant there and killed him in a rage. Not long after this Úna died and was buried on Castle Island. Tomás swam out to the island the night after her burial and, throwing himself down on her grave, he spent the night watching and weeping. He did the same on the second night and again on the third night. These are two verses of a beautiful forty- four verse poem he composed for her. The melody of this song is hauntingly beautiful.

> A Úna Bhán, is gránna an luí sin ort
> Ar leaba chaol árd i measc na mílte corp,
> muna dtaga tú faidh orm, a staidbhean
> a bhí riamh gan locht,
> Ní thiocfaidh mé chun na háite seo go brách
> ach aréir is anocht.

> (O fair-haired Úna, ugly is your lying place
> on a high narrow bed among thousands of corpes ;
> give an answer to my call o stately lady
> who was ever without fault;
> I shall not come to this place ever
> but last night and tonight.)

> Tá an Bhothuille faoí bhrón
> is Máigh Luirg ar fad
> o d'éag an Péarla, plúr na mban;
> in Oileán na Naomh
> i Loch Cé na mbád is na mbarc
> tá sínte i gcré
> O an deighbhean
> mo rún is mo shearc.

> (The Boyle is saddened
> and all of Moylurg
> since the Pearl of all women (Úna) died;
> in Saints' Island
> in Lough Key of the boats and ships
> the goodly lady, my darling and love,
> lies in the clay.)

As soon as he said these words, Úna appeared to rise up and give him a light blow on the cheek and he heard her voice whisper 'come not'. At that he was satisfied and departed that place forever. No trace of the Ford of Donóg is now to be found but it may have been at the point where the Boyle river flows into Lough Key, one of the most beautiful places in the west of Ireland.

The rest of Tomás Láidir's life was as romantic and tragic as this story. The people of north Roscommon and south Sligo have many stories about him even to this day. The Dillons are supposed to have given a reward to a man named Ruane to kill him. He shot him from behind a clamp of turf and Tomas lay there mortally wounded for three days. He was buried in the same graveyard on Castle Island as Úna. Indeed the two graves were said to have been side by side and tradition has it that there grew an ash-tree out of the grave of Úna and another out of the grave of Costello, and they did not cease growing until they met and entwined around each other. Dr. Douglas Hyde in the 1933 edition of his Amhráin Ghrádha says that the late Jasper Tully, editor of the Roscommon Herald, claimed to have seen the two trees twined over Tomas' and Una's graves when he was touring the area in the year 1865. Surely there is an international folk-motif here. The story and song live on in our hearts today.

According to records in the Genealogical Office, Dublin, Dudley Costello was the son of Jordan Boy Costello of Tullaghanrock. His sister married William Costello of Castlemore. Their son Charles married Giles, daughter of James Farrell of Cloonyquin, Co. Roscommon. Their son in turn, Edmond Costello of Edmondstown, was a Dublin Counsellor at Law. He married Mary the third daughter of Francis Bermingham, the twenty first Baron of Athenry. When Edmond died in 1748, Mary married John Metag, MP for the borough of Ratoath, Co. Meath. Edmond Costello and his first wife Mary had seven children: Francis who died at one year, Edmond who lived only a short time, Charles, who married Mary, daughter of MacFarrell King of Dublin, Mary who died an infant, Alice who lived to the age of twenty one, and Margaret Louise who married Arthur French, son and heir of Arthur French of Frenchpark, Co. Roscommon.

Another family from the vicinity of Sliabh Lugha which featured prominently in the ranks of the Wild Geese were the Mac Donnells who were of Scottish origin and came to Ireland in the later middle ages as mercenaries (gallóglaigh or 'galloglas') in the service of Gaelic and Norman lords.[14] In the 17th century Alexander Boy Mac Donnell owned 211 acres in the parish of Knock while Cahir McTurlogh Mac Donnell owned 448 acres in the parish of Meelick. In the following century a branch of the family were Catholic landlords living at Palmfield House, Carracastle, probably from the mid-1770s.

Anthony Mac Donnell died there in 1851. His son Mark Garvey Mac Donnell (1807-89) will feature in a later chapter. In the *'History of the Irish Brigades in the Service of France'* we find that James MacDonnell of the Mayo MacDonnells died in the Austrian service on 4 October 1766. He was a Count, A General, an Imperial Chamberlain and an Inspector General of the Guard in Camp. He was very generous to his relations in Ireland during his life and his descendants gained pecuniary advantages from Vienna under his will as late as the 1840s.

LANDLORDS, RAPPAREES AND WILDGEESE

James Mac Donnell was succeeded in his countship by his nephew, Francis Mac Donnell, who was related to some of the principal Irish chieftain families, such as the O Rourkes of Breifni and the O'Conors of Connacht. His first cousin was the Franciscan Fr. Tadhg O Rourke, chaplain to Prince Eugene of Savoy before his appointment as bishop of Killala in 1703. He served his people faithfully for over thirty years during the harshest period of the Penal Laws. He lived incognito for much of the time in the house of his grandnephew, Charles O Conor of Bellangare, the most renowned Irish scholar of the 18th century. Charles, incidently, was also a grandnephew of Fergal O Gara. Francis Mac Donnell fought with exceptional gallantry under Eugene of Savoy, the greatest military leader of his age. It is interesting to note that Prince Eugene was a close friend of King William of Orange and that the Irish Wild Geese who fought for Austria often faced their countrymen and even neighbours, such as the Dillons and O Conors, who were fighting for King Louis of France. Francis Count Mac Donnell's father, Henry, was reported to have died in 1772 at the age of 118.

The Mac Donnells were connected with Benada Abbey. A sister of Joseph Mór Mac Donnell of Doocastle married Daniel Jones of Benada Abbey. She left the whole estate to the Sisters of Charity before the turn of the century. This is a very interesting story the details of which are little known. Joseph Mór Mac Donnell was the candidate whom Lord Dillon's agent, Charles Strickland opposed in the election of 1847 (see the chapter on the famine). Joseph Mór's father, Myles Mac Donnell, had replaced the MacPhillips family in Cloonmore House. The latter, as we saw earlier, were an offshoot of the Mac Costelloes. In the Mayo *Book of Survey and Distribution* Moyler Keogh – Maoilir Caoch – Mac Donnell is shown as owning the lands of Cloonmore, as well as land in surrounding parishes. The last member of the Phillips family to live at Cloonmore House was Thomas Phillips (1797-1872). The estate was offered for sale under the Encumbered Estated Court and was bought by O Conor Don and the Powers. When Bishop Mac Nicholas was bishop of Achonry and lived at Brooklawn House there was no proper college for the retraining of priests. Thomas Philip had obliged the bishop by letting him have rooms for six priests in Cloonmore House. Fr. Patrick Durkin from Maynooth, a brilliant scholar, came to guide and train these priests. He succeeded Dr. McNicholas as bishop and set about building the cathedral at Ballaghadereen.

A native of Barroe, now aged ninety five and living in Wrexham in north Wales, tells how her father, James Henry, was taken by his father when he was about nineteen years old to the 'Big House' to be interviewed by Mr. MacDonnell in the hope of being accepted as a recruit by the Royal Irish Constabulary. After the interview he did an exam and was accepted. 'But' she says, 'he was in love with my mother and he followed her to America where they got married, and they came back and forth five times with my brother and sisters as my father always had a soft spot for old Ireland'. His parents felt very let down. The young man had chosen emigration rather than join the R.I.C. So it is clear that there is a wealth of history connected with the Mac Donnells of Palmfield, of Cloonmore, of Doocastle, of Benada Abbey, as well as those who left to seek their fortunes on the continent.

ABBEY OF BALLYHAUNIS

CHAPTER 3

THE PENAL DAYS

AND

THE YEAR OF THE FRENCH

Irish Catholics in general gave their allegiance to James II and his son, styled James III and popularly called 'The Old Pretender', down to the latter's death in 1766.[1] It was only when the Pope refused to recognise James III's son, Charles Edward (Bonnie Prince Charlie'), as king of England on his father's death that Stuart nomination of Irish bishops ceased. This helped to bring a measure of relief to Irish Catholics as it gave the Protestant Establishment less of an excuse to maintain the Penal Laws. Without the threat of foreign invasion, or at least interference in Irish affairs, those laws became less and less defensible. No amount of pretence could disguise the fact that the penal code was directed against the great bulk of the country's population. When agrarian troubles in the west of Ireland in 1711-12 were blamed on the Catholic clergy and a certain Colonel Coote received instructions to commit all priests to jail, he replied to the secretary, Mr. Dawson, that 'the papists are so numerous in this country that, without the assistance of the army, there is no good to be done'.[2] Nevertheless, there were some who adopted a very hardline attitude to the subject of Catholic rights. A Protestant gentleman and clergyman named Rev. Thomas Campbell who toured Ireland declared that 'there was a limit to the degree in which papists should be indulged in a Popish country such as Ireland. They should not be allowed to hold any civil employment or vote as freeholders'.[3] Many believed for a time, in the early 18th century that Catholicism was losing ground. The mass of Irish Catholics were so utterly prostate from a combination of overwhelming military defeat and grinding, degrading poverty that it seemed inconceivable that they could ever again raise hand or voice on their own behalf.

Bishops were appointed by Rome even though they were 'on the run'. Protestant bishops were appointed to practically the same area as Catholic bishops. In the diocese of Achonry, which covers a large portion of the barony of Costello and Coolavin the following bishops were appointed:

THE PENAL DAYS AND THE YEAR OF THE FRENCH

CATHOLIC BISHOPS[4]	PROTESTANT BISHOPS[5]
1707 Hugh Mac Dermot	1691 William Lloyd
1725 Dominic O Daly	1717 Henry Downes
1735 John Harge	1720 Charles Cobb
1739 Walter Burke	1727 Robert Howard
1758 Patrick Robert Kirwan	1730 R. Clayton
1776 Philip Phillips	1736 Mordecai Carey
1785 Boetius Egan	1750 Richard Robinson
1788 Thomas O'Conor	1759 Samuel Hutchinson
1803 Charles Lynch	1781 William Cecil Perry
1809 John O'Flynn.	1784 William Preston
	17- John Law
	1795 J. Porter
	1798 Joseph Stock
	1810 John Verschoyle

During this period the Protestant diocese of Achonry was united to the Protestant diocese of Killala as it still is today. The peasants were called 'our aborigines' by the wealthy, wrote the Rev. Richard Woodward, Dean of Clogher, in *'An argument in Support of the Poor to a National Provision 1768.'* 'Their living conditions was an argument against window tax.[6] Their hovels were generally six feet by seven feet with mud floors and a bundle of furze for a door.' Only someone who had visited these areas could appreciate the dreadful conditions with their attendant ignorance and the savagery of that time. The exorbitant rents, the hearth money and the tithes accentuated all of this. Conditions in the barony of Costello were as bad as anywhere in the west of Ireland.

At this period wool was a powerful source of wealth. In Roscommon large landowners had 'sheep walks' and the wool from thousands of sheep sheared each year was sent to Cork to be spun and exported. The Rundale system of agriculture was used– potatoes, flax, barley, oats were sown in that order each year. Grass seeds were not grown. Flax mills and corn mills situated on rivers, dotted the West. Women and children did the hardest work, quilting, warping, carding and winding. All required hard labour and care. Cottiers were not allowed to keep sheep in case they might think of becoming farmers.[7]

Lord Middleton in writing to Townsend in August 1775 said that a Repeal of the Penal Laws would give Catholics an interest in the peace of their country and would stop frequent uprisings and give them an incentive towards industry.[8] Charles O'Conor of Belanagare decried the want and weakness brought about by the Penal Laws and called for the

THE PENAL DAYS AND THE YEAR OF THE FRENCH

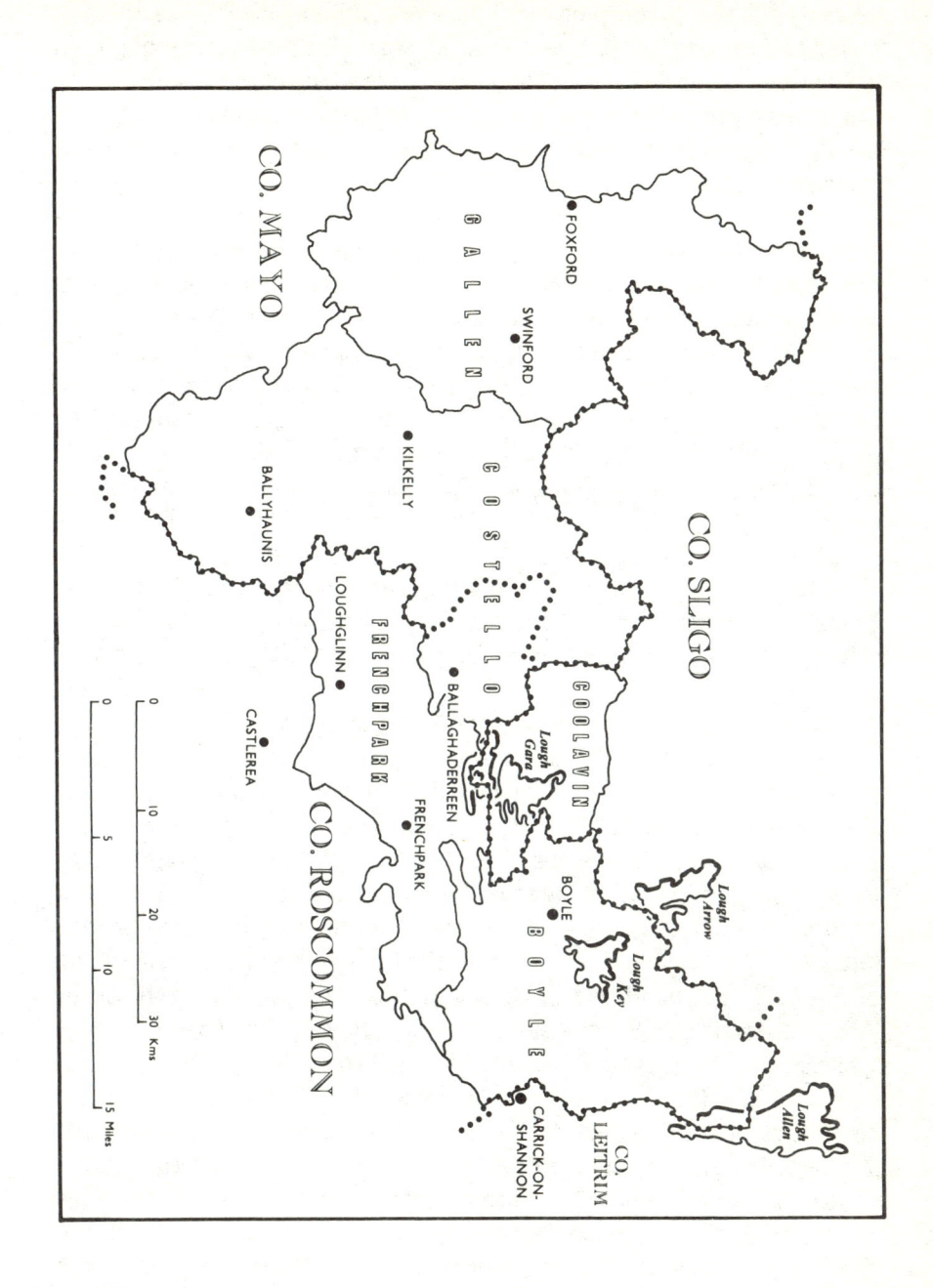

removal of restrictions on Catholic enterprises. Preachers and writers saw no early solution to the problem. The Protestant landowners were determined to hold on to their property at all costs. Elections were fought on local issues rather than National ones.[9] So the bulk of the Irish House of Commons were of the landlord class. Great landlords could and did influence large groups of people. For three quarters of a century the Catholic voice was not heard. There was no leader.

By the mid-seventies Dublin Castle was growing alarmed that the United Irishmen were getting a grip on the country and were looking for help from France. General Abercrombie ordered all arms to be taken from the Irish peasants and inhuman atrocities were committed throughout Ireland while this was being done, by a brutal and indiciplined soldiery. By about 1780 many of the Penal Laws had been repealed or had fallen into abeyance. Catholics were able to hold unprofitable lands in their own names under 'the Bogland Act' and enter long leases, and they could practice their religion with comparative freedom. But they had no political power – all offices of state were still closed to them. They could not vote for a Protestant representative let alone a Catholic one.

The founding of the Catholic Association by the 'elite' of the Irish Catholics in order to bring about constitutional change in 1752 heralded a change of mood. Charles O'Conor, Dr. Curry and Mr. Wyse were the instigators and they sought Repeal of the Penal Laws against the leading Catholics who were no longer prepared to be as supine as heretofore. The formation of the Volunteers and the petition for redress of Catholic grievances were viewed with suspicion by the Government. A later development was the establishment of the Catholic Committee of which Lord Kenmare was one of the leading members before 1790. He was afraid of offending those in power so he suggested that Catholics were satisfied to remain in a position of inferiority and only wanted the most pressing of wrongs removed. The Catholic Committee disagreed strongly and Lord Kenmare resigned.[10] The foundation in Belfast in 1791 of the United Irishmen by Wolfe Tone and others gave strength to the party who opposed Kenmare. Wolfe Tone soon became assistant secretary to the Catholic Committee.

Up to now the Catholic Committee could hardly be said to represent all the Catholics in Ireland. Its members were chosen by selection rather than election and represented only the aristocracy, the wealthy and the educated classes. A complete reorganisation began in 1791. Resolutions were passed promising allegiance to the Crown while seeking full participation in commercial pursuits. Denis O'Conor of Belanagare received a letter from the Committee stating that it was important to show that the Irish Catholics were with them and not divided. He called a meeting at

Tulsk, Co. Roscommon, on January 18th 1792. There they pledged their allegiance to the King but 'taking note of the degrading position in which they existed and noting the work of the Catholic Committee to which they sent delegates, recognised the right of this Committee to speak or act in the name of the Catholics of Ireland'. Another meeting was held at Elphin and a further one at Roscommon where similar resolutions were passed.

Strengthened by the number of resolutions which came in from all over the country the Catholic Committee presented a petition to Parliament. It was rejected on the grounds that the Committee was self constituted. The Committee appealed to the Catholics of Ireland to have delegates elected. They then held a Convention in Dublin in 1792 at which Owen O'Conor represented Co. Roscommon and to which Charles O'Conor, brother of Denis, and his nephew Mac Dermot of Coolavin were also sent as delegates. In 1793 an Act was passed giving many of the rights and privileges sought including the right to vote, but not to sit in Parliament.[11]

Loyalty to the Crown was reiterated in addresses to the Lord Lieutenant. In October 1793 Denis O'Conor again presided at a meeting in Roscommon and a letter was given to Lord Viscount Dillon of Loughglynn to be passed on to the Lord Lieutenant. The enemies of Lord Dillon slandered him for being friendly with the Catholics. Further meetings were held in Roscommon and O'Conor presented an address for the Lord Lieutenant to Arthur French, MP for Roscommon. Owen O'Conor eldest son of Denis had joined the Irish Volunteers and subsequently he became attached to the yeomanry of Roscommon and was second in command of that contingent. Owen was on very good terms with the United Irish leaders, including Tone. He probably was a member of the Society but it is clear from his correspondence that many of the leading figures in the Society had never seriously contemplated a Republican Government.[12] They believed that only by constitutional means could redress for the Catholics be got. When the United Irishmen were driven underground in 1794 O'Conor Don and many of the members of the Catholic Committee disowned it.

The United Irishmen increased in numbers. Enrolment of the militia was met with great opposition in the 1790s and rural Ireland rose in groups called Defenders.[13] They first appeared in Co. Louth and spread throughout the country. They armed and drilled openly and made collections outside chapels. They were 'all of the lower order of Catholics' and they plundered for arms. Their threatening letters were published in Dublin and Belfast. In August 1794, Viscount Lord Dillon of Loughglynn reports to Dublin Castle on the state of the Barony of Costello – 'A deep impression had been made on the peasants and lower classes by the

French Revolution. There were constant uprisings. They committed the most atrocious acts when they imbibed spirits and they were less industrious than any of their class in Europe. Clergy and landlords had lost all influence over them. A great many foreigners as well as natives were endeavouring to stir up rebellion, under the pretence of imaginary grievances and the hopes of plunder and an equal division of property. 'Their object was to destroy the landlords' property'.[14] Dillon appealed to the Lord Lieutenant, the Earl of Westmoreland, to set up a cavalry force at Loughglynn for the protection of the area. For the next two years letters of appeal reached Dublin Castle from all parts of Ireland concerning the raising of Volunteer corps to help secure the internal peace of the country.

In 1796 Viscount Dillon again notified the authorities of the spirit of republicanism and revolution that was on the increase in the barony of Costello.[15] William, Earl of Camden, was now Lord Lieutenant and it appears Dillon had fallen out of favour in Government circles. 'I have never made a trade of politics', he said in a letter of 1 September 1796. 'I have been easily used; public faith has been abused to do me an injury. I have been deprived of my right when my expertise would have been as useful as it is honourable.[16] A preference has been given to the lowest jobber who has defrauded the public treasury by raising regiments composed of young boys and old beggars. There is no sacrifice that every honest man should make to preserve our existence as a nation.'

It appears that Viscount Dillon believed he had been promised by Westmoreland that he would be recommended to be made Knight of the Garter, but he was passed over in favour of some other person. Dillon lost no time in stating his feelings to the Lord Lieutenant. He felt threatened on all sides. On 28 May he received a letter from Edmund Dillon of Holywell near Ballyhaunis enclosing threatening letters written by a new secret society called Ribbon Men. They threatened to burn the village of Loughglynn and the town of Ballyhaunis and to kill the yeomanry of about three to four hundred and seventy men and they made it clear they would 'no longer obey the tyrant Dillon'.[17] Dillon immediately sought reinforcements. He got those in 1797 and in the following February and March he submitted a bill to John Davis of Dublin Castle for his Corps of Loughglynn cavalry. It came to £132.13s.7d.[18]

We have no definite figures of how many of these Ribbonmen were members of the United Irishmen. They were both secret and illegal societies. Rumours reached Dublin of a French fleet being sighted off the west coast. Landlords were raising volunteer corps for the protection of their baronies. Militia were being moved into small towns in increasing numbers. Irish agents in France – Tone, and others, were urgently pressing the Directory in Paris to send an expedition to Ireland early in 1798. General Humbert finally set out for Ireland in three frigates with a small body of 1,000 men, and 3,000 muskets.[19] He landed near Killala only to find the popular outbreak in Leinster and Ulster had been crushed for some time. He determined to challenge the overwhelming British force because he had further hopes of help from France. He was joined by large numbers of young men from Mayo and Sligo. At this time the whole of Connacht was in the control of the English under General Hutchinson who was quartered at Galway. On hearing the news he marched northwards to Castlebar with 15,000 cavalry and 1,000 infantry. To make victory more assured for the English, an officer of high military reputation, General Lake, had just arrived in Castlebar with extra forces. The French arrived across the mountains along the western shores of Lough Conn.

The English fled to Tuam thirty miles away, and many of them continued on to Athlone. By evening the flags of France and Ireland were flying from the chief buildings in Castlebar, and bonfires blazed on the hills of Mayo. Humbert stayed at Castlebar to await reinforcements from France. On the morning of 3 September, matters approached a crisis when a report reached Humbert that Lord Cornwallis, the English Commander in Chief was steadily advancing and within a day's march of the town. Humbert realised too late that he should have immediately pursued the enemy after the victory the week before. A general movement towards Connacht of all available units then in Ireland had already begun General Lake who had remained in Tuam after his defeat, now moved with 14,000 troops towards Frenchpark. There General Taylor, who was at Boyle joined him. With their united force they had instructions to move cautiously. General Nugent at Enniskillen was ordered to move south towards Sligo with 1,000 soldiers. Cornwallis left Tuam with 15,000 men for Hollymount.

Humbert had a high opinion of his own wisdom and did not take the advice offered by various Irish and French officers. All the Irish officers were against inaction. When Humbert received word that General Lake was bivouacking at Ballaghaderreen with 16,000 men, having come from Frenchpark, he decided against a sudden night attack on them there and he and his men moved towards Tubbercurry. The previous day the English commander had sent out a reconnoitering regiment of the Coolavin and Leyney cavalry under the charge of Colonel O'Hara, MP for Co. Sligo. After the first flush of the first few heroic weeks, the might of the English army crushed the Irish and French, and no help came from France. The French were forced to surrender at Ballinamuck and were treated as prisoners of war while the Irish were slaughtered without mercy.

THE PENAL DAYS AND THE YEAR OF THE FRENCH

BALLYMOTE CASTLE

CHAPTER 4

EAST MAYO IN THE EARLY NINETEENTH CENTURY

A work entitled *Statistical Survey of County Mayo* drawn up in 1801 for the Dublin Society (later the R.D.S.) by a medical doctor named James McParlan (and dedicated to the Marquis of Sligo) paints a revealing picture of the life and work of the people, and above all, of their dire almost unimaginable poverty. His observations on the barony of Costello are reproduced here in sequence to give a picture of conditions in Sliabh Lugha and in the neighbouring parishes to the south just under two centuries ago.

> The soil and surface of the whole barony, with a few exceptions, is either bog, reclaimed moor or mountain. These exceptions are Edmondstown, the seat of Mr. Costello; about the town of Balladerrin; at Lung and Cloonmore, where some good grounds are to be seen. Between Ballyhaunis and Donmacreeny there are some green grounds; and in that line towards Becon and Clare, there is a green aspect; but the soil is very light, of a moory quality, and seems to have been reclaimed. [p18]

> There is in this barony some little degree of improvement in its mode or tillage. But still the implements of husbandry, and execution of work, are both of a very inferior kind; in the mountainy parts being too soft for horses, and also in many other parts, which are too rocky, the spade is used; the plough in the open parts of the country, which are not very many. This very bad description however does not apply to Mr. Costello, and a few other gentlemen, residents of this barony. [p.27.]

> The only extent of agriculture is now in potatoes and oats. Formerly this was a great barley country, but the prohibition against malting, which prevented the gentlemen from taking from their tenants barley in payment of the rent, has completely stopped the culture of that article, and materially hurted the tillage of this barony; as, before that act, the tillage was double as much as now. Edmondstown alone is, perhaps, the only place where wheat is grown. [p.30]

[Course of crops:] In the best parts, suppose at Edmondstown and Balladerrin,1.potatoes; 2. potatoes; 3. flax; 4.wheat; 5, and 6, and sometimes 7. oats. In the mountainy and less fertile parts, when well manured with limestone gravel and dung and drained 1 potatoes; 2 potatoes; 3 oats; if fallowed 4 flax; and then laid down with grass it becomes good pasure or meadow..[p.33]

[use of oxen – how harnessed:] They had been used at Edmondstown; they are now disused, Mr. Costello having moved to Glasnevin; and none in the barony. But he has experienced so much of their utility, that he is again getting into the use of them.[p.35]

[Use of green food in winter] It is not used in this barony. Mr. Costello feeds his sheep with hay, and gives each one a pint of oats per day; they not only keep up their fat in high perfection, but fatten on this food, as do his cows and bullocks, by feeding them abroad on hay and potatoes. [p.39]

[Pasture – nature of it:] The few good grounds which this barony exhibits, are of a remarkable for fattening, and return of tallow. Those only make part of one half of the barony, the other being mountain, and the remainder is a light, moory, or reclaimed pasture. [p.42]

[Breed of cattle, how far improved – how far capable of further improvement:] It is now, and only now, in a commencing state of improvement; and, though a few spots of the ground are of excellent quality, yet one half of the barony being mountain, and much of the greatest part of the remainder only either very light or moor ground, does not promise a great capability of improvement in the breeds of either sheep or neat cattle. [p.42]

[Markets or fairs for cattle:] Balladerrin, Ballina, Costello, Kilkelly, and Ballynavness. [p.46]

[modes of feeding – how far housed in winter:] The cattle housed here are generally milch cows, which are brought in to make part of the family during the winter; the others are fed abroad in hard weather, frequently on the dunghill. which is always at the door. [p p 57-8]

The method of haymaking here is very good; it is picked, shaken, and put into lapcocks from the swarth, the day it is mown, and shaken out daily, and cocked before night, till saved; by which process the substance and colour are both preserved. [p.61]

The common price of wool here is sixteen shillings per stone; hides three pence per pound, and tallow eight shillings and eight pence per stone. The quantities sold are not considerable, the hides and tallow being only from the home consumption of beef, and all the wool bought up by the poor of the country for their clothing.[p.61]

The farms here being set at a bulk rent, and great pieces of mountain generally attached to them, are of considerable extent, from one to four hundred acres, mostly in the possession of villagers. [p.64]

[Farm houses and offices:] The richest of the yoemen farmers have not a second hearth, nor windows to subject them to that tax, although paying an annual rent of from one to two hundred pounds; the houses are built of stone, and dashed with clay-mortar, and seldom in any of them a chimney. [p.66]

[Proportion of working horses or bullocks to the size of farms:] The villagers here, who are in partnership, divide themselves, according to their numbers, into four or eight parties; each party keep a horse, the joint property of the whole, which horses do in common the work of the village. By this method it turns out, that every two villagers, holding about ten or twelve acres of green ground, will have one horse. [p.70]

The only fences here, with little exception, are bad stone walls. [p.73]

The poor of this country, none indeed but the gentry have got into the practice of hedging ditches with thorn, or anything else; where they are put down they thrive prosperously, which is the case of all the gentlemen seats.[p.75]

[Nature of manures:] In the north-east of the barony limestone-gravel is found everywhere; in the north-west mostly marle; in the southern parts gravel is the principal manure; it is sometimes of limestone. The inhabitants here are just getting into the mode of paring and burning; those are all they they have, and use beside composts and dung. [p.80]

[Habitation, fuel, food, and clothing of the lower rank – their general cost:] Habitations in general, though bad, not the worst in the country. Fuel, plenty of turf; food, potatoes, oaten bread, milk, flummery, cabbage mixed with salt and butter, thin gruel. The cost (and this computation too may stand for the county) of six in a family will come to about twenty seven pounds, calculating on the average price all, that the potatoes, meal, milk, and butter they consume, at two

cows to a family, if sold would bring. But although the articles, if sold, might bring prices to make up that sum, a more reasonable calculation might be from fifteen to twenty pounds – clothing very good; the men wear friezes, and some a finer cloth, thickset breeches, and red coating and pressed cloth waistcoats; the women too are neatly dressed, many of them in cottons and red cloaks.[p.90]

[Price of labour and provisions:]... the general price of labour all through the country... is eight pence per day without food, six pence per day and dinner; the cottiers have about six pence per day short and long, but have good bargains of house, land,and turbary. ...Occasional workers, such as shearers and mowers get from ten pence to twelve pence with food. Provisions are now (December) a drug: potatoes fell at 1s. 1d. per hundred weight, and must be cheaper when the armies are reduced; good beef three pence, and mutton three pence halfpenny per pound, and a proportionate cheapness in all other sorts of provisions. [p.91]

[Use of beer and spirits – whether either or which is increasing:] The dearness of provisions for the last three years, the suppression, or rather the suspension of the distilleries, and the act against malting, have completely over-ruled the use of both beer and spirits throughout this country in consequence of the dearness of price, to which those causes have raised them. In the barony of Tyrawley, and the interior of the county, the viligance of the revenue- officers has kept down private distilleries, but in the remote and mountainous parts they went on in the worst of times, and are now working in full plight in the baronies of Clanmorris, Costello, and in many other places; so much so, that now once more, as they have plenty to eat, they are resolved to have plenty to drink. There is a deal of beer brewed in Castlebar; a great deal has been brewed in different parts, for instance, in the barony of Costello, until the act had been made against malting, which in a great measure prevented the growth of barley, the use of that innocent and nourishing beverage beer, and checked in some degree the career of agriculture. [pp 92-3]

[Of navigations and navigable rivers:]...The river of Lung, which runs into Lough Gara, is navigable for eight or ten miles, from above the bridge of Crenan, for boats of ten ton, except in a few spots,not amounting in all to a mile. Lough Gara is ten miles long to Carrowmore, within a mile of Boyle, and navigable for boats of any weight; from Carrowmore to Lough Key, by the river of Boyle, a distance of about one mile and a half, could at an easy expense be made navigable; and from thence to the Shannon, a space of about five miles, by the excavation of about one mile, could also be made navigable. Lough Gara, near Boyle, touches on the borders of Roscommon, Sligo and Mayo; it is in some places five miles across; its banks are for the most part excellent for tillage and fattening; those banks are likewise in the neighbourhood of coal and iron ore, consequently opening this navigation might eventually prove an extreme public utility. [p p 94-5]

[Of fisheries:]... Probably all the lakes and rivers of the county abound with all sorts of fresh-water fish, and many of them are the depots for all the salmon to deposit their spawn in. Cloonlomley river, in the barony of Costello, is the chief nursery for the Ballina fishery, and is now in the care of bargers, Those bargers, or persons appointed to watch the rivers where the salmon come up to spawn, are extremely troublesome, in entering the houses of peaceable inhabitants at late hours, abusing and beating them when not in bribe. This I write by desire of a gentleman of Carra, who is ready to prove it. ...Fresh-water fish of every kind, and the best qualities, abound in all the lakes and rivers of this county.[p p 96-7]

[State of education, schools, and charitable institutions:] Petty schools, kept and paid for by the poor, are the only source of education here, except Mr. Costello's school, supported by him for the poor of his estate in this barony. I am desired by good authority to state, that there is not one school of the 40s. endowment in any or either of the eight parishes of this barony; and I am sorry to observe that few, very few of them are kept in this or any other county I am acquainted with. No charitable institution. [p.100]

[Of absentee and resident proprietors:] Resident: Costello, Charles, *Edmondstown:* Bettagh,– *Mannin*; Dillon,John, *Lung*; Dillons, Miss,*Cottage*; Dillon, Luke, *Anna*; Hughes, James, *Balladerrin:* McDonnell Myles *Cloonmore:* O'Malley, Alexander, *Eden*; Nolan, John, *Logboy*; Ormsby, *Bowen*; Taffe, Henry, *Woodfield*; French, Fredrick.

Non-resident: Bermingham, John, *Dalgan;* Costello, Patrick, *Galway*; Dillon, Colonel, *Hazel-hill*; Dillon Lord; French, Arthur, *French-park:* Knox, William, *Dublin;* Knox, Arthur, *Woodfield.* [p.106]

[Of manufactures – whether increasing:] The flax and yarn are here

in very brisk plight; large quantities of both are sold raw and in linens. [p.110]

At Ballina, Costello, and different parts of the county, is abundance of fuel and water, and consequently every aptness of situation for bleach-greens, many of which are still necessary in this county, so extensive and considerable is grown the linen business; and every branch of trade could be here promoted, which requires fuel, water. An abundant provision country, and conveniently intersected and indented with good roads and safe harbours.[.p.111]

[Of mills of every kind:] Here are common corn mills in abundance; rape-mills, from the quantity of the grounds, and number and course of the river, call here for encouragement. [p.113]

[Plantations and planting:] None here of any note but on the demesne of Edmondstown, which is extensively planted and wooded, and a little at Mr. McDonnell's at Cloonmoore. Lord Dillon had a small wood near Balladerrin. [p.116]

[Quality of bog and waste ground:] Thirty miles by twenty; bog, mountain, and waste, fifteen by ten. [p.121]

Possibility and means of improving it — [Baronies of Burrishool, Murrisk, Carra Galen and Costello:] The mountains and bogs of all those baronies are every foot reclaimable, by the already mentioned and well known means of burning and sanding after draining, where necessary; but vast tracts of those mountains are naturally dry and absorbent, and the best manures no where unreasonably inconvenient; so that in fact the work only requires hands and encouragement. In one of those baronies Mr. Costello twenty one years ago set a large mountain farm, at 130s 1d. a year, to a number of tenants, with certain allowances for draining and sanding. At November last the lease expired, and they renewed at 400s 1d. annual rent, with the like clauses for improvement. [p p 121-2]

The following illuminating description was published in 1834:

Costello, a barony, on the western border of Co. Mayo, Connaught, is bounded on the north by Co. Sligo, on the east by Co. Sligo,and Co.Roscommon, on the south west by Clanmorris, and on the west by Clanmorris and Gallen. Its greatest length from north to south, is nineteen and a half miles; its greatest breadth from east to west is fourteen and a half miles and its area is 144,462 acres. A very large proportion, particularly along the north and east, is bog a considerable proportion is moorish upland, and a very small proportion presents an inviting or pleasing aspect. Much of the interior may be regarded as elevated table-ground, having in its centre the summit-level between the basins of the Moy on the north west, the Corrib on the south west, and the Shannon on the east. The declination towards the Moy comprises more than one half of the whole area, and sends off its drainage by the Owen-Garrow and the Guishden rivers; the declination towards the Shannon supplies the main head-streams of the Gara or the Boyle; and a patch of bog in the extreme north east declines towards the basin of the bay at Sligo. Lough Gara briefly touches the eastern border; and a number of shivering, boggy lakes expand cold bosoms in the interior. This barony contains part of the parishes of Kilcolman, Kilturragh, Castlemore, and Knock and the whole of the parishes of Annagh, Aughamore, Becan, Kilbeagh and Kilmovee.

Four townlands of Castlemore and two of Kilcolman, with a population of 949, were transferred by the act 6 and 7 William IV, to the barony of Frenchpark Co. Roscommon. The chief town is Ballahadereen. The population of Costello in 1831 was 44,985. Houses numbered 8,655. Families employed chiefly in agriculture, 7,543; in manufactures and trade, 1,039; in other employment, 326. Males at and above five years could read and write numbered 1,313; who could read but not write 184, who could neither read nor write 17,334.

Castle-more, a parish partly in the barony of Frenchpark, Co. Roscommon, but chiefly in the barony of Costello, Co. Mayo, one and a half miles south east of Ballaghaderreen: and eighteen miles north- west by west of Strokestown, Connaught. Length south eastwards, two and a half miles; breadth two. Area of the Frenchpark section 2, 107 acres; of the Costello section 6,807 acres. Population of the whole. In 1831, 3,532. Houses 615. Population of the Costello section, in 1831, 3,194. Houses 504. The land has of four distinct qualities; but the general appearance of the surface is moorish and bleak. The interior is traversed by the road from Longford to Swinford and Ballina. The castle whence the parish has its name was built, some say by the Dillon family, others say by the Costelloes and is a ruin of no note. Their parish is a vicarage in the diocese of Achonry. The vicarial and the rectorial tithes are each compounded for £69. 4s. 7.1d and the latter are impropriate in Viscount Dillon. The vicarages of Castle-more, Kilmovee and Kilcolman (see these articles) constitute the benefice of Castle-more. Length, fifteen miles; breadth three; population in 1831, 12,355. Gross income, £274. 13s. 3d (nett income £228. 17s 1d.). The church was built in 1798, by means of a gift of £461. 10s. 9d. from the late Board of First Fruits.

There are two Roman Catholic chapels in Kilmovee, and two in Kilcoleman. In 1834, the inhabitants of the parish were all Roman Catholics. In the same year two daily schools in the parish: [one of them which was aided with £10 a year from the National Board, and had emoluments worth about £4 from Lord Dillon] had on their books one hundred and two boys and forty girls.

In 1840, the National Board had within Castle-more parish one school at Brusna and another at Aughalusta. In Kilcolman parish in 1835 the population was 5,427. There were no widows or children without relations to support them. All labourers went to England, for periodical employment.

Many of them were married. They were called spalpeens and often left provision for their families for the time they were absent. When they were short they often went a-begging for provisions. No payment was accepted for lodgings. All the farmers and cottiers gave lodgings without any charge. No one died of destitution in the three years previous to the Report.

An interesting report of the poor of Connacht 1835 states that Castlemore had a population of 3,094. On inquiry there were no deserted children and none had died of neglect. One child was being supported by charity. Between one hundred and two hundred were poor and were supported by the charity of neighbours and relations. About six hundred men were in the habit of going to England as labourers for periodical employment. Half of these were married and some owned their own houses. About one hundred and fifty had to beg from door to door for provisions in the summer but they never sought money. No one in the area took in lodgers. Local people took in strolling beggars and gave them lodgings gratis. None died from destitution in the three previous years 1832-34, except by the gradual effect produced by want.

A report furnished for Samuel Lewis's Topographical Dictionary in 1837 describes Kilcoleman and Ballaghaderreen:

> Kilcoleman, a parish, partly in the barony of Coolavin, Co. Sligo, but chiefly in that of Costello, County of Mayo, and province of Connaught, on the new mail coach road from Longford to Ballina. containing, with the market and post town of Ballaghaderreen 5,021 inhabitants. It comprises 13,030 stature acres, of which 5.880 are bog; the land is general of very inferior quality, and the system of agriculture un- improved. Limestone is very scarce, but there are some quarries of freestone of very good quality. The seats are Edmondstown, the resident of the Costello family, Clogher, of R. Holmes. Esq,; and Coolavin House, of C.J. Mac Dermot, Esq. The parish is in the diocese of Achonry; the rectory is impropriate in Lord Dillon, and the vicarage forms part of the union of Castlemore. The tithes amount to £190, payable in moieties to the impropiator and the vicar. The church in Ballaghaderreen is a small building, serving for the vicarial union; and the Ecclesiastical Commissioners have recently granted £110 for its repair. In the R.C. divisions in the parish is the head of a union or district, comprising also Castlemore and containing chapels at Ballaghaderreen and Cragaduff. There are six public schools, some which are aided by donations from Lord Dillon, Mr. Holmes, and the incumbent, affording instruction to about five hundred and eighty children, and there is a private school, in which are about eighty children. There are some remains of the old parish church.
>
> Ballaghaderreen market and post town, in the parish of Kilcoleman, barony of Costello, County of Mayo, and province of Connaught, 12 miles (west by

south west) from Boyle, and ninety seven and three quarter miles (west by north) from Dublin, containing 1,147 inhabitants. This town is situated on the new mail coach road from Ballina to Longford, and consists of three principal streets, containing 200 houses, of which nearly all are neatly built and slated. Here are infantry barracks, adapted to the accommodation of four officers and ninety two non-commissioned officers and privates. Many improvements have taken place recently in the town, which is rapidly rising in importance. The markets are on Fridays and fair days are held on March twenty-fifth and twenty-sixth, May first, June twenty-fifth, August first, September eighth and December twenty-second. The market house is a commodious building and and a court house has been erected in which petty sessions are held every Tuesday. A chief constabulary police and coast-guard stations have been established here and there is an R.C. chapel. Within a mile of the town are the ruins of Castlemore.

The half parish of Kilcoleman is in the barony of Coolavin. It contains 4,550 acres three roods and one perch, and is divided into nine townlands, Monasteraden, Clogher, Fauleens, three islands in Lough Gara, Crow island, Shroof, and Townmuckleigh. An ancient burial ground at Tawnmuckleigh has yet to be investigated.

The Mayo historian Hubert T Knox (d. 1921) has the following account of Kilcolman parish:

Kilcoleman– Cholumbain i.e. Celle Columbani signifies the Church of St. Colman whose festival is not now remembered in the parish. There were more than fifty St. Colmans in the Lives of the Saints. THe Annals of the Kingdom of Ireland note that Colman Finn or Colman the Fair was the particular St. Colman who had his church and cell here in the sixth century. The ruins of the Church of Kilcolman lie about a half mile on the Sligo road outside the town of Ballaghaderreen. The ruins surrounded by a venerable graveyard, are on a circular fort, with only a crumbling pile of moss-covered stones to be seen.

Another monument on the left hand side of the Ballaghaderreen-Monasteraden road is St. Attracta's well, a few hundred yards beyond the impressive entrance to Coolavin House. It is bounded on three sides by walls, the centre one being a limestone slab, on which the figure of Christ is sculptured with scenes from the Passion carved on both sides. Tradition has it that the work was done by a 17th century local artist. On 11th August the feast of St. Attracta was celebrated as a double minor Rite of the diocese of Achonry by kind permission of his late Holiness Pious [1X] granted on 28 July 1864 at the request of the Bishop of Achonry, Dr. Patrick Durcan. As a double festival this commemoration of St. Attracta has been extended to the whole church in Ireland. There is no saint of the diocese of Achonry more celebrated after Nathy than Attracta. She and her brother Coemhan were children of Tolan, a chief of the Gregraide of Loch Techet (now called Lough Gara). Coemhan was ordained at Killaraght. He built a church on the smallest of the Aran Islands – Iniseer – and is known as its patron saint: St. Coemhan of Airtne. In ancient times the island was known as Ara Coemhan.

St. Attracta, according to the 9th century *Tripartite Life of St. Patrick* received the veil from St. Patrick at a place called Machaire, which was later renamed Cill Athracht. In the 7th century account of Patrick's missionary travels by the north Mayo bishop Tireachan there is mention of 'Cella Adrochtae' but no reference to the saint who gave name to the place. Attracta established a hospice for travellers which was said to be the first of its kind in Ireland. Her fame was so great that several places in the area were called after her; Cill Athracht, Tobar Athracht, and Clochán Athracht. The Cross of St. Attracta was famed during the middle ages – it is referred to in a document preserved in the Calendar of Papal letters at the year 1413 (vol. VI, P. 451). The Ó Mochain (Maughan) were hereditary keepers of the relic – they are termed 'maoir na Croise Athracht' in a text in the Book of Lecan written about the year 1400. They were in effect managers of St. Attracta's extensive establishment at Killaraght; one of the family, Cornelius, was bishop of Achonry from 1449 to 1473, and two earlier members, both named Gregory were successively archbishops of Tuam from 1372 to 1383 and from 1384 to 1386 respectively. A 'pattern' was held each year at St. Attracta's Well (Tobar Athracht) on 11th August. Such public celebrations of the patrons of holy wells persisted even through the penal era despite government disapproval; in the 19th century the Catholic Church authorities also, discouraged the practice as they considered it had become open to abuse – in many instances it had indeed become become an occasion of excessive drinking, faction-fighting and general immorality. There has been no celebration at St. Attracta's well since the early forties.

The following are the townlands (or 'villages') in Ballaghaderreen/Castlemore Catholic Parish as locally understood. The Ordinance Survey spelling is given in brackets where this differs from the local spelling. Some of the places named, however, are not officially considered townlands; some are marked on the Ordinance Survey maps as subdenominations of townlands while others, though known locally, do not appear on maps or in other official publications.

Cathedral Area:

Aiteentagart [Attiataggart], Aughalustia [Aghalustia], Banada, Bockagh, Boherbee [in Derrynacross], Boleysely, [Boleysillagh], Castlemore [Ballymaging or Castlemore], Clover Hill [?], Crennane [Crunaun], Culadine [Killadangan], Culherin [Killkeeran], Doogra [Doogary], Drumnalasson [Drumnalassan] Icelawn [ishlaun], Knocknacunny [Knockanaconny], Lessine [Lissian], Lung, Raherolish [Raherolus], Rooskey [Roosky], Slievemore [?], Stripe [?], Tomanaghy [Toomanagh].

Monasteraden Area:

Ardvarna [Ardvarnagh in Tullaghanrock], Ballinagreath [in Tawnmucklagh], Ballinaloghane [in Tawnmucklagh], Boleyhely [boleysillagh], Clogher, Clooncunny, Cloonmeen, Creggane {Creggan], Cross [Cross, North and South],Curry, [Curry in Tullaghanrock], Drumacoo, Edmondstown [Tullaghanmore or Edmondstown], Fauleens[Falleens], Kilcolman, Laragon[Largan], Lumcloon[Lomcloon], Monasteraden [Monasteredan and Annaghbeg or Monasteraden], Rylawn [in Tawnmucklagh], Shroof [Shroove], Tallaghan[?], Tobracken [Toobracken], Townabrack [?].

Derrinacartha Area:

Bohalis [Bohalas], Broher [Brogher], Cloonmeen [Cloonmeen East], Dernabrock [Derrynabrock], Dernaslieve [Derrynasleeve], Deeacroma [Derrachroma], Derreen, Derrinacartha [Derrynacartha], Derryawne [?], Salmonford [?] Slievemore [?], Tavanaghbeg [Tawnaghbeg], Tonragee [Tonregee].

Brosna area:

Ardcull [ardkill], Bailure [?], Barnaboy, Boughtiduff [Boghtaduff], Castleard [Sachelard], Kilvaloon [Kilvaloon].

Both Cloontia and Brosna are well known districts in the parish but neither is a townland. The names of the following townlands are not in general use today: Bailure, Glanmore, Rylawn and Stripe.

Mention of Lessine (Lissian according to the Ordnance Survey spelling) in the Cathedral Area list calls to mind the fact that the townland is linked, however tenuously, with a celebrated late medieval Irish manuscript. The manuscript in question, the *Liber Flavus Fergusiorem*('The Yellow Book of the O'Ferguses') – so named because for centuries it was in the possession of the well known medical family of O'Fergus in West Mayo – is a collection of ecclesiastical materials, mainly dealing with saints lives and in many instances, translated from Latin into Irish. It appears to have been written about the years 1430-40. The name of the scribe and the place of writing are unknown, but in a couple of cases an indication is given that earlier writers had been at work on texts which were incorporated into the Liber Flavus. For example, a note which occurs in the middle of the page at folio 23rb – in between the text of a form of service of the dying and a list of twelve articles of faith – reads as follows in English translation: 'Seán Ua Conchobair put these small matters into Gaelic, and Donnchadh Ua Maelchonaore wrote them at Lios Aedháin in Ciarraighe of Airdí (Ciarraighe of Airteach), in the house of Ruaidrí Ua hUiginn, in great haste; and I implore mercy of Christ'. There can be no doubt that the phrase 'Lis Aedháin a Ciarraighe Airdí' [Ciarraighe of Airteach] refers to Lissian which, when Irish was still spoken in the area in the mid-19th century, was known as Lios Aodáin. As for the three men mentioned in the note, the noted Irish scholar Professor Edward Gwynn, sometime Provost of Trinity College, Dublin, suggested three- quarters of a century ago that they are to be identified with three individuals whose respective deaths are mentioned in the annals; Seán Ua Conchobair who died in 1391, Donnchadh Bán Ó Maoil Chonaire who died in 1404 and Ruaidhrí Ruadh Ó hUiginn who died in 1425.

While there are grounds for doubting the identification of Seán Ó Conchobhair with a man of that name who was killed in 1391, the other two suggested identifications seem plausible enough. We can therefore suggest with some confidence that a man named Ruaidhrí Ó hUiginn, described in the annals as a learned scholar, lived in Lissian at the beginning of the 15th century and that his house was a scene of literary activity some time about the year 1400 when another scholar, Donnchadh Bán Ó Maoil Chonaire, member of a great Roscommon learned family, penned the original copy of some religious texts – perhaps having first translated them from Latin into Early Modern Irish – some thirty years before they were preserved for posterity by being transcribed into the *Liber Flavus Fergusiorum.* Thus has Lissian/Lessine (or, more correctly, Lios Aodáin) earned for itself a tiny but honourable niche in Irish literary history. It is one which at least deserves to be brought to the notice of all schoolchildren in the locality.

The townlands of Aughalusta, Lissine and Rooskey are in the barony of Frenchpark. The townland – or 'village' as it was locally called – of Aughalusta is two miles south of Ballaghaderren and is separated from it by the Lung river. The name Aughalasta is derived from two Gaelic words – Achadh, meaning a plain or field and Losaid – genitive Loiste – meaning a trough or kneading trough. Joyce in his work on Irish place names indicates that 'good pasture land' would be an apt translation for Achadh Loiste. We notice that' Achadh' figures prominently in placenames in Longford, Leitrim and north Roscommon. It is generally accepted that Gaelic place- names accurately reflect the topography of the districts in question. Achadh is no exception, for more than 700 acres in that village are comparatively fertile.

In about 1670, the landlord, Dominic French, whose mansion was at Dungar (later named Frenchpark), took possession of the estate of which Aughalusta formed a part. These lands of which he was deprived for being a Catholic were restored to him after the Cromwellian period. A member of the French family built a dwelling on the Aughalusta lands and lived there for some time. Well founded tradition has it that numerous evictions from the lands took place at various times.

With the exception of the Gordon property, given to them in 1840 by Lord French, the rest of the land in Aughalusta and the surrounding villages was poor, consisting mainly of reclaimed bog, and holdings were small. The large families eked out a harsh existence until they were old enough to emigrate. For generations the relentless flow of emigration continued until the middle of this century when the exodus had reached a trickle for sheer lack of numbers.The school built in 1884 was forced to close down for want of pupils. Time was when that two- roomed structure with a minimum of playing area housed 80 pupils from the villages of Rooskey –(Rúscaigh, meaning marshy land), from Lissine (Lios Aodáin), from Liosargool (which is in Irish Lios ar gCúl, meaning the fort at the rear). This Lios or fort in Flannery's field in Lissine is one of a line of forts from Crenane. The school bearing the proud device 'Aughalusta National School 1884' is almost a ruin. Emily Lawless' plaintive lament for the Wild Geese after Limerick could be aptly applied to the youth of Aughalusta and the surrounding villages: *'We tossed them to the howling waste, and flung them to the foaming sea'*. These lines could be applied to almost every townland in the barony of Costello.

EAST MAYO IN THE EARLY NINETEENTH CENTURY

Boyle Abbey

CHAPTER 5

SECRET SOCIETIES

Rural Ireland had been oppressed by landlords, magistrates and yeomen for so long that by the early 19th century agrarian secret societies were thriving; they let nothing stand in their way. The basic cause of the unrest in those years was, as always, 'the land question'. At this time many poor Irish people tried to eke a bare living from the soil in the most abject poverty. The population continued to rise inexorably. There was a desperate demand for land which in turn raised rents and made tenure uncertain. Subdivision by landlords and subletting by tenants left 'landgrabbers' such as agents and middlemen acting as intermediaries between the landlord and the men who actually cultivated the soil. That there was no overall open revolt can perhaps be attributed to the memory of the bloody suppression of 1798. The people were utterly leaderless in those dark years.

English administrators were baffled at the complexities of the Irish problem. A section of rural Irishmen, bound together by oaths and armed with stolen weapons, and sometimes dressed in rough uniforms, formed secret societies called Ribbonmen in many parts of Ireland, including the barony of Costello. They carried out 'agrarian outrages' to avenge grievances against landlords, magistrates, policemen, soldiers and often Catholic clergy. It has been noted that the Irish Catholics in the first decade of the 19th century were in the habit of forming a branch of the Ribbonmen to equal every Orange Club in the country.

Tithes had to be paid by all Irishmen, both Protestant and Catholic, towards the maintenance of the clergy of the Established Church. Tithes were a tenth part of profits and stock of lands. Down to the time of Henry VIII tithes were exclusively the property of the Church. Upon the dissolution of the monasteries, grants of property made to laymen included tithes which the monasteries had possessed as well as their landed estates. Tithes thus came for the first time into lay hands as a new form of property. These lay and ecclesiastical tithes continued to be paid in kind until 1823. When Henry Goulburn was Chancellor of the Exchequer he adopted voluntary facilities for money payments. By the *Goulburn Act,* 4 Geo. IV., c.99, facilities were given for commuting both into money payment for limited periods. In 1832 by 2 & 3 Will. IV., c. 119 (*Stanley's Act*) compositions were made compulsory and universal. The Act passed for the exchange of tithes into money affected tithes in the hands of laymen as well as ecclesiastical tithes. Matters were so bad that Lord Londonderry sought the revival of the *Insurrection Act* and the *Suspension Act* in the House of Commons on 7th February 1822. These were repeated in 1825.[1]

It appears that the religious aspect of the Irish problem in the 19th century meant very little to the poor tenants and rural workers in the barony of Costello. Catholic emancipation had no meaning for them. They were too concerned with their immediate problems of survival. The result was the rise of agrarian societies and the spread of terrorism, to enforce their law over the law of the state. Each autumn brought a fresh series of outbreaks of rural violence. Local factions formed to keep peasant feuds alive, by gang fighting at markets and fairs. After the rebellion of 1798 these societies were driven underground, but in the first decade of the 19th century they appeared stronger and tougher than before. The speed with which the societies could be mustered together, if rents were raised or if produce was overcharged or sold to the military, caused surprise to the administration.

In July 1800 Lord Dillon writing to Dublin Castle said the country was perfectly quiet.[2] He felt he was responsible for this as he had imported provisions which eased the problems of violence and irregularity when people went in search of food. Shortly after this he appealed to Dublin Castle for troops to be quartered at Ballaghaderreen to prevent drunken riots and the robberies of revenues and because of clashes between 'lower classes of individuals which were brought into this country by Humbert. A spirit of incivility, irregularity and turbulence and public disorder of all kinds prevails'.[3] His letter was signed by seven Magistrates – John Dillon. John Nolan, C. Seymour, James Hughes (who was appointed the year before on the proposal of John Dillon), Myles McDonnell, Commissioner Taffe and J.B. Dillon. It seems the peace had not lasted for long.

In 1809 Luke Mannion, who lived one mile outside Ballaghaderreen was 'carded'. 'Carding' involved tearing a person's skin with steel carding combs used in preparing wool for weaving. Carders, the magistrates believed, were a secret society who had a clause added to their secret oath, 'to assist the French and Bonaparte'.[4] They attempted by force the redress of their grievances and caused consternation among peaceful citizens concerned for their personal safety and the safety of their property. Luke Mannion's crime was selling potatoes at the Ballaghaderreen market at a rate exceeding the regulation laid down by the carders. To prevent further outrages the magistrates arranged to meet every Friday to regulate markets and see that the peace was kept. They advised that the granting of compensation was the best preventive of outrage. Carders were intent on forcing a policy of controlling rents, protecting tenants from eviction and regulating the fees payable to the Catholic clergy. Mr Seymour stated that almost all the peasantry of the barony of Costello had a life interest in the baronial and parochial lands and they had a 'hearty dislike of thrashings, burnings and houghing'. In 1807 Mr Seymour reported to Dublin Castle on the destruction of tithe-oats: '240 stooks which was part of the Rectorial and Vicarial tithe oats of the lands of Aghalostia in the parish of Castlemore was scattered about and wasted' At Seymour's request the proprietors gathered the oats again but most of it was burned. He requested that a reward be offered.[5]

The Solicitor General at Roscommon reported the 'prosecution and unjustifiable' acquittals of Threshers.[6] Luke Dillon an informer was sentenced for perjury. Military protection had to be given to Thomas Sanford, one of the prosecutors. Mr Brannick reported disturbances at Ballaghaderreen and requested troops to be sent in. Mr Brannick had come to Ballaghaderreen at the request of Denis Browne, a landlord and brother of Lord Altamont, to inquire into the causes of disturbances.[7] One cause was faction fighting over the taking of a farm at a higher rent, as a result of which four cattle were houghed. Also, negotiators in the provision trade caused people to meet at night dressed in the array of Whiteboys. To counteract this, notices were put up in the name of Mr Browne promising rewards ('secrecy to be kept') for any information of disturbances and he asked the Government to order a company of soldiers from Boyle to be stationed at Ballaghaderreen.

Later we know that two magistrates, Mr Seymour and Mr Hughes, were accused under the Whiteboy Act 1807. Mr Seymour in a letter to Dublin Castle protested his innocence. He claimed that the Hon. Denis Browne 'was much irritated against him for having the presumption in his and Lord Sligo's absence to have written to Dublin Castle explaining the state of that part of Mayo'. He said that in reporting on the state of the poor and of outrages he included the fact that, aided by subscriptions from Mr Charles Costello and Mr Wyatt (agent for Viscount Lord Dillon), he bought up oatenmeal by the ton and hundredweight, which he sold out to the half starving poor by the pound at the wholesale price. They were both accused of aiding and abetting the supporters of outrage and violence. Mr Seymour pleaded their innocence and begged the Government for help. It is to be presumed that they were proved innocent, for two years later they were in charge of a military inquiry with other magistrates at Ballaghaderreen.

It was of course a well known fact that magistrates throughout Ireland often kept on the right side of Ribbonmen or Whiteboys in order that their

SECRET SOCIETIES

own personal lands or families would go unharmed.[8] Under the provision of the *Whiteboy Act* the magistrates had increased powers. The *Insurrection Act 1807* had been renewed in 1810 shortly before it was due to expire. It was such a severe measure that, even though it was never actually applied, it had been regarded as a success. Seven magistrates in special session could inform the Lord Lieutenant that their county was in a disturbed state. Then all people living in the proclaimed area were required to remain in their houses from sunset to sunrise, under penalty of seven years transportation. There was suspension of trial by jury. No proof of outrage was necessary against a person suspected of outrage beyond that of being out of doors after sunset. The court was presided over by an assistant barrister and as many magistrates as he could muster (no less than six). Apparently a provision of the Act was that anyone found in a public house after 9 p.m., was liable to transportation. If a person could show 'just cause' he was released.

In the early years of the century there were rumours and letters to Dublin Castle of another French invasion.[9] In 1811 one unsigned letter said 'the French are landing an army near Newport, Co. Mayo. A relative of Major Colonel McDonnell landed on the coast'. The letter goes on 'If the above proves true, I will put my name on the next communication'.[10] But the might of the British sea power made further French invasion of Ireland unlikely. Still letters poured in at various intervals to Dublin Castle. George French reported that in the event of a French invasion it would be necessary to keep a strict watch on a man called Hurley who was a steward for Mr Thomas Phillips of Cloonmore in Co. Mayo beyond Ballaghaderreen. He was very active before and in 1798. He had escaped from Ballinamuck.[11]

Assaults and murders were a common occurrence. Charles Costello, reported the murder of a soldier of the South Cork militia on the road from Ballaghaderreen to Boyle on 10th December 1811. Also two men were arrested, Richard Hanlon and Timothy Leane, both of that regiment, for the murder of Thomas Solan of Castlemore parish.[12] On 12th July 1812 a party of Threshers supposed to number from fifty to one hundred men attacked Solan's house: broke down his door, seized him, swore him to secrecy and obedience to their laws. They then carded him in a cruel manner and inflicted several severe wounds on his body with a blunt instrument. They then dragged him outside and made him kneel down. One of the party shot him in the back and, not satisfied with that, they broke his back with the butts of their guns. Then they attacked the man next door, cut off one of his ears and carded him severely. On the following Saturday the wife and two daughters of Thomas Solan swore evidence before magistrates Costello, Hughes and Seymour that Richard Hanlon was one of the party, and another daughter gave evidence that Timothy Leane was also one of the party. Both were committed to Castlebar jail. Not a shadow of evidence was given against any other person. It was an unwritten rule that people never gave evidence against each other.

It was noted that Thomas Solan was the only poor farmer who regularly brought potatoes to the market at Ballaghaderreen and supplied the militia there with provisions at a low cost.[13] A military inquiry was heard at Ballaghaderreen under Lieutenant Goodsall. The militia were reinforced with soldiers from Boyle, as well as some Dutch soldiers from Carrick-on-Shannon.

Charles Costello enclosed three threatening letters to Dublin Castle which were found on the chapel door at Gurteen.[14] One signed 'God save the King' the other 'Captain Conscience' and a third 'Fair Play'. The lives of Mr Costello, Mr Higgins, Mr McDonagh, Matthew Callaghan, and Mr Hehir were threatened and they were called extortioners for raising prices at markets and for buying poor people's land. A list of prices for vegetables and corn was made out, and, anyone who overcharged or was found breaking the Ribbonmen's Law would be made an example of in the whole country; have their cattle houghed and maimed and their houses plundered. In many places oaths were administered to prevent the inhabitants enlisting in the militia. Notices were posted on chapel doors against the prices charged by the Catholic clergy, fixing a price in their own law – 11s.4d for a marriage: 1s. 2d for an anointing, 1s 7d for a baptism and 5s. for a Mass. Tithes were to be as in 1782– not more than £6 per acre to be paid for dunged ground. A publican was not to get more than 4p per naggin for spirits or brandy.[15] The first two or three decades of the 19th century were beset with these disturbances.

Daniel O'Connell who was called to the Irish bar in 1798 and went on his first legal circuit 1799, became aware of the needs of the Irish poor Catholics in his daily attendance at these courts. He became in 1814-1815 the leader of the popular wing of the Irish Catholic Movement. On 29th April 1815, writing from his home at 30 Merrion Square, Dublin, to Owen O'Conor Don, Belanagare, Co. Roscommon, he named two of the most important promoters of the Ribbon system in that county– Pat Byrne (Paddeen or Patcheen) and a man called Fitzgerald.[16] It was against all the principles of the popular Catholic movement to condone the activities of the Ribbonmen against Protestant landlords or Catholic clergy.

In Boyle, Charles Costello certainly did not make himself the idol of the poor tenants. In 1817 he led a group of constables into Coolavin to beat off a gang of robbers who had infested the area.[17] He spent his time seeking information and arresting suspects and then appealing to Dublin Castle for advice. Houses in his area were broken into. In 1819 he sought the signature of the Lord Lieutenant on a warrant to search for arms on two occasions. He said the Ribbon system was spreading and that these men were organised in groups. Arms were taken forcibly, mostly in Coolavin, and money was robbed.

In 1818 Jarrard Edward Strickland came to Ireland as agent to the estates of Lord Dillon in Mayo and Roscommon in succession to Matthew Wyatt (an English barrister) who was agent from the last quarter of the previous century.[18] He had been an ensign in East India Company's Cavalry 1801-1813. Viscount Lord Dillon was an absentee Landlord by this time having been completely disillusioned by Irish politics. Mr Strickland was a magistrate and a well meaning Englishman. He thought at first that he could persuade the inhabitants of the barony of Costello to live peacefully and keep free of the Ribbonmen.[19] He talked to the people immediately around the estate and got promises of good behaviour from them. His naivety soon changed to incredulity. On 2 December 1819 he wrote to William Gregory in the Civil Department, Dublin Castle, concerning the state of the area. The alarming state of the barony of Costello and the borders of Galway had to be seen to be believed. Ribbonmen continued to carry on their misdeeds without check. They entered fields and stables and stole horses, every one they could find. Mounted two on a horse they went from parish to parish and dragged people from their beds and compelled them not only to take their oaths but to join them on the next night when they proceeded further.[20] Two weeks before this they had been in Ballinlough. The terror of their names travelled before them. The general message was that Ireland would rise again in rebellion and woe to those who did not join them.

In parts of Mayo roads were in such bad repair that horses could not travel on them. Being badly made through bogs the foundations of these roads sank into small lakes of marshy, muddy bog. The Ribbonmen stuck notices on the doors of the villages swearing vengeance if these roads would not be ready for them. The whole population turned out and did the work even though they appeared terrified. Yet they were more terrified not to do it.

Mr Strickland had taken out, on the Thursday before this, the party of militia from Ballaghaderreen. They journeyed out towards Ballinlough. A horseman challenged them and galloped off. Half a mile further on, ten to twelve horsemen challenged them and fled. They did not catch up with them. The following Sunday night these men entered Ballyhaunis and visited the home of a resident magistrate, Major O'Flaherty. They threatened the whole town if they would not take the oath. There were between one hundred and two hundred horses with two men on each and they were joined by fifty-five more horses. Major O'Flaherty did not have to take the oath. Three

SECRET SOCIETIES

nights later Mr Strickland took the party out again from Ballaghaderreen. They found Ribbonmen actively swearing-in all the villagers. If a rebellion were to start it would be difficult to put it down. He begged Mr Gregory to send a force to be stationed at Loughglynn where there was ample room for men and horses. It was impossible for the militia at Ballaghaderreen to be effective because of the distance, and indeed Charles Costello on many similar journeys had need of them and they were quite close to him.

Mr Strickland's letter arrived in Dublin after one from Charles Costello of Edmondstown who complained of armed meetings held at night in his area and of the military garrison at Ballaghaderreen being insufficient. Whenever he looked for them they were out on magisterial duty with Mr Strickland of Loughglynn. On one occasion the barrack was protected by two or three pensioners and two petty constables. People were seriously injured as public meetings were held, cattle were killed and haggards were burned. Houses were forcibly broken into at night. The borders of Sligo, Mayo and Roscommon were in a dreadful state.

Arthur French of Frenchpark reported house-breakings in his area and offered rewards for information. Armed men carried out outrages calling themselves 'Right' and 'Captain Dudley'. Two brothers in the Frenchpark area were in terror when their house was broken into by a band of armed men on 14th October 1817. They were given a book to swear the Ribbonmen's oath but they refused and were beaten. In Banada, Terence McDermot gave information to Arthur French of an attack on his house of about thirty to forty men on 24th December 1817 seeking guns. Armed men patrolled the area at night in disguise. He lived half-way between Ballaghaderreen and Frenchpark. They demanded and took arms for the people and caused terror in the neighbourhood. Arthur French sought extra military from the authorities to combat this situation.

The reasons for those dreadful disturbances in the areas along the borders of Mayo and Sligo may mostly be blamed on the landlords. They did not make any effort to deal with the abject poverty of their tenants. There was a scarcity of fuel. Landjobbers and middlemen were merciless in satisfying their own greed. The poor who were of a different religion to the Established Church, did not want to pay tithes to anyone. Collectors of tithes took care to pay themselves well from the produce of the county. This was one great cause of disturbance, dissatisfaction and rebellion. The poor Catholics wished to have this system changed and to pay the clergy by a general land tax – not as it had been up to then, a tax on the industry and labour of the Roman Catholic people. This was stated by one of the landlords himself – Denis Browne.[21] He said that he was not brave enough to state these things openly, as he would lose his standing in the

SECRET SOCIETIES

community of gentry. But he had secured a seat in the new parliament where he hoped to put forward as many of his opinions as he could.

Never before was there such a scarcity of fuel and fire. The comfort of a fire was an Irishman's haven when food was scarce. But in 1820 the landlords of Mayo and Roscommon closed their eyes to this need. The system of land letting was atrocious. The tenants might get a piece of mountainous bog to live on.[22] When they reclaimed a few acres the landlord put grass on it and they had to break more mountain ground. The conacre as it was called was another complaint. The inhabitants were so poor, they were unable to purchase food for their families. The big farmers had old pastures which they set out for tillage, but limited this so as not to glut the market. They charged ten guineas an Irish acre for ploughing this land. The poor were so desperate they often paid more than the value of what was produced, and were then at the mercy of the land jobbers. They also had to pay towards repairing churches, making roads and bridges. As many landlords were by this time absentees, great fortunes were made by bailiffs and middlemen. The laws were entrusted to the magistrates and commissioners of the peace, thus giving considerable advantage to the men of power. 'The law does not protect the people; it works against them. Laws break the poor and rich men break the laws'. So wrote Denis Browne M.P. on 5th February 1820; he saw the situation as it was but feared to speak publicly.[23] It is small wonder therefore that this state of affairs was being dealt with by the ruthless methods of the Ribbonmen, Whiteboys, Carders, and Molly McGuires.

On 7th February 1820 Mr Strickland wrote to Dublin Castle giving a lengthy statement of the area under his control – from Loughglynn to Ballyhaunis, from Swinford to Belahy and along the mearning of Sligo, back to the mearning of Roscommon beyond the town of Ballaghaderreen, which was most of the barony of Costello, and an angle of Roscommon – a distance of about twenty miles, thickly inhabited by a very poor population. There was not he said 'a single gentleman of property or influence residing near him to co-operate in the preservation of the peace'. Denis Browne of Cloone was twenty three miles away on the borders of Mayo and Sligo, and Mr Costello and Mr French of Edmondstown and Frenchpark were the nearest resident gentlemen. Soldiers were stationed at Ballyhaunis, Swinford, and Ballaghaderreen, and they assisted Mr Strickland in patrolling the country at night with him. He continually rode among the villages and encouraged the people to oppose the Ribbonmen. In this way he said he had formed a chain of villages from Ballaghaderreen to Ballyhaunis, a ten mile route whose people had all pledged to unite and oppose the Ribbonmen.[24] But he realised that the people were too miserable and helpless to be firm for long. He blamed the lack of interest taken by the landlords. He repeatedly requested help. Ribbonmen assembled 300-400 men at a time beside Loughglynn to attack the house in order to get arms. He arrested two of them and found two papers, one with the Ribbonmen's oath and the other with signs by which they were to know each other.[25] The papers, he said, proved that nothing short of rebellion was their object. On calling to houses along the roadside in the daytime he found the men to be absent, they being out with the Ribbonmen.

Mr Strickland eventually succeeded in getting eight dragoons and one sergeant stationed at Loughglynn to remain until the peace of the country was maintained. He got allowances from Colonel French, the General Quarter-Master in 1820, for billet money, stabling and forage. Peel, the Chief Secretary in Ireland had introduced a Peace Preservation Force in 1815 which had proved itself to be of value in the struggle against agrarian crime. The enormous expense in maintaining the force resulted in 1817 in *Peel's Amendment Bill.* By 1820 the cost was being divided evenly between the proclaimed area and the Irish Government. This force became known as 'Peelers'. During the winters of 1818-1820 and again from 1821-1823 a considerable portion of rural Ireland was swept by terrorism. On 15 November the entire county of Roscommon was placed under the *Peace Preservation Act* on the representation of twenty nine magistrates of that county. But it was not really the Government who put an end to the activities of the secret societies but the famine of 1821, when in Sligo, Mayo and Roscommon (and many other counties) the potato crop rotted in the ground and the Catholic poor were faced with starvation, and an epidemic of typhus broke out. The people were utterly exhausted and there was scarcely an outrage until 1822. A County Constabulary was established, and it remained in place, side by side with the Peace Preservation Force until 1836 when the latter was disbanded.[26]

Tithes were an important source of contention in Ireland in the early years of the 19th century. The *Tithe Composition Act* of George IV provided for the establishment of Composition for Tithes in Ireland for a limited time. It entitled the Lord Lieutenant to give orders, on the application of the Rector, for a special vestry to meet to carry out the Act.[27] The persons of that vestry should be living on tithe-lands and should have paid county cess charges and grand jury rates in respect of those lands in the previous year. The years from 1829-1831 were famine years complicated by economic distress. In 1830, under the leadership of Bishop Doyle of Kildare and Leighlin (the celebrated 'JKL') the Catholic clergy began a campaign against the tithes. O'Connell and his followers encouraged this. It began as a passive resistance. Tithe law provided that personal property could be taken if a person defaulted. It also provided that personal property in the form of livestock could be seized only between sunrise and sunset, and that animals behind locked doors could not be taken. Livestock of defaulters were hidden during daylight and locked up after dark. Sales of livestock taken were boycotted, but passive resistance did not last long. Constabulary detachments supported by troops were sent to collect the tithes. Between 1830 and 1834 several bloody encounters took place between police, soldiers and peasants. (The returns of Constabulary Stations within a radius of 12 miles of the town of Ballaghaderreen are in Appendix No.2. For parish returns see Appendix no. 3.)

At Ballaghaderreen, Henry D'Alton was sworn before the Commissioner on 23 September 1831 and powers of a Commissioner were vested in him in the parish of Kilcolman to collect tithes. Joseph Sandford was the Commissioner in question. Rev. Joseph Seymour, Rector, living in Glebe House, Castlemore, on twenty acres of land received a letter from the Bishop on 17th February 1832 enclosing a Certificate of Composition for the parish of Kilcolman to be included in the Composition Applotment Book for that parish.[28]

Lord Dillon Rector's part £95
Vicar's part £95
Total £190 (see Appendix for Tithe Applotment Books)

In 1830-31 agrarian secret societies again made their appearance. They were opposed to rent increases as well as tithes. There was the usual enforcing of oaths, raids for arms and brutal outrages to secure compliance with their laws. The presence of Orange lodges in a number of regiments caused some embarrassment to the Government. Faction fights reappeared. The disturbances developed into the so-called 'Tithe War' which lasted from 1830 to 1838. The establishment of the Irish Constabulary later the Royal Irish Constabulary in 1836, headed by an Inspector general under new regulations, saw the beginning of impartiality of police in dealing with the citizens.

The British government, by its Tithe Act of 1838, transferred the responsibility for payment of a new tithe rent charge (reduced by 24%) from the tenant to the landlord. The landlord had to collect from all tenants and he paid the parson out of this. This new shift made the parson dependent on the landlord. If the landlords failed to collect from the people, the Established Church clergy felt the pinch. It was clear that the landlord, the parson and the poverty stricken Catholics were caught up in a system centred around land, which has always been and always would be the most important question in Irish affairs.

CHAPTER 6

'THE BAD TIMES'
1830s and 1840s

An increase in the population, economic difficulties and a scarcity of food led to the formation of the Irish Poor Law system in 1838. Ireland was divided into Poor Law Districts, each with a workhouse under control of a Board of Guardians. But the greatest need of the Irish at this time was work. Had the Government set up public works before the famine to develop the natural resources of each province, matters might have been very different.

Daniel O'Connell opposed a Poor Law for Ireland, considering it a landlords bill which would increase pauperism and leave absentee landlords untouched.[1] Poorhouses would bring moral degradation on the inmates. It was not an economic policy as Irish tenant farmers could ill afford poor rates.

O'Connell supported the Commission of Inquiry which sat between 1833 and 1836 and recommended land improvement, agricultural education and a programme of public works.

It was no doubt due to hunger and desperation that many crimes were committed in the 1830s. The 1837 register of county jails lists the persons awaiting punishment – either of transportation or life sentence, depending on the crime– the names of convicts, age, offences of which they had been convicted, length of sentence, date on which they had been tried, name of the presiding judge, the name of the ship on which they were to be transported and the date of sailing. In one case in the barony of Costello a man got a life sentence for stealing a sheep. For larceny, sheep stealing, robbery with violence, horse stealing, forgery, pig stealing, the sentence was generally seven years. Many were transported on 18th April 1837. More were transported on the Clyde in May 1838.[2]

With the setting up of the Repeal Movement the question of civil and religious liberties came to the fore. The role of The Catholic Church was seen to be on the side of the poor and oppressed, although the secret societies did not trust the Church. Bishops and priests had little power at the beginning of the 19th century, but the Church had been given a tremendous boost by Catholic Emancipation in 1829. A massive pro-

'THE BAD TIMES'- 1830s and 1840s

gramme of building churches, schools, seminaries, monasteries and convents was provided for by legacies from the prosperous members of the Church and subscriptions and dues from all classes of the community. But to reconcile the religious and political problems was not easy. The passion of the tenants to become owners of their farms, especially in Mayo, Sligo and Roscommon, led to individual Catholics being caught up in secret oath bound societies and they committed acts of outrage or engaged in open armed rebellion. It was to some extent at least, a conflict between the descendants of former owners of the land and those who had dispossessed them and reduced them to the status of tenants and labourers.

Tithe collectors were murdered, cattle were houghed, sheep were driven over cliffs. Drink was a major problem. Men, stupefied with 'poteen', were seen staggering around the streets in every town. The temperance movement under Fr. Matthew and the Repeal Association under Daniel O'Connell probably mutually aided one another. But in the west Fr. Matthew's movement was unacceptable to Archbishop John MacHale of Tuam especially. In September 1841 in a letter to Dr. Cullen, Fr. Matthew claimed that Dr. MacHale had denounced him at private dinner tables where Dr. Durcan, and the Rev. Dr. MacNicholas, Bishop of Achonry, were present, 'as a vagabond friar traversing the Diocese of Tuam vending bits of Birminghan pewter and administering a pledge without the consent of Dr. MacHale'.[3] Dr. MacHale was also opposed to holding political meetings in chapels but he publicly favoured Repeal of the Union.

The census of Ireland of 1841 (the first one for which detailed returns are still available) gives us a perspective of the rural population – 46% of families lived in single rooms. Two thirds of families in Connacht lived in rooms totally unfit for human habitation. The census for the parishes of Kilcolman and Castlemore in 1841 indicate the large population and the problems the people must have faced.

'THE BAD TIMES'- 1830s and 1840s

CENSUS FOR KILCOLMAN and CASTLEMORE

KILCOLMAN TOWNLANDS

	Houses	Families	Males	Females
Attiantaggart	5	5	15	13
Ballaghaderreen	21	22	51	60
Ballyoughter	9	9	24	35
Bockagh	18	18	56	55
Boleysilligh	4	4	11	9
Brogher	10	10	30	38
Cloonlumney	105	105	342	303
Coollaghtane	5	5	16	16
Coollena	7	7	25	27
Creganne	24	24	74	82
Cross North	–	–	–	–
Cross South	22	22	56	56
Derynacross	17	17	48	47
Derryaogur	3	3	9	10
Doogara	8	9	16	20
Drumacoo	49	49	133	134
Fallsolus	6	6	15	13
Frasnadeffa	4	4	15	13
Hawksford	37	39	109	102
Islandmore	5	5	10	13
Kilcolman	4	4	15	15
Largan	24	24	63	76
Magheraboy	13	13	42	38
Toobracken	26	26	77	74
Tonregee	15	15	52	47

(Tullaghanmore or Edmondstown demesne)

Tullaghanrock	39	39	110	109
Banada	26	26	96	78
Keelbanada	40	40	84	103
Ballaghaderreen Town	202	289	673	669

Total Population 4,525

'THE BAD TIMES'- 1830s and 1840s

CASTLEMORE TOWNLANDS

	Houses	Families	Males	Females
Ardkill	41	41	99	90
Ballymaring (Castlemore)	33	33	107	104
Barnaboy	25	25	77	73
Boghtaduff	34	34	99	105
Bohalas	36	45	130	117
Castleard	17	17	58	52
Cashelcolaun	21	22	70	63
Cloonvallaun	2	2	7	10
Crunaun	49	49	144	120
Doogara	12	14	27	31
Drumnalassan	48	50	139	125
Friarshill	-	-	-	-
Glebe	1	1	4	3
Ishlaun	33	33	89	95
Killadangan	25	25	61	60
Kilvanloon	19	19	48	54
Kilkeeran	23	31	68	76
Lung	35	36	107	93
Poolboy	14	14	52	44
Toomanagh	8	8	40	27
Aghalustia	69	70	154	166
Cappagh	2	2	8	13
Lissian	13	13	44	34
Rooskey	27	27	97	72
Knockanaconay	29	33	89	87

Total Population 3,745 [4]

To feed eight thousand two hundred and seventy-three people in times of acute distress was a major problem. In Castlemore the Rev. Joseph Seymour of the Established Church, who had come to the parish in 1811, worked unfailingly with Dr.MacNicholas, Catholic Bishop of Achonry (who resided at Brooklawn House) and with Fr. John Coughlan, the Parish Priest, and Fr. P. Groarke, his curate, in alleviating the plight of the poor.

Thirteen times in Ireland before the Famine of 1847 the potato crop rotted in the ground. The distress caused to a people who depended completely on this crop must have been horrific, quite beyond description.

'THE BAD TIMES'- 1830s and 1840s

Remembering back to the late thirties myself, I can still recall the donkey carts full of potatoes heaped to a pile, as the little donkeys trudged up the hill to pass our house on the way to the market each Friday. We knew then that these small farmers depended solely on the return they received for the produce of their toil, for the purchase of their groceries and bare necessities of life. And if the prices were poor the farmer returned with his produce unsold. Those were fearful days.

But to go back to the period 1800 to 1847 and view the tragic happenings is well nigh impossible. It was only later that it was realised that the tragedy was caused by a disease which now appears was carried on ships from the United States and not only affected Ireland but spread right across Europe. We now call it potato blight. Growing the potato required little attention except at springtime and harvest. The fate of the potato crop meant literally the difference between life and death. In 1845, within a few days of digging the potato crop, the fine-looking tubers became a stinking mess of corruption. Alarm turned to terror. The Government relief for distress came too late. All I can do here is relate from records the situation as it was then in the barony of Costello.

The Catholic priest Fr. John Coughlan writing to the Quakers, praised the help given to him by Joseph Seymour in visiting fever-stricken cabins. He approved of Rev. Seymour representing the Catholic parish in Dublin when he went there to seek outside help for the Castlemore and Kilmovee people.[5] But Fr. Coughlan was very bitter against the landlords of the area – notably Lord Dillon and his agent Charles Strickland. He denounced the landlords in the columns of the *Evening Mail* and the *Sligo Champion* as ruthless rack-renters, especially Lord Dillon. The *Mayo Telegraph* 21st September 1836 had reported a popular demonstration in favour of Lord Dillon by the people of Ballaghaderreen for his kindness to his tenants in the barony of Costello. The same paper expressed concern for Mr. Strickland when he was ill. A Quaker, Joseph Crossfield, visited Lord Dillon's estate at Loughglynn in 1846 and spoke warmly of Charles Strickland and his sisters to the Central Committee, when he saw the help they were giving to the poor at this time. And the Quakers sent more relief aid to Mr. Strickland, than to any other applicants because of his good work.[6]

The letters continued from Fr. Coughlan and it is worth noting that some Catholic clergy came to the defence of Mr Strickland – the P.P of Ballyhaunis, and the clergy at Knock, and Aghamore. They said he did everything possible to assist local relief committees protect the people. They also made it known that Fr. Coughlan was an old enemy of the Strickland family. Charles Strickland had opposed a local politician, Joseph Miles McDonnell, while Fr. Coughlan supported him.

'THE BAD TIMES'- 1830s and 1840s

In the midst of severe poverty and hunger, outrages continued. At Barnaboy on 1st January 1843, Pat Towey's turf was set on fire and all burned.[7] At Ballindoo the oats of Owen Flannery and James McGovern was scattered and their lives threatened. A public reward was offered to bring to justice those who damaged property. The life of Dan Gallagher was threatened at the same time. On 2nd April a filly was killed belonging to Luke Prendergast in Fauleens. In Barroe a notice was hung up at a local church threatening persons who paid the priests dues on the old scale. In June a horse was killed belonging to Mr.Coll McDonnell at Hagfield. In Carrigarriff, Thady Fleming's mare's legs were broken. In September Bartholomew Casey's pound was broken open and Thomas Hanley's turf was set on fire. In May 1843 Pat Phillips was assaulted and died later. Pat Reid was set upon bailiffs while they attempted to destroy his property. At Ballyglass persons were threatened with vengeance who did not keep the pledge of curtailing the priest's dues. At Fauleens John Sreehan's turf was burned by mistake instead of Thomas Cotter's; the latter was accused of paying dues on a marriage at the old high rate.[8] These are only some of the outrages reported to Dublin Castle in 1843. On 21st August a letter was sent to Lord Lucas, Under-Secretary at Dublin Castle, from the Petty sessions at Ballaghaderreen written by Inspector John J. Kelly. A Repeal meeting was to be held at Ballyhaunis on Monday 28th August. Because a pattern was also being held on the same day (as it had for centuries) and hundreds of people generally attended it, an additional force was sought in case a breach of the peace occurred. The general state of excitement in that area over a Repeal meeting resulted in a force of cavalry being sent from Athlone under Major General Guy Campbell.[9]

An extraordinary movement among the people in the barony of Gallen which spread into the barony of Costello was reported to Lord Lucas. About 700 people gathered together on the Ballaghaderreen-Foxford Road. They did not believe they were breaking the law. Their priests were overcharging them and they would not submit to it. They prepared to go into Sligo across country in various directions. The Magistrate Mr. Green, saw crowds of people – about 2,000.[10] They explained when confronted that their object was to reduce the exorbitant charges of their priests. They had been sworn as a secret society to walk two days from sundown to sunset in the parishes adjoining them and to put up notices and give instructions to the people in those parishes to do likewise, until the message had spread all over Ireland. They refused to give any information as to those who had sworn them. They determined to carry on. They also objected to the high price of conacre and the high rents charged to them. One of the notices put up on the chapels read as follows:

'THE BAD TIMES'- 1830s and 1840s

> No 1 for marriage 10 shillings and certificate
> No 2 baptising one shilling
> No 3 for reading masses for the dead one shilling
> No 4 to give no oats to the curate

No 5 for wages five shillings a year; no money or potatoes to be given to a clerk; if the clergy employs servants let them pay them; confession to be heard in the chapel and likewise all children to be baptised in the chapel. You good men are to travel for two days from sundown to sunset. Any person or persons disobeying our orders to report to him for the Tubbercurry market and likewise Belaghy, Ballymote and Ballaghaderren. You are to go from parish to parish and spread this law into execution by the orders of Thomas Phillips, Joseph McDonnell, Mr. Jones Strickland. For your own sake don't ye neglect your duty.[11]

(All these notices were written without capital letters or punctuation. It appears to be written like this on purpose to disguise the fact that whoever wrote it was educated.)

The constable reported that similar notices were posted up at Tubbercurry, Swineford, Foxford and Killala. It appears that support for the Repeal Movement and the behaviour of the landless Catholics were not compatible. The Catholic clergy or the majority of them throughout the land backed O'Connell's Repeal movement, but in this area the people and the clergy were very much at loggerheads. Outrages continued in 1843. Grassland was turned up for tillage around Ballaghaderreen and many parts of Roscommon. The people who did this were called 'Molly McGuires'. On appeal to Sligo a stronger force of soldiers was sent into the town. Threats on the life of Mr. Strickland, allegedly by Patrick Duffy of Loughglynn, led to a notice being posted up around the area. Strickland sent a copy to Dublin Castle and explained that Loughglynn had been quiet for a while and almost all the inhabitants had arranged this meeting. The following is a typed version of the notice which was published by J. Siggins, Main Street, Boyle.

NOTICE

A LETTER having been written

And sent through the Post Office at Ballaghaderreen, addressed to Charles Strickland, Esq. J.P. as agent to Lord Viscount Dillon, threatening to take his life, if he did not comply with the writer's wishes.

'WE THE UNDERSIGNED, deeming such an act in this hitherto peaceable Country, as likely to lead to further outrages, unless checked in time REQUEST A MEETING WITH THE MAGISTRATES, GENTRY, AND CLERGY, and all other inhabitants of the barony of Costello who wish for and are interested in the preservation of the public peace at the COURT HOUSE of Ballaghaderreen on Friday, 19th April 1844 at the hour of twelve

'THE BAD TIMES'- 1830s and 1840s

o'clock noon to take such steps as may be deemed advisable not only for bringing the writer to justice, but also to adopt measures to prevent a reoccurence of such an atrocious act'.

This was signed by the following:

W.H.Daniel,J.P. James Beytagh, Michael Connell, John Caulfield, J.Seymour, J.P. Dominic, J. Betage, William Costello, Edward Kilgarriff, John Holmes J.P., Luke Fitzgerald, Thomas Higgins, Pat Peyton, James Dillon J.P., Edward Fitzgerald, Ferdinant Kelly, John Peyton, Francis R. O'Grady, Patrick O'Grady P.P., Patrick Duffy P.P., John Caulfield junior, Edward P. McDonnell, D.Cosgrave surgeon, O.P. Dalton, Thomas Kelly, Richard O'Grady, Thomas Dalton, Richard Dalton, John Cox, John O'Grady, Oliver Dalton, G.C. Dalton, Pat Gallagher, Henry Seymour, Thomas Gordon, Thomas Flannery, Thomas Towey, William J. Kelly, J.H. Byrne, Michael McCormick, Edward Jordan, Richard Gaffney, Patrick O'Regan, Patrick Dougherty, John Roddy, John Burke, George Gilligan, John Clancy, John Keegan, Pete Dockery, Thomas Costello, Hugh Burke, Michael Brannan, and James Rogers.

DATED 13th APRIL 1844.[12]

Duffy had been arrested but was let out on bail even though there was strong circumstantial evidence against him. Mr. Whelan, the local magistrate, attended the meeting and heard all the evidence. Enough evidence was available to bring Patrick Duffy to justice. Mr. Strickland had taken a portion of land from one of the tenants of Viscount Dillon's estate (of which he was agent). The record does not state that Patrick Duffy was evicted (see Appendix No.3).

This Charles Strickland was a son of Jarrard E. Strickland who came to Loughglynn on 5th August 1818 and continued to live there as an agent for Dillon after his father's death in 1844. His mother Anne, died at Loughglynn on 15th January 1829 and is buried in a vault in the cemetery of the old church at Ballaghaderreen. He managed the estate for forty years. He was regarded, by all accounts, as a very fair man and he devoted himself to the welfare of all around him with unswerving patience. There were no evictions on the Dillon Estate, hence the large population of the very poor.[13]

During the famine 1847-1848 he saved many of the tenants from starvation when the Government relief works had provided the people with money for food but there was no food to be had in many districts. Mr. Strickland in this emergency purchased large cargoes of Indian meal and corn and set up depots at different parts of Lord Dillon's estate. He worked day and night to battle against the famine. He often sat up whole nights with the dying during the famine fever. His wife Maria, daughter of

'THE BAD TIMES'- 1830s and 1840s

IRISH SKETCHES: BOG-TROTTER'S CABIN, BALLINTOBER BOG, ROSCOMMON.—SEE PAGE 245.

'THE BAD TIMES'- 1830s and 1840s

Richard Farrell, Q.C. Dublin, worked equally hard to help the destitute all around. Charles had five brothers, William and Jarrard who became Jesuits, Edward, who like Charles had no family, and Walter who was the father of Lord Strickland of Sizeragh and Thomas. Thomas was born at Loughglynn on 30th December 1826. He had two sons and one daughter: Walter George, born in 1850, Gerard, who was born at Brooklawn, Co. Mayo, on 29th November 1852, and Annie who was born at Loughglynn and became a nun of the Order of the Assumption. Charles had four sisters, Cecilia, Harriet, Katherine, and Annie.[14] Descendants of this family of Stricklands live today in Malta and have just completed a history of their family. Jarrard E., father of Charles, and Mr. Edgeworth, father of Maria Edgeworth, were close friends. Both were interested in the improvement of land for agriculture.

Relief committees were set up in the 1840s. Requests were sent from various Unions to the Government for famine relief and all the policies followed by the Government in providing relief are on record. Once a Union collected a fixed sum the Government were prepared to back it with an equal sum. Charles Strickland was Chairman of the Gallen and Costello Relief Committee; it included the Castlerea Union, and the Swineford Union. Relief Committees of Ballaghaderreen, Kilkelly, Frenchpark, Loughglynn, Ballyhaunis, and Clogher reported to these Unions who in turn informed Dublin Castle as to the state of the people.

In May 1846 it was noted that Castlerea workhouse was not open and vacancies in Boyle workhouse were 499.[15] An amount of £2537. 3s. 2d. was laid out for public works in the barony of Frenchpark, in the areas of Artagh, Loughglynn, Frenchpark and Breedoge. Half the crops in these townlands were lost, and in Loughglynn and Ardagh there were no idle labourers, while in Breedoge and Frenchpark half the labourers were idle. Forwarded to the Board of Works on 23rd May 1846 by G. Vaughan Jackson, Chairman, Co.Surveyor, was a statement showing that £10,300 was available for the execution of work in the barony of Costello.[16] Mr. Strickland and Mr. O'Grady had inspected the works to be done. There were six hundred and eighty-eight vacancies in Swineford workhouse and Castlerea workhouse was still not open. The parishes of Knock and Aghamore had lost four-fifths of their crops and Kilmovee, Kilbeagh, Castlemore, and Ballaghaderreen had lost one third.

All the labourers at Knock, Aghamore, Kilmovee, and Kilbeagh were idle. But there were none idle in Castlemore and Ballaghaderreen. On 26th May 1846 these works were sanctioned by the Treasury Chambers, Dublin. The Lord Lieutenant of Ireland had given the necessary direction to the Commissioners of Public Works to proceed with the works recommended by them to His Excellency in the barony of Frenchpark, Co. Roscommon and in the barony of Costello Co. Mayo. One moiety was to be advanced by loan and the remainder by way of grant.[17] Six hundred and forty eight perches of road from Frenchpark to Loughglynn and eight hundred and twelve perches of proposed road from Castlerea to Swineford were to be built. Three hundred and twenty five perches of road were to be constructed from off the main road from Frenchpark to Boyle, and to Ballymote, between the end of the part now made at Tournagee and the ford at Lough Gara opposite the road through Clooncunny – £475 was available.

On 21st January 1847 the Chief Secretary, Sir Randolf Routh, was asked to furnish full particulars to the Lord Lieutenant as to what steps had been taken for the relief of distress in the districts of Ballina, Swineford, Foxford, Crossmolina and Ballaghaderreen. This reply came from Routh:

> 'A depot has been formed at Ballina for supply of these districts and Relief Committees can obtain there any meal which their funds will purchase.[18] There has been a Relief Fund in Swineford District since the commencement of November. On the fifth and thirteenth of which month grants of £31. 10s were on subscriptions amounting to £63. On December twenty eight a grant of £17 was made on subscriptions amounting to £17 and on twenty-third instant a grant of £100 was added to subscriptions of £72. In Foxford district a Relief Fund for the present season has not yet been formed. At least no subscription list has been forwarded with a view to obtaining a grant. In Crossmolina there has not been a local subscription. A remittance has been made to it by the Lord Lieutenant. A subscription has not yet been received from the Committee at Ballaghaderreen District but a Fund has been collected and food provided. At Ballina District a fund has been formed consisting of £758. 14s.0d subscribed to which two grants of £480 and £150 have been added making a total fund of £1,388. 14s 0d. Assistant C.J.Adams has received his instructions to proceed to those districts and report the actual state and wants of each. The Ballina workhouse for 1,200 inmates contained according to the last Return received at the Commissariat Relief Office 1,151 persons and the Swineford Union workhouse for 700 contained at the same date 722 inmates. It will be observed that the deaths in Mayo have occurred wanting means to purchase food.
>
> Signed R.I. Routh, January twenty-ninth 1847 [19]

Meanwhile, people were dying of hunger as discussions were taking place on paper. Mr. Strickland on 15th February wrote urgently to Dublin Castle enclosing the subscription list from Ballaghaderreen and begging for a grant equivalent to the £90 collected for the relief of the starving population.

> 'If a grant of boilers could be made to us it would be of infinite service in provid-

'THE BAD TIMES'- 1830s and 1840s

ing a cheap, warm and nutritious food as well in the town of Ballaghaderreen as in the country districts. It would be waste of time for me to say anything of the terrible distress among the lower classes of that densely populated district'.[19]

£90 was forwarded on 2 February 1847. It appears that the full subscription from Ballaghaderreen Relief fund amounting to £203 had been collected and Charles Strickland was not slow to reply stating this and enclosing the full list and asking for the remainder of the grant.

The list was as follows:

British Relief Association, Southsea House	£25
Central Relief Association to Rev.D. Tighe	£75
Society of Friends	£10
Lord Dillon	£30
Waldron Esq.	£5
Cogan Esq.	£1
Costello Minors by Holmes Esq.	£15
Rev. D. Tighe	£1
Andrew Dillon M.D.	£1
Charles Strickland	£2
Total	£165
(Deduct the amount contributed by the Central Relief Association)[20]	£75
	£90

In March, Charles Strickland sent in a further letter begging and beseeching help for the starving people, and requesting grants for the £61.13s. 7d. collected in Loughglynn. One of the subscribers was his brother Walter. Priests in Catholic churches and ministers in Protestant churches were only too aware of the dire need for food and sought help from the pulpits. A sermon was preached at Castlerea by the rector William Baker Stoney in December 1847.[21] It speaks for itself (see letter in Appendix 5).

It must have been apparent to the Rev. W. Stoney how hopeless the situation was at the time and his awareness of dealers taking advantage of the poor by raising the price of corn makes it clear to us how widespread those dealings were. Sickness and death followed the potato disease, and fever from eating diseased potatoes was widespread. Evictions by landlords followed and while these tragedies continued it is noted that up to February 1846, 450,000 quarters of wheat, 701,000 hundredweight of barley and 1,000,000 quarters of oats were exported to pay the rent. These figures were produced in the House of Commons. Help began to arrive slowly after that.

Panic in the areas of hunger replaced outrages. Food was a priority. It would be several weeks before the oat crop would be ready. Extra Government depots were needed and additional quantities of Indian and oatenmeal made available, otherwise the prices would unavoidably rise in the markets and the poor would be unable to purchase. Reports that Government stores were closing led to a rise in the price of meal from fourteen shillings to eighteen shillings a hundredweight.[22]

It is clear from the records available that Mr. Strickland did his utmost to waken the conscience of the Government. The following letter indicates the harrowing experiences of the poor in the barony of Costello and the near desperation reached by the Chairman of the Costello-Gallen Relief Committee. In this case he writes from Loughglynn seeking first of all supplies for the Ballyhaunis Relief Committee.

September 16th 1846
Loughglynn,

'I am much surprised by your letter of yesterday's date just received, that that you can give me only four tons of Indian meal for Ballyhaunis Relief Committee. Finding the supply of meal in the barony of Costello so much less than was absolutely required, we formed a Relief Committee at Ballyhaunis and entered into subscriptions to the amount of about £100 for the purchase of Indian meal for that very distressed locality from ten to twenty five miles from any depot. It gives us now the greatest possible alarm to find that we have taken this onus upon ourselves and with our money ready to pay we cannot be supplied with food in sufficient quantity to keep the poor alive. The heart-rending accounts I have heard and what I myself have frequently seen, show, beyond all question of doubt, that if this supply cannot fully be kept up the poor will starve with money in their hands to pay for provisions.

You can see the state of public opinion as to the want of provisions for this locality when private subscriptions; four of £20, to £3 and even ten shillings each has been given to bring in meal for sale only, and thus supply what we have long but uselessly sought from the Government. The markets have not been supplied with the usual quantity of meal. Persons with capital are afraid to buy for fear of its being taken from them at the outbreak which they consider inevitable. Those who have any store are afraid to own it for the same reason. I have been so pressed on one or two occasions to buy meal from one or two persons who were found out to have a few hundred of meal for their own use that I have bought under the market price for the purpose of selling again in small quantities to the poor at cost price. Many would rather sell at any price than keep even a small quantity in their houses when they were known to have it.

The supply must really be kept up for two months until the poor small landholders can get their corn ground. This country is entirely in the hands of small occupiers without any potatoes and milk from half an acre to three or four acres of oats. The population of the barony is about, as well as I now recollect, above 66,000 souls with an extent of about 150,000 statute acres and with but one depot at one end of it.

Mills are but very few not above ten in the barony and but half of those worth speaking of, and you may calculate how it must then take before any general relief can be felt from these mills when every small landholder gets his own small quantity of ground. It cannot be sooner than six or eight weeks and in the meantime Indian meal is the sole support of fully one third and, I might say, half the population.

I entreat of you to let me know when I can send the carts again for more and for what quantity. From eight to twelve tons a week is as little as we could do with to give the necessary relief.

*Trusting for an early reply,
I am Sir,
Your obedient servant
Charles Strickland
To: Mr. Stephens Esq.*[23]

In October 1846 a call upon the Government had been made by the Gallen-Costello Relief Committee. The merchants and traders had taken advantage of the poverty of the people and had raised food prices even beyond famine prices.[24] A depot was requested for Kilkelly Relief Committee by Fr. Coughlan. Ballaghaderreen Relief Committee directed Fr. Denis Tighe to implore help from the Government as some people had died. Fr. Tighe said many men were unable to walk from hunger.

The Union around Lough Gara was called the Union of Killaraght. The Coolavin Relief Committee was part of this. The Established Church clergyman at this time (1836-1876) was the Rev. E. Powell. An application for Quaker relief came from the committee in 1846-47 while Rev. Powell was ill. It showed how important the parson was in local society at the time. Without the Protestant clergyman to act as chairman of the Relief Association it seemed impossible for the others to work together. When the application came to the Quakers they were unsure of how to handle the situation. While they looked around the people starved. Without Rev. Powell they refused to work together. Then the committee elected the local Presbyterian, Mr. J.A. Holmes as chairman, and two soup kitchens were set up. The soup pot, a large cast iron pot of over three feet in circumference and the same in height, with ten inch high cast iron legs, leaving enough space to light a good fire beneath it, is still there in the home of the Prince of Coolavin. One can picture the thousands who were once fed from it.

Various cheap recipes for soup were proposed. The following one by Alex Sayer, one of the Quakers, was widely used: 2 gallons of water, one quarter pound of leg beef, 2 ounces of dripping, onions and other vegetables, 7 pounds of flour, 3 ounces of salt and seven ounces of sugar. The total cost was one shilling and four pence. Boilers sometimes held up to

'THE BAD TIMES'- 1830s and 1840s

300 gallons. The following letter from Mr. Holmes makes it clear how bad the situation was in Monasteraden also.

> Clogher House
> Ballaghaderreen
> March 17th 1847.
>
> Sir,
> I have the honour to enclose you a list of subscriptions received by the Coolavin Committee, Co. Sligo, and to request that the Government will grant a similar sum – all the money has been paid into my hands as Chairman. I regret very much to state that district is in a very wretched state. We have two soup kitchens established and I trust by the Government granting a similar sum to what we have received that we may be able to supply the soup gratuitously, which as yet we have not been able to do.
> I have the honour to be
> Sir, Your obedient servant
> J. A. Holmes   Chairman.

The Society of Friends did much to alleviate the plight of the hungry as may be seen from the records they kept for the period.[25] Fr. Denis Tighe, P.P. Ballaghaderreen, sent £419 to Sligo for ten sacks of Indian meal and ten sacks of barley meal. Mr. Holmes sent an order for one ton of Indian meal and ten bags of biscuits for distribution at the usual terms. In Frenchpark Matt Conmee ordered a boiler of forty to seventy five gallons. Francis Kelly of Ballaghaderreen said at a meeting of Castlerea Union that clothing was very scarce and assistance to any extent could not be given. But he asked could food be given in payment for work done. The parish priest of Cloonloo said that on May 19th, 1847 no grant had been made in Coolavin because the inspector's opinion was unfavourable.

Joseph Seymour, rector, Ballaghaderreen, ordered two tons of Indian meal for joint disposal by himself and Dr. McNicholas, the Catholic bishop. Mr. Holmes ordered one ton of Indian meal and five bags of biscuits from Sligo. Denis O'Conor of Mount Druid, Frenchpark, sent an order to Sligo for one ton of rice and four bags of biscuits and an order to Castlebar for one ton of Indian meal on the usual terms. Mr. Holmes ordered in Sligo one ton of Indian meal, half a ton of wheaten meal, one ton of rice and five bags of biscuits. His wife Elizabeth asked that two tons of the best rice be sent for the sick and to keep the Sligo rice for common purposes. Denis Tighe ordered half a ton of Indian meal and a quarter ton of barley meal. John Gallagher reported that Carracastle had got no grant. Mr. Holmes again ordered one ton of rice from Sligo for the sick. His wife ordered half a ton of rice, half a ton of Indian meal and five bags of biscuits for the school.

Mr. McDonnell, Swinford Union, promised to distribute cooked rice.

Elizabeth Holmes ordered half a ton of Indian meal, a quarter ton of rice and three bags of biscuits for the school. J.A.Holmes ordered from Sligo half a ton of Indian meal, half a ton of rice and and five bags of biscuits for the support of Elizabeth Holmes's school. On 18th May 1848, Elizabeth Holmes ordered two bags of biscuits, a quarter ton of rice for the children and five extra bags of biscuits. Mr. Holmes ordered from Sligo depot one ton of rye meal, a quarter ton of Indian meal, three bags of biscuits, half a ton of rice for the school. It is also noted that Charles Strickland gave £30 for relief on 4th July 1849. Mr J.A. Holmes gave £30 for the relief of small farmers, and in July he gave another £30 for the Claremorris poor. The Central Relief Committee of the Society of Friends was based at Fleet Street Dublin.

By the summer of 1847 soup kitchens were operating in almost every poor law Union in the country but this failed to prevent disease and fever. Temporary fever hospitals were set up, but it was well nigh impossible to combat the disease. Thousands had died, over a million emigrated. Overcrowding in jails and workhouses led to further misery and deaths. Some Unions were too poor to pay for their relief programme so the Government was forced to intervene, first by loans and then by levying a special rate on all rateable property to help clear the debts of the poorer Unions. This created another problem. The landlords were liable for the entire rates on holdings under £4 so they began to evict smallholders and demolish their cabins. Another reason for eviction and misery was the 'Gregory Clause' in the 1847 Act by which anyone with a holding of more than a quarter of an acre was not to get relief. So further outrages were committed: rate collectors were assaulted. *Outrage Papers* in Dublin Castle preserve records of the happenings of those cruel sad days.

In 1848 G. Knox was the Magistrate at Tubbercurry and Ballaghaderreen. The 'Molly McGuires', a previously mentioned secret society, had in February broken into a house in the area and seriously wounded one man and killed another. Two men, Peter and John Costello, were convicted at the Castlebar assizes and sentenced to transportation for life. Later the house of James Costello of Derrynabrack, six miles from Ballaghaderreen, was attacked and broken into by a party of 'Molly Mc Guires'. They killed Pat Callaghan with a loy and beat up John Towey in the next house. He died later. Police protection was demanded. In Ballaghaderreen one hundred infantry and twenty cavalry and one hundred police were available for the poor rate collection. On 23rd March 1849 George Knox reported that he was attending Petty Sessions at Ballaghaderreen from the 19th, enforcing rates in Coolavin with a strong military and police force. Only £25 was collected. The people had removed their cattle and the rate collector begged the military not to continue the collection. The feeling in this locality against the collection of rates was, he reported, violent, and the collector and his men could not leave the presence of the police without being attacked. Some of the locals had been arrested and sent to Ballymote for trial.

Mark McDonnell of Ballaghaderreen complained to the Earl of Clarendon, Lord Lieutenant of Ireland, that the tenants of the farms of Magheraboy refused to pay rates or rent and had assaulted himself and his bailiffs. He requested that Mr. Knox accompany him. McDonnell had come from Strokestown to take up his employment. Molly McGuires had threatened his workers and labourers with severe punishment. His cattle were allowed to stray. His brother Anthony of Palmfield brought over a party to do his tillage but they were attacked by a mob and driven away. Some were injured. On four occasions the constabulary helped McDonnell on the Magheraboy (Machaire Buí– The Sunny Plain) property.[26] Small wonder there was a bitter hatred by the smallholders in the area against bailiffs and rate collectors. This lasted right down to the end of the century. Outrages continued, murders, arrests, rate collections, disturbances. In 1851 a lighted candle was maliciously thrown in the letter box of the Post Office at Ballaghaderreen where Mrs. Monica Duff was the postmistress. Because she did not report it for four days the constabulary had to report it to Dublin Castle.

Harrowing events like these created further bitterness and steady emigration continued to drain the country for many decades after the Famine, and a deep hatred of England increased as the root of Ireland's misfortunes was blamed on England. The picture that emerges from this period is of three classes, the landless men of the secret societies, the middle class Repealers, and the landlord class who had to resort to the authorities at the least whim. Many of these were resident magistrates to whom the poor went, cap in hand, when they had to. There is no appearance of co-operation between all classes.

Ireland's history could have been very different. Lord Chatham had delivered a speech in the House of Lords at the time of the American Revolution. 'If I were an American as I am an Englishman, while a foreign troop remained in my country I never would lay down my arms; Never; Never; Never. The inhabitants of the Thirteen Colonies had organised resistance to their mother country; the principle 'No taxation without representation'. The American colonists were at that time, only about three million in number. The Irish were a little more numerous, but the four-fifths of the population who were Catholic had, by the operation of the Penal Laws, been effectively disarmed and reduced to a state of utter helplessness.'

'THE BAD TIMES'- 1830s and 1840s

CHAPTER 7

EDUCATIONAL DEVELOPMENTS OVER TWO CENTURIES

Severe legal restrictions were imposed on Catholic education by the Penal Laws in the late 17th century. The Irish poor resorted to Hedge Schools. By the time the Penal Laws were abolished towards the end of the 18th and beginning of the 19th centuries, the hedge schools or pay schools had come generally to be regarded as a community responsibility.[1] That they were so numerous shows that Catholics in spite of their meagre resources valued education highly. In the early 19th century the population increased dramatically, resulting in increased rents and deterioration in the already depressed standard of living of the Catholic Irish poor. Educational Societies began to make their appearance aided by state grants. Of these the Incorporated *Society in Dublin for Promoting English Protestant Schools in Ireland*, founded in 1733, and the *Association for Discountenancing Vice and Promoting the Knowledge and Practice of the Christian Religion* founded in 1792, were proselytising agencies. Because the *Kildare Place Society*, established in 1811, appeared for a time to promote a non-denominational system of education, the Catholic clergy initially welcomed it. Its method was to make grants towards the maintenance of schools and the publication of textbooks and the training of teachers.[2] This society proved also to be biased towards Protestantism and in the long run unsatisfactory to Catholics.

The tenacity of the Catholics in securing their childrens' education despite the obstacles of the Penal Laws can be seen in the way they developed their own schools – 'day schools' run by parish priests and supported by parish contributions, girls' schools attached to convents and boys' schools started by Christian Brothers. But the bulk of children were not educated in these well organised schools but in the so called pay schools, deriving for the most part from the hedge school of the 18th century, started and maintained by private individuals. 'They were frequently undertaken by persons ill-qualified to discharge the duties of school masters'.[3]

A Commission on Education was set up in 1824 and it noted that only about two-fifths of the population of school age were attending school.

This meant about a half million children, Catholic and Protestant. In the diocese of Achonry 1731 there were eight Popish schools, so that a Protestant school master 'were he to be had, cannot get bread'.[4] Also vagrant friars went about prophesying to the poor people for reeks of barley and handfulls of flax. In a complete review being carried out by the Commissioners they found that fifty eight Charter schools were administered by the *Incorporated Society for Children of the Very Poor*. But they were badly run and the children were neglected. Bible Societies abounded. Sixty three Baptist schools were set up in Connacht. The number of schools financed by various societies numbered 1729 out of a total of 11,823. The findings of the Commissioners made it clear that the Educational Societies did not succeed in establishing themselves as a promoters of popular systems of education. British mishandling of Irish affairs arose from a lack of knowledge of the country itself, of its people and their ways and thoughts. The Commissioners reviewed the whole scene of Irish education. In 1824 the Catholic bishops sent a memorial to the British Government stating their needs for an acceptable system of education and claiming the right of some measure of control over Catholic teachers, the staffing of schools and the right to a veto over all books used by Catholic pupils.[5] The first official intimation of the scheme was given by the Chief Secretary for Ireland Mr. Edward Stanley to the Commons on 9th September 1831. He said that the £30,000 previously paid annually from public funds to the Kildare Place Society would in future be placed at the disposal of the Lord Lieutenant for the creation of an educational system 'in which the most scrupulous care should be taken not to interfere with the peculiar tenets of any description of Christian pupils'. The Duke of Leinster who was a member of the Established Church was appointed first President of the National Board of Education which included seven members.

It appears then in contrast to Presbyterians, the Catholics tended at first to look favourably on the experiment of mixed education and Dr. Murray, the Catholic Archbishop of Dublin became one of the seven members of the Board[6]. A letter was sent from Mr.Stanley, Chief Secretary for Ireland to the Duke of Leinster.[7] It stated clearly what the aims and new systems were. By 1831 Dr. John McHale Archbishop of Tuam objected to the new Board as he claimed it was an invitation to proselytism. The result was a controversy within the Catholic Church. The Irish Christian Brothers saw it as being inconsistent with their conception of a Catholic education. Taking into account the previous monies spent on education in Ireland on only a section of children this new Board was emphatic in promoting the education of all children. The system was intended to be non-denominational – children of all faiths to attend the same school and religious material of a dogmatic nature to be excluded. Suspicion and wariness was natural to the Catholic hierarchy especially in the west. History had taught them a bitter lesson in repression, penal laws and hangings. The National system of education being a creation of the Whig Government would have been disapproved by the majority of Church dignitaries no matter what its structure was. By 1850 the alternative to mixed education was generally seen to be Government grants for separate Catholic schools.

In the Abstract of Parochial Returns the result of an enquiry gives interesting details for the barony of Costello.[8] In Kilbeagh there were six schools and six teachers:

Carracastle: Patrick Gallohar; *Larga*: Michael Kelly; *Baroe:* Charles Shrihane; *Rooskey*: Patrick Doherty. In *Gragaghduff*, Michael O'Hara taught one hundred and twenty Catholic pupils in the Chapel for thirty shillings a quarter and he also taught thirty Catholics in *Monasteraden* for eleven shillings per quarter. In *Deranacarta* sixty pupils were taught in a thatched house for four shillings per quarter. In *Kilmovee Parish*, Andrew Duffy taught sixty children in a small cabin. His patron was the Londonderry Hibernian Society; £8 per annum was his fee. At *Rodestown*, Patrick O'Gara taught twenty pupils for £10 per year in a miserable cabin. At *Culgarriff*, Bartholomew Spelman taught forty nine children in a small stone barn. At *Raherrolis*, John Beirne taught fifty eight pupils in a miserable cabin. In the parish of Coolavin there were six schools:[9] *Gurteen:* Patrick Beirne taught twenty pupils in a thatched cabin for £10 per year. There were no patrons. *Kilfree:* Bartholomew Finn taught twenty four pupils in a thatched stone cabin for £9 per year. He had no patron. *Kilfree*: John Lee taught twenty four pupils in a thatched stone cabin for £7. He had no patron. *Sraigh*: John Nangle taught twenty pupils in a cow house. His pay depended on the parents of the pupils. *Lisvallally*: Michael Clarke taught sixty eight pupils for a £10 fee from the London Hibernian Society and was promised a gratuity from Mr Ellwood. Both versions of the Prayer Book were received. *Cloonloo:* John Scanlon taught thirty six pupils in the parish chapel. Lord Lorton the owner of Rockingham Estate allowed the teacher two acres of land valued at seven shillings and six pence per acre. All of these children were Catholics.

In Mayo forty two schools existed before 1831; four were replacement buildings, twenty seven were privately built before 1831 and thirty five were newly built by the National Board.[10] In east Mayo Viscount Dillon contributed sites for schools. It had been noted that many teachers previously employed in local day-schools made the transition to National Teacher status along with their school. Evidence as to the quality of these teachers is scant. In Mayo there were many free proselytising schools and many parishes were too poor to raise the money to get the qualifying grant. Despite the general statement in Parliamentary Papers that pay schools were run by private individuals for gain, the fact emerges that many of these schools were receiving patronage and some financial support from local Catholic clergy. A record of the state of religion in Ballaghaderreen in 1838 shows that a school had been established before 1826 in the parish under the auspices of the clergy, for the education of the poor[11]. There was a diocesan seminary here also; a classical school under the patronage of Dr. McNicholas, Bishop of Achonry, where young men were prepared for Maynooth, and for the medical and legal professions. Two curates, Dr. P Spelman and Fr. Denis Tighe, attended the unfinished church—a steeple, spire and bell needed to be added to it, but the parish was too poor to contribute the necessary funds.

From an early date a Latin School flourished in *Ballaghaderreen*. It seems to have supplied the needs of a wider field than Achonry diocese for many years. Three famous priests of Elphin in the late 19th century were educated there; Dean Kelly of Athlone, Canon McDermott of Croghan, and Canon Casey who was known as the 'Bard of the Suck'. This Latin school was conducted in a wing of the old church which stood on the site of St. Mary's Hall.

In 1831 two schools, *Brusna and Aughalustia,* were endowed with four acres by Lord Dillon.[12] One hundred boys and one hundred girls were instructed there. There was also a pay school where fifty boys and fifty girls attended. There were public schools at *Ballaghaderreen* and *Castlemore* which were aided by donations from Lord Dillon. Mr. Holmes and the incumbent, afforded instruction to about 500 children. There were 144 Protestants in Castlemore Parish and 13,132 Catholics. Prior to 1826 Dr. MacNicholas assisted Viscount Dillon in the building of school houses. John Melan taught in one of them and his salary was £26 for one year. In *Crenane* school the teacher was Charles Shryane with thirty pupils and in *Rooskey* school John Donohue taught thirty pupils for £10 per year in a small country cabin. In *Kilcolman* Edward Daly had a pay school in a good slated house which held one hundred pupils. His salary was £24. In *Ballaghderreen* Malachai Dowd held a pay school in his house. He had seven pupils of the Established Church and twenty eight Catholics. His pay ranged from £1.1s. to £1. 8s. per quarter.[13]

The greatest increase in enrolment occurred among female students. There is some evidence that students who were segregated by sex may have received an inferior education because many female teachers seemed incapable of teaching arithmetic.(This is what the report says). The most interesting finding of the Commissioners of Irish Education was the degree to which the Catholic Church was involved in education prior to 1831 in spite of all the Acts of Parliament passed in the two previous centuries.[14]

> In 1837 there were one hundred and forty five pupils in *Castlemore* school and one hundred and forty pupils in *Kilcolman* with one teacher for each school.[15]
>
> In 1839 *Castlemore* had one hundred and forty pupils and *Kilcolman* had one hundred and eighty five.[16]
>
> In 1843 *Kilcolman* school had one hundred and seventy eight male pupils and one hundred and seventy two females, with one teacher for each, and *Castlemore* had one hundred and eighty three pupils.[17]
>
> In 1844 grants were made to *Kilcolman–Ballaghaderreen* school where one hundred girls attended. £7. 10s was paid for fittings. Local contributions were £7. 1s. 8d. In 1846 this school was struck off the National School Roll. There were one hundred and seventy two pupils altogether.[18]

By 1845 the number of National Schools had doubled and so had their attendance. At this time no child was required to be present at any specific religious instruction. *Castlemore* had one hundred and sixty eight pupils in a one teacher school. *Kilcolman* had one hundred and ninety six pupils with one teacher.[19]

The diminishing attendance in 1846 may be fairly ascribed to the prevailing famine which compelled parents to obtain employment for their children in the public works.

In 1847 the *Ballaghaderreen* school roll (no.3956) lists the division of classes into first, second and third class, totalling one hundred and sixty five boys and one hundred girls. The headmaster was James McAuley and there was a probation teacher and an assistant. In 1846 there was a fourth class roll.[20]

In *Kilcolman-Monasteraden,* school Number 47, Roll No.1099 there were in September 1846 one hundred and forty seven boys. In school No. 48 there were twenty eight girls. In *Ballaghaderreen-Kilcolman* School No. 61 there were one hundred and eighty seven boys, and a teacher who had a salary of £24 and a paid monitor. The patron was Mr. Charles Strickland. In *Castlemore-Brusna* school No. 38 there was a total of one hundred and seventy two children with one teacher who was paid

£15 per annum. Fr. Tighe was the patron.[21]

All the Parliamentary Reports lay stress on Castlemore-Brusna's poor land, its large stretches of bog and mountain and the extreme poverty of the people, as well as the density of the population. This last, however, changed markedly between 1841 and 1851. There were 1,420,705 people living in Connacht in 1841. By 1851 this had dropped by 9% to 1,012,479. By 1861 the population had dropped a further 10%.[22] The percentages of illiterates in Connacht in 1841 were 59.4% Catholic and 13% Protestant. So despite the hedge schools, and the free schools and the activities or various societies, education was severely lacking in this deprived part of Ireland.

In the 1851 Census in *Kilcolman* (including *Ballaghaderreen*) there were three hundred and twenty persons who could read and write, one thousand and fifteen who could read only, and one thousand nine hundred and seventy two who could neither read nor write. In *Castlemore* three hundred and nine persons could read and write, two hundred and twenty one could read only and one thousand nine hundred and seventy two could neither read nor write. A Presbyterian School was established at Clogher in the Parish of Kilcolman in the early 19th century. Mr. J. A. Holmes looked after this school and children of both denominations, Catholic and Protestant attended.[23]

The Education Report 1853 deals mainly with the supply of books by the Commissioners of Education to National schools. These were supplied to each school in proportion to the numbers attending and were renewed every three years. Roman Catholics forbade their children to use any books, at any time, containing Scripture lessons or lessons containing the truths of Faith.[24]

In 1868 a census was taken of the children present in each school on 25th June – this was published in 1870. In Ballaghadereen the National Agricultural College had no connection with the National School Board. One hundred and eight boys were present. All were Catholics. Ballaghaderreen had no girls' national school; eighty girls attended a non private school. An infants' school had nineteen children. In 1886, according to a census by Bishop Francis MacCormack, there were over twenty-four thousand children attending three hundred and sixty five primary schools in the diocese of Achonry.

As the population of Ballaghaderreen increased in the second half of the 19th century, it is easy to see why the successor to Dr. MacNicholas, Dr. Patrick Durcan, was determined to have a convent in the town. For many years he had tried to meet the needs both religious and secular, of a large poverty-stricken population. He consulted with Mr. Strickland and succeeded in getting from Viscount Dillon the site at Cnocán na mBráthar – Friars' Hill, near Castlemore. The site consisted of 15 acres, three of which were leased for five hundred years for buildings at a merely nominal rent. The remainder was to be held by the nuns after 1877 for £15 per annum. As this land was given for educational purposes it had to be leased in trust to the bishop for the time being, with a priest of the diocese, Fr. Finn, and Mr Strickland acting as joint trustees. Dr. Durcan decided finally on inviting the Sisters of Charity to set up a foundation at Ballaghaderreen.

In building the convent he employed a Mr. Callaghan from Dublin as architect, Mr. McGlynn from Ballaghaderreen as contractor and Mr. Troy as clerk of works.[25] The convent and schools were built of coarse sandstone and local limestone. It was sad that Dr. Durcan was unable to be present due to illness (he died a year later) when the foundation was laid on the Feast of Corpus Christi 1874 by his coadjutor and successor, Dr. Francis MacCormack. The building cost £6,500. Part of this was collected by subscriptions. £500 was donated by Dr. MacCormack. Fr. Loftus and Fr. Spelman went to America to collect funds. A bequest was added to the funds from the estate of the late Colonel Gore Ousley Higgins of Co. Galway for £3,000. The foundation was endowed by the life interest of the sister of Colonel Higgins, Sr. Mary Aloysius Higgins in the estate at Glencorrib, Co. Galway: the rents from the tenants went to support the convent. However when the land war began in 1879, the tenants of the Ousley Estate withheld their rent and the convent suffered accordingly.

The convent and chapel were not completed until 1877 due to the contractors defaulting. A great friend of the sisters at this time was Mrs Deane of the Square, Ballaghaderreen. When the furniture for the convent arrived before it was completed she stored it away on her premises. She remained a constant friend during her lifetime. Many days of airing and unpacking were spent when the sisters did arrive and everything possible was done by her to brighten those first days at Friar's Hill and flitches of home-cured bacon were suspended from hooks in the convent kitchen. Hardly a week passed for the first year without some substantial help towards the larder being sent up. For four years Mrs Deane gave a weekly help of £1 for the poor until the famine and agitation of 1881.[26]

Bishop Durcan travelled to Newtownforbes in Longford to meet those 'ladies from Dublin'. On reaching Ballaghaderreen he introduced them to various well wishers. Never in the lives of the local people had anything like this happened. Thousands turned out to greet them, lining the route through the town, along the Station Road, turning left to the top of the town and right up the Castlemore Road, where bonfires were lit en route. Excitement was intense. A new era in the history of the barony of Costello had arrived.

CAROLAN,
The Celebrated Irish Bard.

To His Excellency the Marquess Wellesley, K.G.
LORD-LIEUTENANT of IRELAND &c. &c.

This Print (by Permission) is most respectfully Inscribed by his most Obedient Servant
John Martyn

Ballaghaderreen's first prioress was the celebrated Mother Arsenius (formerly Agnes Morragh-Bernard) who is best remembered for her foundation of Foxford Woollen Mills.[27] She and her faithful sisters set up house and for fourteen years struggled, worked and slaved for the thousands of people in the town and surrounding area. Viscount Dillon did not carry our evictions; as a result the population, which decreased all over Connacht during his time, increased in the barony of Costello. So the task of setting up schools and coping with a poverty-stricken people was undertaken valiantly by those nuns. When the Sisters of Charity moved into Friar's Hill they lost no time in setting to work. Boys and girls in the area had reached the age of eighteen to twenty without making their First Communion. So the sisters had large classes of boys and girls to prepare for the Sacraments. There was a great demand for their help. During the summer season the priests from outlying parishes sent their broughams to convey the sisters to the churches where they brought the children to undergo a six-week course of instruction. During the first year of their stay in Friar's Hill five hundred people were confirmed – all adults.

The year 1880 saw the poor suffering from the effects of bad seasons with a shortage of fuel and food. If the turf-saving season was wet then the poor had no fires. A large turf fire on an open hearth was the only luxury people had. They worked when the weather permitted to ensure that this at least they would have. When winter came it was sad to witness the pale, pinched faces of the many ill clad barefooted children who came to school without breaking their fast. Mother Arsenius decided to provide a stirabout (porridge) breakfast for them with £2 sent to her by the blind children in Merrion, Dublin, (saved from their Christmas sweets). Many donations came from America, England and even Australia to pay for the meals. From seventy to one hundred children were provided with as much as they would eat of a daily breakfast of porridge and sugar that winter. There was no milk but the children were happy.

Mother Mary Arsenius set up a dispensary on the right-hand side after you enter the Gate Lodge. It was called St. Martin's. Here people were treated and looked after in their hundreds. With the help of an Englishwoman, Mrs. Grehan (Sr. Mary Oswald), the Rev. Mother and her sisters made themselves almost indispensable. Some cases of fever broke out in the year 1880. The sisters burnt the beds and bedding to prevent its spread. The local people had such a terror of the disease that they fled from their nearest and dearest once the disease was confirmed. In one case the panic was so great that after the sisters had performed the last acts of charity for a poor mother and laid her in her coffin they had to drag it down the stairs and with some difficulty had to get the remains carried to the nearby churchyard by a few men who were less cowardly than the lookers on. In 1881, on the first Sunday of Lent, four hundred children made their First Communion at the children's Mass in the cathederal. They came from the surrounding National Schools of Tondragee, Brusna, Benada, Cross, Coolavin, Cloontia, Derrinacarta, Townebrack, the boys national school in the town and the convent school. The convent school had been built in 1879 at a cost of £3,400, on borrowed money. Mother Mary Arsenius had not joined the National School system at this time and was therefore not entitled to state aid. A laundry, a dairy, a kitchen, and teachers' apartments were also built. Of housewifery the local girls were grossly ignorant. Grown girls were taught to read and write, do a little cyphering and needlework and were prepared for service by doing some months' work in the laundry. Many of these emigrated to America and letters of gratitude poured back to Friar's Hill in appreciation of knowledge acquired there which enabled the young women to earn twice as much as they would otherwise have done.

A bazaar was held in 1879 followed by two amateur concerts to liquidate the debt on the schools. This was the beginning of the fulfillment of a social need in the area. People were happy to meet and help each other. The convent became the the hub of community life in the district. A library was opened in the convent. It opened on Sundays after last mass for two hours. Businessmen, bank clerks, railway officials and women joined. Soon there were seventy members. A separate library was started for schools, Children of Mary and the teachers. These libraries were the first of their kind in the west of Ireland. On market days – Fridays and Tuesdays – people came, slowly and hesitantly at first and then in flocks, to borrow books to assuage an aching thirst for knowledge.

A grant for an Industrial school was certified in 1886. £4,500 was raised by the sisters for this. Seventy five girls were taken from different parts of Mayo, mostly from workhouses. Many brought the seeds of sickness with them and it was months before they were well. An infirmary was set up. The nuns had more work and worry than ever. In 1887 the Rev. Dr. MacCormack was transferred by the Holy See to the diocese of Galway. The Sisters of Charity regarded his going as one of the greatest trials to befall the convent. As the founder and benefactor of the convent he had spent over £2,000 in various sums in the ten years. It was not so much what he gave as the way he gave it. He lived at the 'Abbey' on the Sligo Road, and had a large orchard and gardens. Many a basket of fruit and crock of home-made butter found its way from the Abbey to the convent. No Christmas passed without a well-filled hamper. If the sisters were short of milk for the convent he had always some to spare. His cheques for the stirabout breakfasts or for clothes were always so welcome. The parishioners in both parishes were sorry to lose him.

As yet there were no Christian Brothers in Ballaghaderreen. So the sisters were asked to look after the religious instruction of the boys who went to the convent two or three evenings per week for instruction in reading and writing. In 1885 the Christmas crib was a source of joy to the poor in the area: they came from all parts to visit the crib erected in the infants' school and sang hymns, recited the Rosary and listened with avid attention to the instruction. In 1888 a little cottage hospital with 10 beds was opened on 24th September. Rev. John Donohue of Portland sent £30 per annum for three beds. Dr. MacCormack, the former bishop, and his successor Dr Lyster, and Mrs Deane each paid £10 for a bed and the local doctor Dr MacDermott, gave his services gratis. When measles broke out in 1889, thirty children were in the infirmary at the same time.

In 1890 a handloom was erected in the convent. An old weaver from Cork spent three weeks teaching the sisters and girls how to work the fly-shuttle looms. A Mr. Fox came from Manchester and brought one of the newest makes of hand-looms for cotton and fine materials. There were five or six knitting machines in the same department. Several poor people were employed during the trying winter of 1891 knitting socks. The looms were eventually transferred to Foxford where Mother Arsenius opened a new foundation in 1891. Foxford tweed is renowned today. That is another debt we owe to the Sisters of Charity. A velvet-cutting industry was set up in the convent by 1891 by Dr. Lyster. Twenty girls were employed from September 1891 to January 1892. When the industry closed in England it faded out in Ballaghaderreen while hosiery and knitting continued. According to a contemporary account :

> 'the Sisters of Charity opened a knitting factory at Ballaghaderreen, Co. Mayo, at which ninety two hands are employed and the Board has advanced £3,000 on like terms to the Community. The loan is secured by a mortgage on real estate property possessed by the Sisters of Charity in Co. Dublin. It is also under consideration whether this factory might not be further assisted by capitation grants for boys and girls instructed in the respective industries'.[28]

Poverty was kept at bay from many a home in Ballaghaderreen at this time by the employment provided by the factory. In September a branch factory was opened in Monasteraden and, soon after, another in Derrnacartha. The workers coming a long distance were boarded in the little hospital on the convent grounds. After the factory closed each evening classes were held for writing and arithmetic for those wishing to learn. The registered trade name of the business was 'Mater Admirabilis'. Only by trust in our Blessed Lady did the sisters surmount all difficulties. The factory continued during the late 1890s even though the tide of emigration took many of the trained hands. The sisters set up a poultry yard without grants from the Congested Districts Board and bred a better type fowl.

Dr. Lyster's Silver Jubilee provided one gleam of bright relief in the gloomy year 1897. The heavy summer rains of 1897 and 1898 ruined the crops, the sole support of the farming poor, and brought disaster and near starvation in their wake. Many would have died of starvation but for the timely aid afforded them through the convent. Friends from overseas in America, England and Scotland generously gave the means of relieving three hundred families weekly, all through the winter and spring until the Lord sent a plentiful harvest in 1899. Two journalists – past pupils of the sisters were responsible for help from England and America; Conor O'Grady from Manchester and Patrick J. Coleman, whose pens were ever at the service of the sisters and their good works. Funds were raised to help complete the new cathedral in 1900. A monster draw and bazaar were held. There was excitement in the united effort to help. The poverty of the district was shown very plainly; the greater part of the money was collected in coppers. Tickets were just one penny each and the prizes were unusual– a magnificent fat pig, a bicycle and a wedding cake. Concerts and dances were held, and Dr. Lyster was presented with £200. Mrs Deane was still to the forefront in helping although many of the earlier friends had passed away. In January 1911 Dr. Lyster died after twenty-three successful years ruling the Achonry diocese. The new bishop was Dr. Patrick Morrisroe, a native of Charlestown. With a gradual increase in affluence, the urgent needs of a poverty-stricken people were easing. The industry for the making of underwear, started in 1906, had to close: many of the local girls were by now in more comfortable circumstances than they were formerly, and did not need the employment; many of the remainder emigrated to America.

The Pioneer Abstinence movement was introduced to the town in 1914 after a retreat and 200 men and women became pioneers, thereby promising to abstain from alcoholic beverages. In 1918 a dreadful epidemic of influenza swept over the land – not a home escaped. The mission sisters were out from morning till night with their simple remedies. One of the sisters wrote out a list guidelines to treat 'flu victims and made several copies. So helpful did it prove that the parish priest of Gurteen had it posted up at the church gates for the benefit of all. Schools closed. Five sisters and the doctor were victims. Mr. Jack Gordon, a town businessman, sent a man on a bicycle to Tubbercurry for help. Every winter after that brought illness, whooping cough and measles. In March 1921 the death of Mrs. Grehan

(Sr Mary Oswald) was a great loss to the community. To rich and poor, young and old Mrs.Grehan's name was a household word. Sr Mary Leydon of the Sacred Heart convent, Mount Anvile, Dublin, born in Fauleens, Monasteraden, in 1894, recounted how Sr. Oswald and another sister came to Coolavin School on a side-car every Sunday and gave religious instruction. She had a deep love of Ireland. As a young sister her heart was saddened by the sight of the vast number of boys and girls departing every year from the west to America. She devised a plan for keeping in touch with the many at the same time helping their younger brothers and sisters at home. She employed numbers of boys and girls to pick shamrock, make it into artistic sprays and pack them in neat little packages. She composed touching little messages and these were packed and posted to foreign countries. She was anxious to put on paper 'The Life of St. Patrick' and during her illness she asked a young sister, Sr. Mary Martin MacLoughlin of Dublin, to help her with this. Sr. Mary Martin wrote the book for her and worked through the small hours of many nights to complete it, even when she had to rise early and do her own work each day. Sr. Martin was as thorough as Sr. Oswald was exacting, and it was a great joy when the book was published by Dollards of Dublin.

There is an item recorded in the Sisters of Charity Annals in 1922. The factory of St. Francis Xavier in Ballaghaderreen went on fire. An old lady going to Mass ran back to the Barracks where the Black and Tans were stationed at the time and begged for help. The officer in charge said he would not allow women and children to burn to death so he gave a helping hand. Hoses could not be found so they had to carry buckets of water. The work-room and a year's supply of wool were destroyed. The officer got his hands burned saving a statue of Our Lady. Almost £4,000 of damage was done but £3,000 was received in insurance. This is the only record I have come across where the Black and Tans helped anyone! The officer's name is not on record, unfortunately.

An interesting point at this time was the Irish language course which was conducted at the convent at Ballaghaderreen. Sisters came from Dublin, Clonmel and Foxford for this. Sr. Mary Martin had a big part to play in the course. It was she who taught the language to teachers as well as pupils and her after-school hours were spent in school doing tremendous work for the Irish language.

In 1927 the Golden Jubilee of the foundation of the Sisters of Charity at Ballaghaderreen was celebrated. They made a presentation to Mother Arsenius, now at Foxford, of £100. Concerts and operettas were performed by the children. 'Maritana' was put on in St. Mary's Hall. Bunting was put up and bonfires lit. Altogether it was a happy time. One little shadow fell across the celebrations – the absence of Mother M. Arsenius Murrogh Bernard. Fifty years before that she had toiled up Friar's Hill to begin that great work in such unpromising surroundings. Now in 1927 there stood a noble pile of buildings – splendidly equipped schools, a convent, a beautiful chapel, and sacristy, a dispensary a large workroom a laundry and industrial school. Mother Arsenius was too old to come to the celebrations from her 'Providence' home beside the Moy in Foxford. But she insisted on all the sisters going to Ballaghaderreen to rejoice.

Great improvements were made in the laundry; new machinery was bought; washing came in large baskets on horse-drawn carts from Castlerea, Frenchpark, and Charlestown. Later on a motor lorry was bought to collect and deliver from these towns. At one stage even Maynooth College sent their laundry down to Ballaghaderreen convent. Twelve acres of land was purchased for £420. More cows were bought. Concerts were held by the children to cover costs. Sodalities of the Children of Mary flourished in the convent and in Carracastle, Gurteen and Kilmovee. Retreats were well attended. No one wanted to miss out on these wonderful occasions.

In 1932 a new St. Martin's was built. The dispensary became known to the poor of the countryside. Since the closing of the American ports to emigrants the girls of the district were in a sad plight as little employment was to be had. Situations in Ireland were insufficient for the number of girls seeking them. With their limited knowledge of domestic science they were ill-prepared for abroad. So the sisters had a busy time dealing with the situation. A great number were sent as maids to convents and hospitals for a year or two to get training. Those waiting for a 'call' spent much time at St. Martin's where demonstration lessons were given in cookery, laying tables, cutting out etc.

In 1933 St. Joseph's Intermediate School was opened by Dr. Morrisroe, who had long looked forward to this development. This marked a great improvement in educational facilities in the area. Many parents who could not afford to give their children a secondary education in a boarding school welcomed this day-school with appreciation because only a small fee was charged. St. Nathy's College was for years catering for the boys of the diocese. St. Joseph's was to cater for at least 51 girls. On 1st July 1944 the Mother General of the sisters, on the advice of Sr. Mary Martin and under her direction caused St. Joseph's Secondary School to be amalgamated as a 'Secondary Top' to the primary school. The reason for the change was the sheer poverty of the people in the area who were unable to pay £8 per year for education. Under the constitution of the Sisters of Charity their help was only for the poor. Hence, Sr. Martin's great contribution to the education of the girls at Ballaghaderreen. Pupils of ability, even those in poor circumstances, now had the advantage of secondary education free of charge. At the beginning of the school year 1946, over one hundred pupils were enrolled in the Secondary Top. Nine girls sat for the Leaving Certificate that year and twenty five did the Intermediate Certificate.

The work of the Sisters of Charity carried on through the years 1941-1959. Bishop Morrisroe died in 1946. 1947 will go down in history as 't '47'. On 1st February a fall of snow unlike any in living memory was accompanied by intense cold and bitter wind from the east. Blizzards carried in drifts mountains high. Houses in lowlands were completely covered. The convent was cut off for over ten days from the outside world. All roads were impassable, no buses, no telephones, and worst of all no water. The men of Ballaghaderreen displayed a splendid spirit. Over two hundred volunteers cleared the roads and the railway line. Although the snowfall affected almost the entire country, the west got it heavier than any other part.

In May 1947 a new bishop, Dr. James Fergus, was consecrated and formally opened the new school building. Most of the girls attending the Secondary Top were from the outlying border-districts of Sligo, Mayo and Roscommon. During the 1960s the numbers attending the schools remained constant. The Department of Education now had school buses taking children from outlying areas into the convent as the small country schools had closed. In 1969 the laundry finally closed just as the term of Mother Mary MacLoughlin as Reverend Mother came to an end. By this time the sisters of Charity had decided to leave Ballaghaderreen. The convent was taken over by the Sisters of Mercy. It had been officially closed on 30th June 1971.Its schools today are busy and lively with the voices of children of all ages, and the new sisters are doing wonderful work. Ballaghaderreen was now a thriving community, with new houses and factories being built. Gone was the poverty, illiteracy and lack of employment of the 19th century. The Sisters of Charity had done their work well.

Ballaghaderreen was fortunate in 1890 that Bishop Lyster invited the Brothers of St. John the Baptist de La Salle to accomplish for the boys what the Sisters of Charity founded by Mary Aikenhead were doing for the girls. The Brothers of the Christian schools as they are called were founded in May 1684 by John Bapist de La Salle in Rheims in France. Irish Lasallians undertook educational work, adapting themselves to the circumstances in which they found themselves. Many Irish had been educated in France. When King James II, driven from the throne of England, had sought the protection of the king of France, some 25,000 Irish soldiers followed him and were received into the French Army as the Irish

Brigade. Among the refugees were Irish boys of school age. King James approached Cardinal Noailles of Paris, who recommended De La Salle. So fifty Irish youths were taken in and educated. This was the beginning of the link with Ireland.

In 1879 an Irish Relief Fund was launched by Cardinal Guibert of Paris who appealed to all religious orders in France to come to the assistance of famine stricken Ireland. The Superior General of the brothers, Brother Irilde, contributed 2,000 francs. He said in a letter that thanks to Ireland the Institute of the Brothers of the Christian schools had been able to supply teachers to the New World and open schools, orphanages and colleges where some 400,000 children were receiving a Christian education. On the list of deceased brothers is one Eliseus MacNicholas, of Ballaghaderreen born 1863, entered the novitiate in Baltimore and is buried at Ammendale twenty six miles south of Baltimore and fourteen North of Washington. After the 1847 Famine many sons of families who had emigrated to the United States from their famine stricken homes in Ireland had joined the de La Salle Brothers and contributed greatly to their educational establishments.

The Brothers had recruited boys in Ireland itself, and a house had been opened at Cobh in Co. Cork, in 1862 as a recruiting centre for those Irish De La Salle Brothers destined for the United States. It lasted two years. In 1880 the De La Salle Brothers came to Ireland to establish a novitiate. This was set up at Castletown in 1851. It was on 2nd October 1890 that Brother Francis Griffin, Director and Principal, Dominic O'Callaghan, Baldwin Fitzpatrick and Finbar Barry took charge of St. John's Monastery school in Ballaghaderreen which had just been built at the top of New Street. On the rolls were the name of 130 pupils between the ages of eight and fourteen. The Brothers' first home in Ballaghaderreen was Beechmount House (now the home of the Cryan family) on the Dublin Road. It was old, damp, poorly furnished and had no proper sanitation and was unhealthy. When Brother Andrew Dowling (1874-1894) died of typhoid fever, they moved to Chapel Lane while awaiting a new house promised to them by the bishop, Dr. Lyster. In 1920 they moved to a house directly opposite the school and remained there for the long productive years they spent in Ballaghaderreen. This house was purchased from Sarah Flannery of Landsdown Road, in Dublin for £600.[29]

Down through the years the De La Salle brothers have played a large part in the education of the youth of Castlemore-Kilcolman. Many scholarships were won to St. Nathy's College. Historical tours were organised. Games also played a large part, football, hurling and handball mostly. Young boys were trained as altar boys. Music was taught. There was much dedication by the Brothers. One great man who was in charge of the schools in the forties was Br. Cassian. He started evening classes for those who wanted to work towards scholarships for St. Nathy's College. The school provided well- instructed candidates for secondary studies from the poorer families of Ballaghaderreen and neighbourhood. A fife and drum band came into being in the 1930s instructed by Mr. P.J. Giblin who lived in Charlestown. Classes for violin were provided for both boys and girls, directed by the same Mr. Giblin who was a keen traditionalist. Today the band is still carrying on the tradition of earlier years and appears at Fleadhanna Ceoil throughout the country. The foundation of the Brothers of the Christian Schools in Ballaghaderreen eased the heavy burden placed on the shoulders of the Sisters of Charity, and they worked in co-operation with each other down through the years. The sisters took the infant boys and educated them until they made their First Communion. Then they went to the De La Salle Brothers for the remainder of their National school training. Among the many well- known past pupils to attend Ballaghaderreen (St. John's) is Bishop Thomas Flynn of Achonry, successor to Dr. James Fergus. Dr. Flynn had been diocesan instructor and professor in St. Nathy's College of which he became president in 1973. Another past pupil of note is John Towey (Br. Nathy) who joined the De La Salle order in 1935. He received a B.A. Degree in U.C.D. in 1935 and Higher Diploma in Education in 1958. He worked in almost every province of the Christian Schools throughout the world. He was awarded the degree of M.Ed.in the South African University of Witwatersrandt in 1975 for a thesis on Latin language teaching in South Africa. He was awarded a Ph.D by the National University of Ireland in 1980.

St. Nathy's College, as far as can be established, was founded in 1810 and was known as the Diocesan Classical School. It was managed by the bishop and clergy. By 1832 it was known as Achonry Diocesan School and had twenty three pupils.[30] The course of instruction was comprehensive, and the answering in school subjects satisfactory. Instruction included a course prescribed by the Intermediate Educational Act.[31]

One of the earliest records available gives many famous men who should never be forgotten in the west. Canon Thomas Judge was a student in St. Nathy's College in the late 1830s and matriculated at Maynooth on 1st October 1840. He was ordained a priest in 1844 and became P.P. of Killaser from 1881 to 1900. Archdeacon Terence O'Rourke was a contemporary of Canon Judge. He was born in 1819, attended St. Nathy's in the 1830s and like Thomas Judge, matriculated to Maynooth in 1840. He was a historian and an orator. To him we owe one of the two great histories of Co. Sligo. (The other, a rather different point

DOUGLAS HYDE

of view, is by Colonel W.G. Wood-Martin.) Attending the fifty-years celebrations of these great men in 1884 were Dr. Durcan and his brother Dean Durcan, Canon Judge, Dr. Nulty Bishop of Meath, Dean McGuire of Manorhamilton, Canon Furlong of Ferns, Dean Flynn a contemporary of Canon Judge and Archdeacon Terence O'Rourke.[32]

At a sermon preached at the Mass mention was made of the achievements of that era particularly Fr. Tighe and his trojan work for famine relief. Dr Lyster, later Bishop of Achonry, Dean Staunton, D.D. Canon Loftus, P.P. Frs.T Judge, John McKeown, Denis O'Hara, John O'Grady, Patrick Durcan, J. Connington, P. Quinn, P. Burke, John O'Donnell and P.Gallagher, were all present on this memorable occasion.

St. Nathy's College had various homes since 1810. It was first said to have been established on the old road to Castlemore. After 1865 it was based in the old Catholic Church. By 1875 Bishop McCormack had bought two houses on the square; numbers 66 and 67. The bishop was consecrated coadjutor bishop with Dr. Durcan on 4th February 1875. In the rate-books of 1891 Dr. Lyster and students occupied numbers 67 and 68. The numbers of these map plots changed and 67 became 23. Rate-books for 1894 indicate the occupier of 23 was Dr. Lyster. But from the evidence of Canon T.P. Gallagher PP Bohola, only students lived there. His information was that study and meals were in the house on the square. Classes were held near the site of the present St. Mary's Hall, perhaps part of the old Catholic Church at that time.

An earlier student of St. Nathy's College was Fr.William Brennan, born in 1798. He stayed at weekends at the house of his cousin in Strokestown, B.J. Duffy. He was from the Elphin Diocese. He matriculated to study Rhetoric in Maynooth in 1832 and was ordained in 1836. Rev. Dr. Gillooly, later bishop of Elphin (1885-95) also attended the classical school at Ballaghderreen as did his brother Abbé Gillooly, president of Summerhill College, Athlone. Both stayed at weekends at the same house in Strokestown. Bishop Lawerence Gillooly was born in the parish of Roscommon in 1819 and was educated in Roscommon and Ballaghaderreen. He studied Latin in Paris, Geneva and Mount Pelier. He was ordained in the Vincentian Order in 1847. He was appointed coadjutor to Bishop G. J. Plunket Browne of Elphin in 1856, and succeeded him in 1858. He died in Sligo in 1895.

In 1813 Edmondstown Park House home of A. George Costello became the home of St. Nathy's College. It was conducted there until 1895. Eventually in 1886 Dr. Daly who was its president bought the old military barracks from the War Office. This infantry barracks which was used as college premises from 1896 to 1916, cost £400. The present college was built

1914-1916 at a cost of £13,061. Thousands of priests and laymen were educated at St Nathy's College and its fame has spread all over the world. Among its past pupils in recent times were, the celebrated journalist John Healy, a former Minister of State Ted Nealon T.D., and Dr. Thomas Mitchell, recently elected provost of Trinity College, Dublin.

In a pastoral letter Dr. Lyster, said that the 'parish of Ballaghaderreen already contributed to the Diocesan Fund for an equipped seminary'. This probably referred to the purchase of the military barracks. An appeal for funds was extended to all the parishes in the diocese. Many of the clergy helped in the building of St. Mary's Hall which opened on 13th February 1900. Dr. Healy, Archbishop of Tuam spoke at the opening.

We can safely say that our traditional music and airs kept the soul of the west in harmony in the humble homes of the dispossessed despite hunger, hardship, poverty and oppression. The plaintive 'sean-nós' airs are a reflection of those times. Yet the people had their moments of joy in song and in story. They met in their cabins and danced to jigs, reels, hornpipes, marches and polkas. A spirit of this lives on today. Perhaps without this the Irish might not have survived. Also in the barony of Costello we have the music of Turlough O'Carolan who travelled this area at the end of the 17th century and the beginning of the 18th century; a blind harper, whose music we are only beginning to tap now. He composed tunes for Mrs Costello of Edmondstown, the Dillon family of Loughglynn, Lord and Lady Dillon, Gerard, Fanny, Luke and Counsellor Dillon, Dr. John Hart, bishop of Achonry, and the daughters of the Prince of Coolavin –The MacDermot and the descendants of the O'Conor kings in Connacht Maurice, John, Denis, Charles, Dr. and Mrs O'Conor.

On his way from Alderford to Turlough, Co. Mayo, (the home of his patron Mrs. MacDermot Roe, before she was married), Carolan spent the night in a humble house between Boyle and Ballaghaderreen. Next morning before he got up he could hear two men talking. He asked his 'giolla' who they were and the answer was 'Priest Cox and his clerk Fox'. When they had eaten their breakfast Carolan said:

> 'Ionadh mór do chonaic mé go
> tréith-lag im' luí,
> Sionnach agus coileach i gcuideacht
> ag bord im' thaoibh.
> Bhí cruinn-mhias uibheacha eatarthu is
> corn maith dighe.
> agus iad ag ithe gan iomaidh gan fearg,
> gan comhrac na glao.

COSTELLO NEW HOME 1867, NOW THE BISHOP OF ACHONRY'S PALACE

> *I saw a great marvel while exhausted in bed*
> *A fox and a cock sat together a-breaking their bread*
> *A round dish of eggs was between then and plenty of liquor*
> *And they ate without anger or strife-not a crow, not a bicker'.* [33]

The Irish language was used extensively then and many of Carolan's poems were written in Gaelic. Forty eight years later Anthony Raftery (1779-1835), blind at the age of five, a native of Cill Aodain Co. Mayo and a fiddler was composing hauntingly beautiful airs. Like Carolan he travelled Connacht but not in the luxury of Carolan. At the end of the 19th century his airs were still being sung but the composer was almost forgotten. Dr. Douglas Hyde the first President of Ireland (1860-1949) heard one of Raftery's songs in his native place – Frenchpark, and wrote down the words. Some years later while studying in the Royal Irish Academy in Dublin he came across the manuscripts of Raferty and the song he had learned – Cill Aodáin. On one of the Ms pages were a few lines penned by James Hardiman: *'Anthony Raftery who composed the following poems and songs, ...was born on 30 March 1799 ...He was a minstrel by profession; and played the violin tolerably; ...and sang his own songs accompanied by music from his violin, I knew him. He was an honest man'.*[34] Dr. Hyde was excited and later travelled Connacht and collected Raftery's works and published them in his *'Love Songs of Connaught'*. We have much to be grateful for to Dr. Hyde. In his youth illness prevented him from being sent away to school so after lessons at the rectory in Latin and Greek he spent all his spare time playing with Irish speaking boys, fishing on Lough Gara and listening to the men on the bog at the Float talk in Irish of folklore.[35] He was the founder of the Gaelic League in 1893. The aims were to preserve and revive the Irish language and encourage Irish art and industry. He wrote at least seven dramas in Irish and both acted in and produced most of them. Educated in Trinity College he became Professor of Modern Irish at U.C.D. Many books and essays are being written about him now.

A scholar whose ancestors were evicted from the De Freyne estate, at Aughalustia was Fionnan MacCartha. He qualified as a teacher and became a friend of Dr. Douglas Hyde who encouraged him to support the revival of Irish. His health was poorly and in 1933 he emigrated to Australia. His book of poems on Coolavin was published in the 1950s. His sadness at not hearing one word of the Irish language in the country of his adoption – Queensland, prompted him to compose poems in Irish called *'Amhráin Dheireadh Domhain'*.[36] His friend Tomás ó Máille published two of these poems in *Irisleabhar Choláiste na Gaillimhe* in 1950. 'Diarmuid na nGall' was published in an Irish paper in Sydney founded by Bishop ó Síothcháin. These poems were all republished by Oifig an tSoláthair, Dublin, 1953.

Another great educationalist was Brother Robert Egan De La Salle who taught in all parts of the globe. A native of Aughalustia, he remembered his grandfather who was born in 1809 telling him that twelve families were evicted in the village by the De Freynes at the turn of the 19th century. The holdings were small and large families eked out a harsh existence until they were old enough to emigrate.

P.J. Coleman, a native of Ballaghaderreen, emigrated to Canada and became editor of the *Catholic Register* in Toronto. His father and two brothers played a large part in the Fenian Brotherhood. His father was arrested and imprisoned. After his release he had to go to America, leaving his young wife alone at home. It was only through the efforts of Dr. Durcan, bishop of Achonry, that he could eventually return home in safety. P.J.'s grandmother on his mother's side was a Mullaney girl from Boyle. He corresponded with the late Dr. Morrisroe, Bishop of Achonry about writing a history of the diocese.[37] (See poem on Castlemore in Appendix 4.)

CHAPTER 8

THE FENIAN MOVEMENT
AT
BALLAGHADERREEN

Black 'forty-seven' left an indelible mark on the west of Ireland. In the mid '40s the young men who had joined O'Connell's constitutional Repeal Movement became impatient with his efforts and formed their own Young Ireland Movement. One of these John Blake Dillon, son of Luke, was born in Ballaghaderreen, in 1814. There can be little doubt that his father's experience of eviction gave rise to strong feelings of nationalism in the young John Blake. He was probably educated in the Classical School in Ballaghaderreen, forerunner of St. Nathy's College before going to Maynooth, where he discovered he had not a vocation for the priesthood. His aunt Monica Duff had made a thriving small business of the shop her brother Thomas had given to her in Ballaghaderreen. She now held the post office in the town and was quite able to provide education for the family.

John Blake went on to Trinity College where he became a great friend of Thomas Davis. Both were active in the college Historical Society. John Blake was called to the bar. Being a Catholic in a Protestant college did not deter him. Both Davis and Dillon had begun to dabble in political journalism and contributed to the *Nation*, a newspaper started by their friend Charles Gavan Duffy.

Considering the plight of the people around Ballaghaderreen in the 1840s it is not surprising that John Blake Dillon should be deeply distressed as he contemplated the needs of the 'industrious poor'. He desired a *'National existence for Ireland, that an old historic state might be raised from the dust and a sceptre placed in her hand and thus might she become the mother of a brave and self reliant race'*.[1] Primarily he wanted to get rid of social degradation and suffering which it wrung his heart to witness without being able to relieve. As early as 1845 the Young Irelanders had proclaimed in their newspaper their definition of 'Nationalism' to embrace Protestant, Catholic and Dissenter, which would be recognised by the world, and sanctified by wisdom, virtue and prudence'. Small wonder that they differed with O'Connell's hostile attitude

O Donovan Rossa

towards Sir Robert Peel's Colleges Bill of 1845, which was to establish three Colleges– at Belfast, Cork and Galway, the first mainly for Presbyterians, the latter two mainly for Catholics. These colleges were to be free from all denominational tests and any religious instruction given in them was to be financed from private not public sources. Since unity between all denominations was the main principle of Young Ireland doctrine there was bound to be a clash. And Young Ireland's most important creed did not rule out the use of arms in the attainment of freedom in certain circumstances. Thus, unable to accept O'Connell's rejection of force, the Young Irelanders withdrew from the Repeal Association. John Blake's health was poorly at this time and he was sent to Maderia to recuperate. Thomas Davis had died of scarlet fever aged thirty one in 1845.

The attempted rebellion of 1848 was a fiasco. The Young Ireland leader Gavan Duffy joined by Fintan Lawlor struggled on. For a time Lawlor advocated in the *'Nation'* that only those landlords who gave adequate security to their tenants could expect to survive. The famine had created a new situation and a secure independent, agricultural peasantry was a necessity. John Mitchell was convinced that a revolution was necessary and he advocated this. He was arrested with O'Brien and Meagher. The latter two were discharged but Mitchell was was convicted and sentenced to fourteen years penal servitude in Tasmania. Whatever hopes the Young Irelanders had of being a serious threat to the government vanished, when they realised the vast indifference of the population who were so occupied with hunger and disease. Dillon escaped to the United States disguised as a priest. Smith O'Brien was sent to Tasmania but returned to Ireland after his release in 1856. The idealism of the Young Irelanders lived on and even though totally out of touch with the world in reality in 1848, the essential message of Davis to recall his countrymen to a sense of pride in being Irish, caught the imagination of the emigrants who left Ireland after the Famine. And hatred of British rule in Ireland was intensified in the United States, in England and in France.

James Stephens and John O'Mahony had taken part in the abortive insurrection of 1848 and had afterwards gone to the continent to avoid arrest. It was in Paris, where they both supported themselves by teaching and translation work, that they began planning anew to overthrow British Rule in Ireland. (Stephens was one of a number of tutors who taught John and William Dillon in that same year). To this end they founded the Irish Revolutionary or Republican Brotherhood, popularly known as the Fenian Movement, in 1865. That John Blake employed Stephens as tutor to his sons was no more than a gesture of goodwill to a friend who had been with him in 1848, for Dillon had abandoned Stephen's radical

Fenianism and played a major part in founding the National Association. This (with the blessing of the Church) aimed to oppose Fenianism, bring about the disestablishment of the Church of Ireland, seek improved conditions for tenant farmers and set up a National University.[2] John Blake Dillon was elected MP for Tipperary in 1865, but within a few months he died of cholera after only a few days' illness.

The Fenian Movement spread rapidly in the United States. From forty members in 1858 the movement grew to 50,000, with perhaps four or five times that number of sympathisers. In Ireland the situation was depressing enough. Stephens walked thousands of miles to every part of Ireland (he was called 'An Seabhac Siúlach', the walking hawk) to organise the movement. He planned to enrol ten thousand men in this new secret society on the continental style. Security was to be preserved by the division of the membership into 'Circles' A Circle contained one hundred and twenty men commanded by a 'Centre' and organised in multiples of nine. Rapid expansion of the movement into the British regiments in the Curragh, Dublin and Athlone facilitated the British Government authorities in infiltrating all sections of the movement so efficiently that all its movements at home and abroad and all activities were known to the authorities.[3] The success of the movement depended on the funds collected in America. It was an enormous undertaking by enthusiastic men. J O'Mahony was the head 'Centre' in America, Stephens in Ireland. Leading men in the movement included Jeremiah O'Donovan Rossa, Thomas Clarke Luby, John O'Leary and Charles Kickham. Stephens estimated that in Ireland and England 80, 000 Fenians had been enrolled by 1865.[4] Insurrection was their goal.

By the end of 1863 and the beginning of 1864 the Fenian organisation was fast gaining ground in Connacht. This was quite an achievement as the province was still the stronghold of Ribbonism. And it was a well known fact that it was easier to turn an Orangeman than a Ribbonman into a Fenian.

The success of the Fenians in Connacht was largely due to a young man named Edward Duffy. Edward Duffy's father had the ground floor of a two storey house in Ballaghaderreen. The second floor was used as a Latin school. This schoolhouse was situated at the corner of what became the Convent Road. The old road led from the 'Shambles' or market where the Vocational School now stands. The road is now the back lane to the Main Street. Duffy's school was said to be an excellent school and it was here Edward and his brother John were educated. They were born in Kilmovee a few miles outside the town.

Edward's devotion to the cause and overpowering fervour was infectious. His ill health (he suffered from consumption) gave him a pale serious appearance. The frustrations and poverty and hopelessness of the area led Edward towards the new movement and he spent his short life dedicated to the cause. John O'Leary's sister who was a sincere friend of his had a high opinion of his ability. James Stephens was also aware of this and he appointed Edward head of the organisation during his absence in America. The west, due to Edward Duffy, became wide awake and Ballaghaderreen became a hotbed of the Fenian Movement. There was much activity in the area as police records of the time show.

A newspaper –*The People* was established in Dublin, within a stone's throw of Dublin Castle, as a Fenian Journal under the editorship of A.M. Forrester.[5] John O'Leary, Charles Kickham, Thomas Clarke Luby and Jeremiah O'Donovan were on the permanent staff.[6] Daniel Ryan, superintendent of the Dublin Metropolitan Police found an informer, working for *The People* who gave all the relevant information needed. It is clear from research in later years that the Government authorities were aware through their spies of even the smallest activities of the Fenians. They were therefore doomed to failure in insurrection even before they began.

Early in 1865, Head Constable Talbot had infiltrated the Fenian movement and he reported that the number of drilled Fenians in Ireland exceeded one hundred and twenty thousand and that arms were being stored in several timber yards in Dublin. Arms were seized which were sent from O'Mahony to O'Donovan Rossa of the Irish People Office. A rising was expected to take place at the end of September. Farmers of the south began to draw their money out of the banks in gold. There was good reason to believe that not only the army but the militia, the Coast Guard, the Dublin Fire Brigade and even the police had many sworn into the conspiracy. The *Irish People* was becoming more daring with every issue. James Stephens was reminding the Fenians that 1865 must be the year of action. Rebel songs were published in the Irish People inciting and encouraging members. Ships were expected to come from America with guns and men so the authorities ordered a cordon of war ships to move around the coast to meet any American aid. On the night of the 14th September a series of raids were carried out on Fenian centres in Dublin, Cork and various places throughout the provinces. The newspaper *'The Irish People'* was suppressed. Many leaders were arrested but Luby, O'Leary, Rossa and Stephens managed to avoid arrest. On November 19th Stephens, Hugh Francis Brophy, Charles Kickham and Edward Duffy were arrested at Fairview House, Newbridge Avenue, Sandmount.[7] Edward Duffy when searched had a bill for £1,525 in favour of George Hopper and a key. Hopper was a brother-in-law of Stephens.

They were all brought before Mr. Strong, J.P. and were committed for trial to the special Commission. Brophy and Kickham were committed for treason-felony and sentenced to penal servitude. Edward Duffy's health seemed to be so much affected while in custody that he was let out on bail.[8] He failed to appear for trial at the Special Commission. Warrants in duplicate were prepared on the 23rd February 1866 and directed, one to the sub-Inspector at Castlerea and the other to Mr. Ryan, Superintendent of Police, Dublin. Mr. Ryan knowing something of the state of Duffy's health dallied before executing the warrant and sent it back for consideration. A new warrant was issued for his arrest on the twenty sixth of February 1866. On the 3rd March 1886 Mr. Charles Strickland J.P. of Loughglynn reported to Dublin Castle that Edward Duffy had returned to the neighbourhood of Castlerea and was spending every day and night spreading the Fenian conspiracy everywhere. 'He was' he said 'out on bail and was visiting all the small towns and doing a great deal of mischief.' But strange to say, the Attorney General did not think that Mr. Strickland's statements on hearsay were sufficient to justify the arrest of Duffy.[9] Evidence against Duffy was accumulated by the authorities. In the month of June 1866 he was reported by Thomas Kelly to have been in Castlebar talking to men in the barrack yard and visited Mr. McMahony's public house in that town. Kelly said he was sworn in by Duffy 'to be true and loyal to the Irish Republic and to levy war against the Queen when required at a moment's warning'. John Moran and Thomas Sweeney of Ballaghaderreen who were members of the North Mayo Regiment at the time, were sworn in by Duffy also. Detective Officer Godfrey Massey said Duffy was 'Centre' for the west of Ireland and he had seen him at his lodgings at Upper Pembroke St. Dublin. John O'Leary said Stephens has often been blamed, wrongly, in relation to his prison escape, for not taking Kickham, Duffy and Brophy, who were in the same part of the prison, out with him.[9] But besides there was the safe keeping of the men once they were out. In any case it was Devoy and the others who planned the escape of Stephens and not Stephens himself, who were to be blamed.

For what appeared on paper to be such a large organisation, funds in the Fenian exchequer were pitifully small. For the first six years, 1858-1864, a little less than £1,500 was collected. From 1864-1866 about £30,000. Of this £7,000 was seized by the Government. It was not ample to conduct a serious rebellion with. Stephens got away from Ireland to Paris and from there to the United States. By now, discontent had become widespread in the organisation. In January 1867 Stephens was deposed and replaced by Colonel Kelly. The official Fenian body sent over representatives from the four provinces to meet Kelly in London –

THE FENIAN MOVEMENT AT BALLAGHADERREEN

Edward Duffy from Connacht, William Harbison from Ulster, Edward O'Byrne from Leinster and Dominic Mahony from Munster. They met on the 10th May 1867 and constituted themselves a Provisional Government. In England was John Joseph Corydon an old and trusted friend of Stephens, formerly a lieutenant in the Federal Army, who had joined the Fenian Brotherhood in 1862. Corydon had been giving information for some time to the police in Liverpool.[10] He reported the proposed attack on Chester Castle, and was instrumental in identifying Colonel Kelly and Deasy at Manchester as having commanded the Fenian Rising at Mill St. County Cork. As Kelly and Deasy were being taken in a police van from the courthouse in Manchester to the county jail, a rescue attempt was made.[11] They escaped but Allen, Larkin and O'Brien went to the gallows for the murder of Constable Brett and ever since have been known as 'the Manchester Martyrs'. The authorities were furious at Kelly's escape as he was a far more important man than Stephens. He was never rearrested.

The following is some of Corydon's evidence about Edward Duffy:

> 'I know Edward Duffy and have seen him in company with James Stephens, O'Donovan Rossa and other leaders in Dublin. The first time I saw Duffy was immediately after my first arrival from America, in August 1865, at Deniffe's house in South Anne Street. Stephens, Rossa, Brophy, Kickham and some American officers were also present. We reported ourselves to Stephens. I saw Duffy on several occasions at different Fenian resorts in Dublin, up to his arrest. I saw him several times after his release from prison. In the month of February 1867, I was directed by Godfrey Massy and Edward Duffy to go to the County Kerry and see Colonel O'Connor, for the purpose of giving him instructions as to the intended rising. Prior to my starting Duffy sent me three pounds for my expenses. Duffy was the 'Head Circle' for the west of Ireland. He had five or six American officers to take command in Connacht at the rising which was to take place on the fifth of March last and in my presence gave them money and directions as to how they were to act. The plan was that there was to be a simultaneous rising at twelve o'clock on Tuesday night, the fifth of March, all over Ireland, save the province of Ulster. Duffy gave these men full directions as to their course of action, in case of reverses or otherwise.[12]
>
> April the seventh 1867.

The indictment of the Fenian prisoners at the Commission court at Kilmainham 1867 charged:

> 'that they did feloniously and wickedly combine, conspire, confederate, consult and agree with each other and with James Stephens, John O'Mahony, Colonel Kelly and divers other evil disposed persons to raise, make and levy insurrection and rebellion against our Lady the Queen of this realm'.[13] They were charged with trying to subvert and destroy the constitution of this realm,

to stir certain foreigners and strangers, and citizens of the U.S.A. with force to invade that part of the United Kingdom called Ireland; to induce and persuade persons to become members of the Fenian society, including soldiers in Her Majesty's service, to desert and join illegal societies of people called Fenians.

Edward Duffy's trial along with that of John Flood and John Cody was brought to a conclusion. When asked what he had to say why sentence should not be passed on him, the following is the speech which by great physical effort he delivered from the dock. His bright eyes and pallid features lit up with a glow of earnest and lofty enthusiasm while he spoke:

'The Attorney General has made a wanton attack on me but I leave my countrymen to judge between us. There is no political act of mine that I in the least regret. I have laboured earnestly and sincerely in my country's cause and I have been actuated throughout by a strong sense of duty. I believe that a man's duty to his country is part of his duty to God, for it is He who implants the feeling of patriotism in the human breast. He, the great searcher of hearts, knows that I have been actuated by no mean or paltry ambition, that I have never worked for any selfish end. For the late outbreak I am not responsible. I did all in my power to prevent it, for I knew that circumstanced as we then were, it would be a failure. It has been stated in the course of those trials that Stephens was for peace. This was a mistake. It may well be that it should not go uncontradicted. It is but too well known in Ireland that he sent numbers of men over here to fight, promising to be with them when the time would come. The time did come but not Mr. Stephens. It may be a very pleasant sight but I would not be in his place now. He is a lost man, lost to honour, lost to country. There are a few things I wish to say relevant to the evidence given against me at my trial, but I would ask your lordships to give me permission to say them after sentence has been passed'. The Chief Justice – 'That is not the usual practice. Not being tried for life, it is doubtful to me whether you have a right to speak at all. What you are asked to say is why sentence should not be passed upon you and whatever you have to say you must say now'. 'Then if I must say it now I declare it before my God that what Kelly swore against me on the table is not true. I saw him in Enniscrone but I never spoke to him on any political subject I declare to heaven I never did. I knew him as a child in that little town herding with the lowest and the vilest. Is it supposed that I'd put put my liberty into the hands of such a character? I never did it. The next witness is Corydon. He swore that at the meeting he referred to I gave him directions to go to Kerry to find O'Connor and put himself in communications with him. I declare to my God that every word of that is false. Whether O'Connor was in the country or whether he had made his escape I know just as little as your lordships and I never heard of the Kerry rising until I heard it in the public papers. As to my giving the American officers money that night, before my God on the verge of my grave where my sentence will send me I say that also is false. As to the writing that the policeman swore in that book and which is not a prayer book but the *'Imitations of Christ'* given to me by a lady to whom I served my time what was written in that book was written by another young man in her employment. That is his writing not mine. It is the writing of a young man in the house and I never wrote a line of it. The Lord Chief Justice; 'It was not sworn to be in your handwriting'. 'Yes my Lord it was. The policeman swore that it was my handwriting.' The Lord Chief Justice; 'That is a mistake. It is said to be like yours'. Duffy continued, 'The dream of my life has been that I might die fighting for Ireland. The jury have doomed me to a more painful but not less glorious death. I now bid farewell to my friends who are dear to me.

> There is a world where souls are free,
> Where tyrants taint not nature's bliss
> If death that bright world's opening be
> Oh who would live a slave like this?

I am glad to be thought worthy of suffering for my country. When I am lying in my lonely cell I will not forget Ireland and my last prayer will be that the God of liberty may give her strength to break off her chains'.

Edward Duffy and John Flood were then sentenced each to fifteen years of penal servitude and Cody to penal servitude for life. Edward Duffy's term of suffering did not last long. A merciful providence gave his noble spirit release from its earthly tenement before one year from the date his sentence had been passed away. On the 21st May 1867 his trial concluded; On the 17th January 1868 the patriot lay dead in Millbank prison, London.[14] The Government permitted his friends to remove his remains to Ireland for interment; and they now rest in Glasnevin Cemetery Dublin.

O'Donovan Rossa was at this time also a convict in Millbank and a few weeks after Duffy's death a prisoner named Lynch whispered through the prison grating in passing Rossa's cell 'Duffy is dead'. Straight away he wrote the following poem. It was sent secretively to *The Nation* and it appeared in the issue of that journal on the 1st January 1870. The editor wrote 'Considered at any time in any light, it is a composition of great pathos, force and beauty, and as the work of a man enduring the daily hardships and indignities of English prison life, it appears to us to be a remarkable effort.'[15]

THE FENIAN MOVEMENT AT BALLAGHADERREEN

A LAMENT FOR EDWARD DUFFY

The world is growing darker to me, darker day by day;
The stars that shone upon life's path are vanishing away
Some setting and some shifting, only one that changes never
'Tis the guiding star, the beacon light, that blazes bright as ever.

Liberty sits mountain high and slavery has birth
In hovels in the marshes, in the lowest dens on earth;
The tyrants of the world pitfall – dig the path between,
And o'ershadow it with scaffolds, prison blocks and guillotine.

The gloomy way is lightened when we walk with those we love
The heavy load is lightened, when we bear and they approve.
The path of life grows darker to me as I journey on,
For the loving hearts that travelled it are falling one by one.

The news of death is saddening even in the festive hall,
But when 'tis heard through prison bars, 'tis the saddest then of all.
Where there's none to share the sorrow in the solitary cell
In the prison within prison – a blacker hell in hell.

To lay your head upon the block for faith in Freedom's God
To fall in fight for freedom in the land your fathers trod,
For freedom on the scaffold high to draw your largest breath
Or anywhere against tyranny, 'tis well to die the death.

That whisper through the grating has thrilled through all my veins,
'Duffy is dead' A noble soul had slipped the tyrant's chain
But whatever wounds they gave him in their lying book will show
How they very kindly treated him, more like a friend than foe.

Still sad and lone was yours Ned, 'mid the jailors of your race
With none to press the cold white hand, with none to smooth thy face
With none to make the dying wish to homeland, friend or brother
To kindred mind, to promised bride, or to the sorrowing mother.

For these are Christian pharisees, the hypocrites of creeds
With the bible on their lips and the devil in their deeds
Too merciful in public gaze to take our lives away
Too anxious here to plant in us, the seeds of life's decay.

THE FENIAN MOVEMENT AT BALLAGHADERREEN

These Christians stand between us and the God above our head
The sun and moon they prison and withhold our daily bread.
Entombed, enchained and starving, that the mind they may control
And quench the fire that's burning in every living soul.

I tried to get to speak to you before you passed away
As you were dying near to me and far from Castlerea,
But the bible-mongers turned me off when at their office door
I asked last month to see you, now I'll never see you more.

If spirits once released from earth could visit earth again
You'd come to see me here Ned, but for these we look in vain,
In the dead house you are lying and I'd wake you if I could
But they'll wake you in Loughglynn Ned in that cottage by the wood.

For the mother's instinct tells her that her dearest one is dead
That the single mind, the noble soul from earth to heaven has fled.
As the girls look towards the door and look towards the trees
To catch that sorrow laden wail that's borne upon the breeze

Thus the path of life grows darker to me, darker day by day
The stars that flashed their lights on it are vanishing away
Some setting, some shifting but that one which changes never
The beacon star of liberty that blazes bright for ever.

This poem shows how highly O'Donovan Rossa thought of Edward Duffy, whom he affectionately called Ned. Indeed death was a relief as prisoners were not treated well. On the 9th February it was noted in the *Freeman's Journal* by a correspondent from London that O'Donovan Rossa himself was subjected to corporal punishment; he received ten lashes of the cat'-nine-tails for being guilty of insubordination.

In March 1867 the constable at Ballaghaderreen reported that a man called Fogarty was arrested the previous night while in the company of Fenian agents. He refused to give a satisfactory account of himself. First he said he was from Boyle, then from Galway and after, that he was from Dublin and was living on his money. He was taken before Lord De Freyne to whom he said that he had come from America. He said he had gone to see a Captain Costello. The sub-Inspector at Ballaghaderreen said that Fogarty had been left there by Edward Duffy to lead the insurgents, and that but for Fogarty's arrest there would have been a rising in that part of the country. It was noted that there was no rising in Connacht as the Fenians there refused to rise unless the Americans took the lead. Evidence was given that Fogarty was a Fenian. He was discharged on condition of his going direct to America on the 24th August 1867.

Many were arrested in Ballaghaderreen and surrounding districts for being members of the organisation and for helping to spread it. James Benson of Ballaghaderreen a draper's assistance was arrested. Denis Bligh a draper was sent to jail in Roscommon. Owen Carney a tailor of Ballaghaderreen held Fenian meetings in his house and was reported for 'doing much mischief'. John Casey of Castlerea head of the Supreme Council in England was arrested in March 1867. Charles Conlon of Castlerea, Andrew Cruise and Joseph Duffy of Frenchpark were arrested as was Patrick D'Arcy of Ballaghaderreen after his return from England, in a house where illegal practices were carried on.[16] John Duffy brother of Edward, was charges with illegal drilling. An order was given for his discharge on condition that he went to America on the 22nd February 1867. He sailed from Queenstown in April. In July 1868 John Duffy (who had returned from America) was arrested for having posted Fenian printed proclamations about the district.[17] He was charged and as there was no evidence against him he returned to America later in 1868. More arrests followed. A clerk named Egan from Boyle, Stephen Farrell of Castlerea and Thomas Gallagher of Aughaherin were arrested. Patrick Curran a labourer, of Ballaghaderreen, who joined the militia was arrested for drilling and dismissed. He had been surrounded by young men at fairs and markets carrying out Fenian orders. James Grady and his brother William of Curry, Edmondstown, both active Fenians, were believed to be 'Centres'. Francis Grady was committed to Castlebar jail. Anthony Grady of Ballaghaderreen, a National School teacher was remanded. A paid informer for the authorities named Thomas Kelly of Ballaghaderreen who was a member of No. 5 Company of the North Mayo Militia gave reports that a number of men in the area were involved with Fenianism. He claimed that on the 10th July 1865 he attended a drill meeting in Corrigeen in County Mayo. There were about four thousand present, and they were put through military movement and drilled by James Hyland who was a National School teacher at Cross National School. Among those present were John Mearan, John Duffy, Thomas Shannon, Thomas Spelman, Frank Grady (shoemaker) Thomas and William Grady, Pat Farrell and Thomas Gallagher of Aughaherin.[18] Thomas Spelman was an agent for the *'Irish People* ' in Ballaghaderreen. His house was a meeting place for the Fenians of the neighbourhood and in his house they were paid. John O'Leary's sister and Mrs. O'Donvan Rossa were in charge of the monies being paid out to to organisers of the Fenians and made frequent visits to Paris and brought back funds for the payment of men and the purchase of arms.

THE FENIAN MOVEMENT AT BALLAGHADERREEN

On the 22nd February Joseph C. Maguire, senior inspector of the Constabulary at Ballaghaderreen arrested Charles O'Hara. The following paper was found on him. 'I solemnly swear allegiance to the Irish Republic, that I will yield implicit obedience to my superior officer, that I will take arms at a moment's warning to defend the independence and integrity of my country'.[19] Most of those arrested were released on bail at the time, or if offences could be proved were discharged on giving an undertaking that they would go to America. It is clear that each member of the Fenian movement understood what was demanded from him and was excited and proud to be a member in spite of the constabulary. Thomas Spelman of Ballaghaderreen was arrested and committed to Castlebar jail on the 10th April 1867. On the 3rd March he hired a car and sent the driver to meet Edward Duffy and bring him to McDermott's hotel in Tubbercurry. On the intercession of the Right Rev. Patrick Durcan D.D., Catholic bishop of Achonry and several other clergymen he was discharged on bail.[20] Thomas Mannion, was arrested on the 13th February 1867 in a house where the Fenians were in the habit of meeting.[21] James O'Malley, a saddler was arrested in the town for endeavouring to administer the 'illegal oath' on the 13th December 1866. It is interesting to find that his sister had married James F.X. O'Brien a young Corkman who who travelled throughout Connacht as a commercial traveller spreading Fenianism.[22] His usual place to stay was in Sligo with Fay who was a stone cutter and a 'Centre'. O'Brien acted with bravery in the '67 rising at Ballyknocker in County Cork. He forced the police to surrender but allowed then to retire to Mallow on giving up their arms. He was later committed to Portland Prison. He found the organisation healthy on his release in 1869. By 1871, however, when he was a member of the Supreme Council he felt the organisation was on the decline and he felt obliged to quit altogether.[23]

Meanwhile, in 1867, arrests continued at Ballaghaderren, including Thomas and John Shenan and Thomas Ross of Mullaghroeon on whom Fenian documents were found. John Mearon was sent to Castlebar jail on the 24th of April 1867 and James McGovern, a draper's assistant was arrested at a Fenian meeting on the 19th of December 1867. In spite of the elaborate planning and the support of the Fenian organisation in America, the men of '67 were no more successful than those of '48. The attempted invasion of Canada was equally abortive. Still Fenianism carried on after 1867. A convention of 'Centres' in the north of England division of the I.R.B. was held in England on the 15th April 1871. Fifty three 'Circles' purported to represent 4817 men. A financial statement of £2963 /19 between money and material was presented. It was reported at the convention that Connacht was improving with moderate speed and that the States promised great assistance. It was also reported

> 'The organisation in Ireland will go on with the good work whether it receives external assistance or not. A great sum of money is waiting to be converted into material as soon as the high prices resulting from the Franco-Prussian War are reduced. In 1869 the Fenians were active in Mullaghroe. A letter sent to Dublin Castle reports information from Charles Costello, Esquire, of Kilfree that Fenianism was about to establish itself in that part of the country with more energy than ever, and 'Head Centres' had lately been appointed in Tubbercurry and Ballymote.'

The constables in Clogher were asked to keep a close watch on all suspicious characters.[24] Charles Costello stated that there was a widespread and deep-rooted conspiracy established in that neighbourhood (Clogher), that they had locations of meetings in the townlands of Knocknashreagh, Moygara, Sreagh and at a place called Everlawn near Buninadden. 'They (the Fenians) proceed from these places by night collecting money, that everyone is bound to give according to his circumstances and that in some cases the payment of these contributions is enforced at the muzzle of a revolver'.

To all appearances, the actions of these men were like those of the Ribbonmen of the 1820s. For example, notices were sent or posted, threatening tenants of one Caddel, a landlord who resided in County Meath, for paying an advance of rent.

> *'Sir, whereas that we were strongly informed that your family and Barrets are connected by marriage, you had the privilege of being favoured with his interest and therefore you hold your lands at a very low rent and the rest of the tenants living on Caddell's property in this part of the country holds you to blame very much for your being so prompt in paying the advance of rent at the last Gale. We now strictly caution against paying at this time. So we hope you will not put us to the trouble of paying you the second visit; if you do so, you will mark the consequence.*
>
> *We remain yours respectfully.*
> *'Men of Tipperary'.*

A second notice similar to the first, warning the tenants against paying in advance was posted and dated 30th of October 1869. A case of arms was sent by the London and North Western Railway invoiced as silk and addressed to O'Donnell, Ballaghaderreen, County Mayo. It was left at Castlerea Railway Station (the branch line to Ballaghaderreen not being finished at that time) and was to be called for by a man named Owen Carney alias 'Mr. Patrick Forde'. The case was opened by the police and

THE FENIAN MOVEMENT AT BALLAGHADERREEN

the arms found. James O'Donnell's house and shop in Ballaghaderreen were searched also without success. Some time later, another case containing arms was opened at Castlerea, addressed to Mr. James Morgan, draper, Castlerea. Large quantities of arms had been coming into the Ballaghaderreen area in this way for some time. It was found out by the constabulary that James O'Donnell who was a shopkeeper in the town of Ballaghaderreen, had a brother-in-law who dealt in old clothes and was active in the Fenian movement. Owen Carney had been at the assizes of Castlebar for having a sword in a proclaimed district. Both men needed to be closely watched. Working on this information it was discovered by the police that the back of the premises of 32, Featherston Street, St. Luke's, London, was used as a workshop by the Fenians for packing arms and forwarding them to Ireland.

A watch was kept on the place. A man arrived in a cab and took away two large parcels containing apparently six or eight rifles in each. He came to a low beerhouse in Bermondsey Walk, kept by an Irishman named Higgins. Opposite Higgin's house was a set of stairs, leading to the river where the Cork boat was lying. Seemingly American arms were packed here and sent to all parts of Ireland, addressed as 'Broad Street Station, London, to Castlerea, Athlone, Ballinasloe, Hollymount, County Mayo. The fact that the police were aware of what was going on made the Fenian activities difficult.

Mention has been made of the advent of the railway to this corner of Connacht. On the 3rd December 1862 the Sligo-Dublin Railway opened.[26] Work started on the Kilfree-Ballaghaderreen line on the 6th August 1869. F. Newell contracted to build it for £4,500 per mile. At the end of 1869 a strike over wages stopped the work. It re-started in early 1870 but on the 29th January the County Sheriff seized all the materials on behalf of T. and C. Martin of Dublin over unpaid bills. In June 1871 the Consett Iron Company took over the railway works. In December 1871 the line to Ballaghaderreen opened. It was operated by the Midland and Great Western Railway. There were three trains to Ballaghaderreen, at 7.50 a.m. 10.55 a.m. and 10.00 p.m. and three down to Kilfree from Ballaghaderreen at 9.00 a.m. 1.45 p.m. and 10.00 p.m. On the 31st December 1875 the line closed. On the 24th March 1876 it re-opened for traffic. It had cost £24,000. In March 1877 the M.G.W.R. took over completely. The first drivers were Ben Partridge and a Mr. Conneely. In 1891 Peter Lambe was the driver. Others over the years were Two Ton O'Brien, 'Slasher' Morgan, 'Muskrat Nestor' and 'Taylor' Byrne.[27] The last train ran on Saturday the 3rd February 1963. The station at Kilfree stands in the middle of a bog but it brought many people on its branch-line to the unknown across the seas.

John Dillon
September 1888

CHAPTER 9

LAND WAR IN THE VICINITY OF SLIABH LUGHA

Mayo had suffered more from the landlord system than any other county. In a period of thirty years, following 1849, twenty five thousand homes were deserted as cattle-raising replaced tenant farmers. People who could not emigrate were compelled to migrate to reclaimed bogland for which they paid rackrents. Small wonder that secret societies sought revenge.

The young Mayo-born Fenian, Michael Davitt, found on a visit to America in 1878 that some of the most advanced nationalists like John Devoy were impatient to launch out in a new direction. By 1879 figures such as Davitt, Devoy and John Dillon had decided that it was on the land question that all their energies should henceforth be concentrated. The first of a series of mass-meetings on this new issue was at Irishtown, Co. Mayo, on 20th of April 1879. Later, the young nationalist leader, Charles Stewart Parnell, attended a meeting in Westport on 1st June 1879 while Dillon attended one in Claremorris. The Land League of Mayo was formally launched at Castlebar on the 16th of August by Matthew Harris, Michael Davitt and James Daly. The enthusiasm of the people knew no bounds. A meeting at Gurteen, Co. Sligo, on Sunday the 16th November attended by Davitt, Dillon, James Daly of Castlebar and Mr. Killeen, a Belfast barrister, was a huge success.[1] Statements were made by the speakers that a coming combination of farmers and others would sweep landlords and rent out of the country. The speeches were taken down by a Government reporter. James Daly, 1835-1900, was the editor of the *Connaught Telegraph* and Secretary of the Mayo Tenants' Defence Association in 1878. He had organised the Irishtown meeting which led to the formation of the Land League. The Gurteen meeting was the largest demonstration held so far in connection with the Land Campaign. Crowds attended from Ballaghaderreen, Boyle, Swinford, Ballymote, Carrick-on-Shannon, the Island and Kilfree. The Gurteen band provided music for those who had arrived a few hours before the meeting was due to begin. It is worth noting that the clergy were there in strength; Canon John McDermott, P.P. Kilmovee, Fr Brennan, P.P. Gurteen, Canon J.McDermott, P.P. Buninadden, Fr. Keehan,C.C. Keadue, Fr. Michael Kearney,C.C. and Fr. Denis O'Hara, Ballaghaderreen.

Most of those who were at the meeting were tenant farmers who were trying to eke out a living from very bad land. The clergy were fully behind their flock in their constitutional non-violent methods of gaining whatever rights nationalist politics and the Land League had to offer. These clergymen and their bishops were unique in that particular time. Dr. McCormack, Bishop of Achonry, living at the 'Abbey', Ballaghaderreen freely allowed his priests to take part. So also did Dr. Duggan, Bishop of Clonfert, who helped out and encouraged the movement [2].

One of the most outstanding men of that period was Fr. Denis O'Hara. He was born about 1851 in Cloonacool, County Sligo, a beautiful picturesque village at the foot of the Ox Mountains. This was a congested district and the famine had taken its toll on its people. Fr. Denis was ordained at Maynooth in 1873 and was appointed as curate in Kiltimagh. Later he was transferred to Curry and then to Ballaghaderreen, where he remained for eleven years. His brother Roger became Archdeacon of the diocese of Achonry and lived for the greater part of his life in Kilmovee.

A branch of the Land League was established in Ballaghaderreen around 1879 and Fr. Denis and a fellow curate, Fr. E. Connington were joint treasurers. They succeeded in getting 'Champion' seed potatoes for the farmers of the parish and also got £30 from the Land League headquarters for distribution amongst the poor. The format of these monster meetings they held was that one of the speakers proposed a motion and another speaker spoke to it. In Gurteen Fr. Denis O'Hara proposed the main motion;

> 'That, as at present land laws are framed in the interests of a privileged class and operate to the manifest injury and injustice of our people and country, we demand their abolition on the grounds of right and justice, and solemnly affirm that Ireland will never be prosperous or contented until its soil shall be declared the property of those who cultivate it, and we promise to support no member who will not vote for peasant proprietorship'. He continued, 'It was all very well for the landlords to say they had given a reduction of fifteen or twenty percent, and had then done their duty. This would only give one or two pounds – and what was a pound to them? Let them come amongst the people and see what they wanted. While the potatoes were rotting in the ground, the oats heated and rotting in the stacks and the cattle not bringing a penny in the markets, what landord would say he would get his rents?'

This was Dr. Denis' first political speech, simple, reasonable and a speech of one well acquainted with the conditions of his people. His motion was replied to by Michael Davitt:

'Fixity of tenure is simply fixity of landlordism, fixity of poverty and degradation. Abolition of landlordism is the only certain remedy. The time has come when the manhood of Ireland must spring up to its feet and say it will not tolerate this system any longer'.

For these words on the 20th November, almost three weeks later, Davitt, Killeen and Daly were arrested and thrown into Sligo jail. Their trial from November 24th to 27th at which Fr. Denis attended, is highly important, as the validity of English law had been challenged and found wanting. The counsel for the defence was a Mr. Rea from Belfast. Michael Davitt writing about the event in 1900, had this to say about Fr. Denis O'Hara:

'Fr. Denis O'Hara spoke at the Gurteen meeting and began there a career of work which has never been surpassed, or equalled, by any priest who has laboured with the kindest of Irish hearts and the most level of Irish heads, for the protection and for the material welfare of the Connacht peasantry'.[3]

The next major meeting after Gurteen was in Ballaghaderreen where Fr. Denis was ministering. Here he protested against the arrests of Davitt, Killeen and Daly. A crowd of fifteen thousand people attended from the counties of Mayo, Sligo, Leitrim and Roscommon. Fr. Denis spoke from the platform on the Square and said,

'That we, the priests and people of Ballaghaderreen, in this public meeting assembled, deeply sympathise with the tenant farmers of the surrounding districts in their great distress, occasioned by the last three unfavourable seasons, the bad prices of cattle and agricultural produce, together with the foul famine and we call upon the landlords of the district to come to the aid of the tenantry by giving substantial reduction in the rent and urge upon the Government to expend some of the public money in works of public utility and so give employment to the people'.

A meeting was held in Curry, where thousands came from Charlestown, Carrowroe, Tubbercurry, Kilmactigue, Moylough and Cloonacool. Here Fr. Denis gave praise to Dr. McCormack, bishop of Achonry. He said at one stage: 'We are expected to preach peace and counsel loyalty, but it is hard to preach peace and instill loyalty when it is a case of empty stomachs and unsympathetic Government'.

By late 1879 the Land League was seen to be so strong that the Government was compelled to recognise the dreadful state of the country, especially of the tenantry in the west. Parnell demanded an autumn session of Parliament to deal with this, but to no avail. Finally the League decided to send Parnell and Dillon to the United States to ask the friends of Ireland for their help to relieve distress, as well as for aid for the

League itself to enable it to overthrow the system responsible. Bad harvests and falling prices in 1877 and 1878 had affected the payment of rent. A complete crop failure in 1879 left the tenants in Connacht desperate, and unable to pay their rents.[4] Many families still depended on the potato as a staple food. Evictions followed and by 1879, six thousand people had been turned off the land. These evictions produced outrages, varying from the maiming of cattle and the burning of haystacks or farm buildings to attempts on the lives of the landlords and agents. Outrages in the west also involved local vendettas of tenants against their neighbours who from greed had become 'land-grabbers'. People were actually starving and bitterness and anger and despair exploded in so many families that even today the remnants of it all are still there. It was John Dillon who urged the people not to touch a farm from which a farmer had been evicted because of non-payment of rent, 'If any man then takes up that land let no man speak to him or have any business transactions with him '.[5]

It is clear with hindsight, that a movement of this kind could not avoid violence for long. All the old agrarian vendettas re-appeared, cattle maiming, intimidations, burnings and shootings in all parts of the country. In 1880 over two thousand families were driven from their homes and over two thousand five hundred and ninety outrages were committed [6].

The area surrounding Ballaghaderreen was very involved in these desperate affairs. Meetings were held by Land Leaguers to prevent the payment of rents. On 31st October 1880 at a meeting in Loughglynn, Matt Harris and several speakers were present [7]. Matthew Harris 1825-1890 was born in Co. Galway. He was a successful building contractor and supported Repeal of the Union, Young Ireland and Fenianism. He agreed to support constitutionalism. He was manager of elections for O'Connor Power in Mayo in 1874, and was M.P. for East Galway from 1885 to 1890. He opposed the papal stand against the Plan of Campaign. Hundreds attended the Loughglynn meeting and James Grogan spoke as follows:

> 'The man who takes a farm from which another has been evicted is worse than a man who evicts, is a powerful weapon in the hands of the landlord, is a traitor to his county and an enemy to our cause, and should be denied recognition of every man. No man should buy from him, no man should lend to him; no man should speak to him on the highway or byway, at Mass or at meeting. Everyman's hand should be against him, his life should be made miserable until he is obliged to surrender his ill-gotten prey.'[8]

At the Loughlynn meeting Thomas Kelly declared – amongst other things:
> 'There is another object of every true and patriotic Irishman, and that is the national independence of Ireland with a native parliament in College

Green. Instead of seeing the young men of the country come in with green ribbons on their shoulders as they have done today, I would like to see them come with something more substantial, something like what was carried by the Volunteers of '72 and then we might say with confidence, 'THE LAND FOR THE PEOPLE OR THIS'.

Earlier, on the 27th June at Ballinlough, J.J. Walsh of Balla said that he had attended almost all the meetings in the west of Ireland since the initiation of this great movement. He had been sent there to enquire into the position of the evicted tenants of Mrs. O'Connor in the neighbourhood. The Land League had not done much for the people yet, but they had no idea of what it would do for them [9]. Another speaker, T. Brennan said he had a good opportunity, from his connection with the Land League, of knowing the position of many of the Irish tenants:

> 'We have prospects of a golden harvest this year and the question will come to be decided whether you will quietly surrender that harvest in order that a few idlers may enjoy the usual quantity of champagne. ('Never') I don't advise open resistance to the law, not because I see anything wrong with it, but because I know it is not advisable. We advised last year not to pay the rent that you were not able to afford. We give you the same advice this year and we say that any man who pays an unjust rent, whether he can afford it or not, is an enemy to the common good. (Cheers) You must starve out the landlords this year until you force them to agitate for a chance in the land laws. If cattle are seized, they should be branded with the word Rack-Rent and if any man is mean enough to take that land I say such conduct should be branded. The destruction of landlordism will be but a commencement of the destruction of foreign rule in Ireland. It is the chief prop of the institution. Remove the prop and the whole edifice will come tumbling in the dust. Ireland as a nation will take part in emancipating the world, in striking off the fetters of men, writing on the tablets of age 'Republican' (Cheers).

The Resolution was duly seconded and carried. Speakers like James Grogan and Matt Harris spoke out strongly and freely at meetings in Roscommon and Mayo against the landlord tyranny and injustice. Lord Clarendon had compared landlordism in Ireland to a felony. John Stewart Mills, Richard Cobden, John Bright, Englishmen advocating reform at this time, all condemned the system in Ireland. Thousands attended these meetings and feelings were roused. The west of Ireland became the scene of great and exciting political meetings. The tenant farmers were being organised at last and a ray of hope welded them together and their cheers and acceptance of the proposals of the speakers gave them a new courage to stand up against landlord oppression. They felt the land was theirs and another idea coming through these meetings was national independence of Ireland, with a native parliament in College Green. Returning to their poor homesteads, the tenants were fired with these new ideas and strengthened by the knowledge that something was being done. People cared enough. Now at last they were not allowing anyone to take 'their' land. It was the beginning of a profound change – not an Ireland for the Irish, but each man's holding to be his for his family for the rest of time. That idea still holds today especially in the west of Ireland. Meetings of Land League members were held at Mount Irvine, Rainsboro, Keash and Ballymote. On 23rd February 1885 Patrick Tansey was evicted from his holding at Cuilmore, Mullaghroe by Lord De Freyne, a Catholic landlord, residing at Frenchpark, Co. Roscommon [10].

On 31st October 1885 Andrew Muldoon of Cuilmore took the evicted farm and on 7th November 1885 a notice was found posted on a tree near his house threatening a visit from Captain Moonlight if he occupied the farm from which a man named Pat Tansey was evicted. After this notice, Muldoon was boycotted, he could not procure provisions in any of the local shops and no person would speak to him or any member of his family. In the spring of 1887, Patrick Muldoon (Andrew's son) brought some corn to be ground by a man named James Bruen who had a mill in the locality and in the Sligo Champion on the eleventh June 1887 the following notice appeared:

> GURTEEN BRANCH. The weekly meeting of this branch was held on Sunday fifth inst. under the presidency of Rev. M. Henry, C.C. Thirty new members were enrolled. James Hannon, ex-policeman, was denounced for having sent cattle to graze on the lands of James Costello, J.P. whose tenants have joined the plan because of his refusal to give any abatement of rent; also James Bruen, for having ground oats for a landgrabber (Andy Muldoon) [11].

On Sunday 15th April 1888 a meeting was held in the Land League room at Gurteen. Rev. C. Fehan, C.C. presided. A certain man named Coffey was boycotted. A man who had been esteemed and trusted by his neighbours had now become a social outcast. He sought compensation for his sheep that had been stabbed, but he was still boycotted. He was only one of many. The plan was working. It was slow, tedious and bitter but the message was getting around: 'touch the farm of an evicted tenant and you became a social outcast and were boycotted'.

Jasper Tully was editor of the Roscommon Herald at this time, a true Land Leaguer he was jailed for his part in the movement. He later was M.P. for the Boyle area. On 30th September 1880 he was found guilty of inciting Her Majesty's subjects. He printed all the Land League notices, he boycotted people who would not join and incited the people against certain landlords.[12] Boycotting in the area was rife; tradesmen were intimidated for selling goods to people who paid rent, *'no rent manifestoes'* were put on doors and the Land League courts were a new feature.

Thomas Towey, a small farmer of Barnaboy, was arrested on 16th July 1881 and sent to Galway prison. A meeting had been called at Brooklawn to draw attention to those who had paid rent. Towey spoke and advised the people to boycott these and he read out their names. Patrick Lavin, Ballaghaderreen, was arrested and sent to Omagh prison in 1882 for posting numerous *'no rent'* and *'reward'* notices in towns and villages of East Mayo.

Patrick Beirne of Ballaghaderreen was arrested at the house of a man named Walsh on the night a small-time Gurteen farmer named Freely was murdered. Men had forced their way into the house of David Freely shouting *'Blood rent payer'*. They dragged him outside and beat him, then let him go back inside the house, but they later took him out and shot him. His father had paid the rent. Michael Beisty was arrested for the murder and committed to Monaghan Prison. All were discharged later.[13] Other men from Ballaghaderreen held in custody were Thomas Towey, Dominic Flynn, Denis Conroy, Thomas Leydon, Thomas Dunleavy, Patrick Cregg, John Sheridan and Michael Lavin. In custody also were Bernard McHugh of Castlerea. These were accused of visiting houses and advising people to give up land. They had held Land League Courts in December 1880 and January 1881; when acting as Magistrate, Bernard McHugh had fined fifteen people five shillings each for paying rent.

The Land War continued. Evictions and outrages occurred, cattle and sheep were houghed and maimed, tenants who paid unjust rents or took farms from which others had been evicted were dragged out of their beds and assaulted. One, Michael Brown of Cartron, Loughglynn, was taken out of his bed and carded severely for paying rent for a bank of turf. The houses of Peter Lavin, Patrick Carty, Thomas Flynn and Thady Carty of Cloonfower, Loughglynn, were attacked and all the men assaulted and shots fired over them for not obeying a NO RENT MANIFESTO posted on their doors [14].

Castlerea, Frenchpark, Loughglynn, Ballaghaderreen, Ballinagare, Gurteen, Tibohine were all meeting centres of the Land League. Davitt remained the active organiser of the League's work and Parnell became its President, so the struggle for 'Home Rule' and 'Land War' went on side by side. Boycotting continued. Stephen and James McDermott, Aughurn, Loughglynn were victims, as were Thomas Reddy from Castlerea and Thomas Synne, a member of the Land League who was expelled.

The suffering of many Irish tenant farmers and day labourers, at this time would be impossible to describe. Thrown out on the roads, often in mid-winter, there is no doubt but that it appeared like a reign of terror. Determination became stronger, in spite of tragic happenings in so many areas. One such tragedy happened at Monasteraden where on 2nd April 1881 two men, Brian Flannery and Joseph Corcoran, were shot dead by the R.I.C. Note the one line given in the Police Report on this: 'there were two civilians shot dead on the occasion'. Their names were not even mentioned. On 13th September 1913, a monument was unveiled to these brave men. In 1981 there were wonderful centenary celebrations at Monasteraden commemorating this event.

On 2nd November 1879, a monster Land League meeting was held at Gurteen, sub-district of Mullaghroe and within about three and a half miles of Monasteraden, at which Davitt, Daly and Killeen made seditious speeches, for which they were prosecuted at Sligo Petty Sessions on 24th November 1879 and the following days.[15] They were returned for trial to Carrick-on-Shannon winter assizes in December 1879, but the prosecutions were subsequently abandoned. A contingent from Tubbercurry numbering some hundreds, some of whom carried imitation pikes, had marched to the meeting in Gurteen. On 6th June 1880 a meeting of the Irish National Land League was held at Mount Irvine, Co. Sligo, five miles from Monasteraden. PJ Sheridan of Tubbercurry and Matthew Harris of Galway were the speakers. Sheridan said that he called upon the people to proclaim with one voice that no one would be got to take land from which a man had been driven by landlord tyranny. Matthew Harris said that one of the greatest points in the Agitation was that it was a great Republican democratic agitation; while trying to raise themselves, they had also to try and crush down their enemy.

> 'We are here to protest against this class of men, and there is no language I could use would be strong enough for these men to denounce them; until you drive this class from society you can never have a wholesome state of public opinion. There is only one way of doing this and that is non payment of unjust rents. You will not be able to refuse paying rents except you combine together; then you will be able to make a strike against rents or unjust rents. We are characterised as Communists, but who are the Communists. They are the men who have sent millions of our people from our land. These are the men who should be crushed and put down'.

On 26th December 1880, James Broder, a process server residing at Cloonsilla, about two and a half miles from Mount Irvine, received a letter through the post, threatening him that if he did not give up serving processes his life would not be long a burden to him. On 31st March 1881 Broder went to the townlands of Shroove and Tawnamuckla, in the police sub-district of Clogher, to serve civil bill processes – some for rent on the property of Arthur French, Esq. of Straffan, Co. Kildare, and some for shop goods for Mr. Flannery of Ballaghaderreen. Broder went first, without protection, to Townamuckla and served three processes. A man named Thomas Sharkey from the locality pointed out the houses to him. Having served the three processes, Broder was followed by a 'mob' who pelted him with stones. He had to abandon the serving of the processes and flee to Clogher barracks where he reported what had happened to Sergeant Thomas Gunnis. The sergeant, together with a constable, escorted Broder towards his home until he was out of danger. Broder said to Sergeant Gunnis that he would make another attempt to serve the processes on Saturday 2nd April 1881 and the sergeant reported the matter to his officer, Mr Gardiner, asking that an escort of twenty men be sent to protect Broder. On that day, Broder went to Mullaghroe Station and Sergeant Walter Armstrong and Constables Michael Donnelly, Patrick McNaughton and Walter Hayes proceeded with him towards Clogher where they were to meet an extra force of police. When within a mile of Clogher, in the townland of Monasteraden, a mob of about eighty people came towards them shouting that the 'Orange dog' (i.e. Broder) would not serve any processes there that day. Stones were thrown by the mob. Broder was struck with one under the eye and severely cut. He was also struck on the knee and shin. He then heard Sergeant Armstrong tell the people to be quiet, but it had no effect. The sergeant then rushed into the crowd which closed in on him. Hayes rushed into the crowd after the sergeant and the next thing Broder saw was Sergeant Armstrong lying on the ground and blood oozing from his head. McNaughton and Donnelly fired two shots each as the crowd were rushing towards them and seeing they were unable to cope with the mob, they retired across the hill, as also did Broder. When about a mile from the scene Broder looked back and saw some of the mob raising their hands and letting them fall as if beating something on the ground. This was at the spot where Sergeant Armstrong lay.

Mr. Harrel, R.M. Mr. Gardiner, D.I. and forty men were all in Clogher Barracks at the time waiting for Broder. Sergeant Gunnis and ten men decided to go to meet him and when about ten yards from the barracks the sergeant was informed that Sergeant Armstrong was lying dead on the road and two civilians had been shot dead. Sergeant Gunnis returned to Clogher Barracks and informed Mr. Harrel R. M. who with Mr. Gardiner, D.I. and all the men went to the scene. Sergeant Armstrong was lying across the road on his right side, unconscious, with a deep wound on the right side of his head. Sergeant Gunnis and a constable lifted him and placed him against the ditch and tied a handkerchief around his head.

Armstrong's rifle, sword and shakoo could not be found. Sergeant Gunnis and ten men proceeded in search of Broder, Constables Hayes McNaughton and Donnelly and on returning to Clogher Barracks they found them there. Hayes had a large cut on the back of his head, his hands were also cut and he was very weak. He was unfit to be removed to hospital for eleven days. Sergeant Armstrong was removed to Clogher Barracks where he remained unconscious until his death on 6th April 1881. That night the country around was lighted with bonfires and the people shouting for 'Watty', a nickname by which Armstrong was known. Dr. Andrew McMunn of Ballymote attended Armstrong and Hayes. Two civilians had also been shot dead in the incident. Shortly afterwards an inquest was held at which the jury returned a verdict of wilful murder against Sergeant Armstrong, Constables McNaughten, Donnelly and Hayes. Thomas Sexton M.P. was present on one of the days of the proceedings. Constable Hayes was rendered unfit for further service and had to be pensioned. On 3rd April a protection party of one sergeant and seven constables was afforded Broder and a hut erected beside his house.

On the next day Broder began to be boycotted: His hired hand Pat Brereby refused to work for him and Thomas Grady, a local blacksmith, refused to shoe his horse, nor could he secure a horse to plough. On 7th April 1881 a mob of about sixty men and women with spades and pitchforks entered Broder's lands and violently drove away his cattle and put other cattle in their place. On 11th April 1881 at about five o'clock a.m. Patrick Moran, Broder's servant man, was returning with a horse he had borrowed from Archdeacon Colter of Masscray, Skreen, and when at Colterane, about one mile from Broder's house, Moran was met by about fifty men who pulled him off the horse and kicked him severely; at the same time one of the party stabbed the horse between the forelegs, inflicting serious injury.

On 1st May 1881 John Cryan of Clogher received a letter threatening him if he did not discontinue supplying turf to the police in Clogher Barracks to prepare to go before his God, 'for that he would be visited before many nights, and to take advice or he would be deceived'. Broder was hooted and booed whenever he left home and on several occasions when he was passing Monasteraden the people rang the chapel bell. Bonfires were lighted opposite his house and the people shouted for 'Broder the murderer'. Broder had the protection of two constables, who remained in the house with him and followed him wherever he went [16].

A report of the affair published in the Roscommon Herald on 13th September 1913, more than thirty years later, recalls how the incident was viewed from a local perspective.

LAND WAR IN THE VICINITY OF SLIABH LUGHA

THE MONASTERADEN MURDERS
A TRAGEDY OF THE LAND LEAGUE DAYS

Sunday's meeting in Monasteraden recalled one of the tragedies of the Land League days. On second April 1881, Sergeant Armstrong of the Mullaghroe R.I.C. Barrack, was killed and two farmers, Joseph Corcoran and Brian Flannery, were shot dead on the wayside, not a hundred yards from where the Catholic Chapel of the district now stands. Sergeant Walter Armstrong was one of the most detested policemen who ever held sway in a rural district. 'Watty' he was called by the people and when it was known by the people that 'Watty', after being responsible for the shooting and deliberate killing of these two young men had also perished in the fray he himself had provoked, a grim feeling of delight overspread the countryside. Many were dangerously wounded in the fierce conflict on that raw spring morning. Many were maimed in that short and hot encounter and some of them carried the marks of the bullets to their graves. Two went down on the people's side, but 'Watty' — whose vicious insolence over a prolonged period culminated in the shooting of these two men was exterminated like a rat and that eased the mourning of their friends. The bloody affray arose out of a process serving expedition of the estate of Major Arthur French, at Tawnmucklagh. He had about fifty tenants in this marshy swampy townland. Their rents varied from £4 to £8. The year 1881 was the culmination of three years of distress. For three years the rain had fallen in the harvest months as it never did before or since. The American cattle and the American wheat were landed then for the first time in England and upset the cattle and sheep trade in Ireland; the big and constant profits of the farmers vanishing like a flash. In the misery of the people, without crops and without stock that they could sell at a profit, the world had to be begged for relief funds by Parnell and the men who acted with him. Major Arthur French who had the reputation of being a good and kindly man, wanted his full rents just as if there had been no famine and no slump in prices. A few days before the tragedy in Monasteraden, he had been amongst the people of Tawnmucklagh and they had received him kindly. Then his lawyers issued processes for the rent that the land had not produced and the people were faced with eviction and extermination.

A week before the fatal day on the slopes of Mullaghchee, which overlooks Monasteraden, there had been a process-serving riot at the big fair of Ballaghaderreen. The Process-server had been repulsed on one of the estates in the neighbouring county and no processes had been served. Sergeant 'Watty' Armstrong was in charge of the police barracks at Mullaghroe and he had proclaimed loudly that, if he had been in Ballaghaderreen on the day of that row, he would have made short work of it, as he would have shot his own officer first for not giving the word to a Resident Magistrate, and shot Fr. Denis O'Hara who was a

C.C. in Ballaghaderreen and is now P.P. in Kiltimagh. This was the frame of mind he possessed when he set out on the expedition of the second of April, when he was hurried to his doom after having accomplished the deaths of poor Corcoran and Flannery. In Mullaghroe he ruled the countryside like a Turkish Pasha.

At that time there was a somewhat eccentric Resident Magistrate in Boyle named Mr. T. Fitzgerald and Mullaghroe was one of the districts in his charge. Mr. Fitzgerald had been in the police force before he became a Resident Magistrate and he was full of the ideas of the wickedness of human nature. All men who are poor and lowly are evil and wicked was apparently his belief. For some reason he took an invincible repugnance to Mullaghrow. In those days a certain number of labourers used to migrate to England every year for harvest work and this contact with English manners and customs tended to brutalise them and when, in the winter months, they returned to their western homes, some of them were not always paragons of perfection. Some of these harvestmen appeared from time to time in the local 'Petty Sessions Court' and Mr. T. D. Fitzgerald never tired in dilating on their wickedness. He used to shriek with passion in Court when he was told a man before him came from that district. 'Oh! another Mullaghroe rowdy", he would scream at the top of his voice and the maximum penalty, a month in jail with hard labour or whatever it was, he invariably imposed. The combination of Fitzgerald and Armstrong in the administration of the law was a sore affliction for any district. Armstrong was a low sized man, too small one would say for the police force. He was a thin poor creature, of a sallow-green complexion. He persecuted the countryside and every monthly petty sessions filled the primitive courthouse with defendants for the most trivial offenses and they always had to pay the maximum penalty when Fitzgerald presided. So odious had Fitzgerald's draconian decisions become that he felt he was a marked man and he always produced two revolvers and laid them beside the order book, in full view of the people, when in town to administer justice in Mullaghroe.

One of Armstrong's pet hobbies was to revive some obsolete statute from the time of Charles the Second, dealing with Sunday sports and Sunday trading. But as the Court was only a monthly one and the 'offence' should have been committed not less than seven days before it sat, there was always a great trial of wits as to whether the particular Sunday charged was inside or outside the limit. With his own men in the police barrack, Armstrong was also a peevish, waspish tyrant and many was the police inquiry he forced into the conduct of some unfortunate constable who was not up to his standard of constabulary rectitude.

On the fatal second of April 1881 Armstrong was ordered by his District Inspector in Ballaghaderreen to bring the process-server, Broder, to Clogher cross-roads and there they would meet the Magistrate and force of police who would go on the process-serving expedition. Armstrong's express orders were to proceed to Gurteen. But he was so full of his own importance and had such contempt for the people that he ignored these orders and he took the shortest way by Moygara Old Castle and then down the winding, hilly road by Mullaghatchee and thus to Monasteraden. He had with him three constables, Donnelly, Naughton and Hayes. Broder the process-server was in the centre, he had an army revolver and army bullets and the police had rifles with buckshot cartridges. Broder had been in Tawmnanucklagh a week before then trying to serve processes and he was driven out with a volley of stones. One of them caught him on the head, looking back he recognised Brian Flannery and calling out he cried, 'Flannery I'll be revenged on you'. On that second of April a bullet went through Flannery's brain, and the only one with ball ammunition that day was Broder.

Armstrong in flagrant disobedience of his officer's orders came along on that cold and musty morning with his small escort and armed process-server. They wound down the broken road that skirts the dark, frowning slopes of Mullaghatchee. The cold and cheerless waters of Lough Gara on the other side of the hill beat in snappy angry waves against the shore. The countryside, desolated by three bad harvests in succession looked wan and wretched. The farmers' houses had no air or comfort, but were sodden and bedraggled by the pitiless rainfall. Armstrong and his armed men stepped briskly out, confident in the death-dealing weapons they carried in their hands to see them through every emergency. A few women spotted this vicious looking squad hurrying along the bad and broken road. They called out to the men who were gathering from all sides in thousands and who were hurrying to Clogher Cross-roads, where the main force of the police was.

No one expected danger by way of the grim, frowning slopes of Mullaghatchee, which Armstrong had selected for the route of his band armed with murderous weapons. About thirty or forty rushed forward groaning and shouting and full of excitement. Without a moment's warning, Armstrong drew a line with his boot on the road and ordered his three men to stand to that line, and then blaze into the few people who were in front of him with buckshot. Broder at the same time fired the ball cartridge from his revolver in quick succession. One of Broder's bullets went through Brian Flannery's head. A full charge of buckshot from Armstrong's rifle tore the life blood out of Joe Corcoran. It was murder pure and deliberate. Armstrong was in that particular place against the orders of his superior officer and he had no authority of any kind to use murderous weapons at a moment's notice on an unarmed crowd. In any ordinary state of the law he would have been sent by an imperial jury to the gallows for his villainous act. Fortunately the manhood of the men in the crowd did not shrink from avenging their dead there and then.

Repeated shots rang out from the rifles of the police and the pistol of Broder. A schoolmaster who, terror-stricken, was peeping from behind some walls fields away, saw the water in the roadside puddles and flashes pumping in the air with the spent bullets and buckshot that hit it. Into this hell of fire two brothers of the Flagherties rushed, carrying their lives in their hands. They grappled with Armstrong, disarmed him, smashing his rifle in two and flung him on the ground. The rest of the crowd, enraged to fury, saw nothing but blood and they finished the tragedy. Constable Hayes was felled beside Armstrong, dying. He pulled out a scapular and appealed to the infuriated people as a Catholic for mercy. A girl of the Birminghams flung herself upon him and in her womanly pity, placed herself between him and three people full of blood-lust. She saved him and when in after months he recovered from his wounds he came out of hospital and married this girl whom he had never known until that day. The other two constables, Donnelly and Naughton, escaped across the fields with Broder and they drove off their few pursuers with repeated charges of buckshot. In the evening one of them, bloody and torn straggled into Clogher where the police and officers and magistrates had waited for hours for Broder and his escort, unconscious of the tragedy that had taken place not a mile away on the harsh and rugged slopes of Mullaghatchee.

The processes that Major French had issued for his tenancy were never served from that day to this in Tawnymuklagh. The people of Tawnymucklagh are now the owner of their lands. Major French met a violent end, being killed in an accident on the hunting field in Roscommon. Broder, the slayer of Flannery, never could face his neighbours again. In his remorse, he fell prey to drink and one miserable morning his body was found in a ditch where he had escaped as a result of a deep debauch.

Mr. John Dillon attended the funeral of the Land League martyrs, Brian Flannery and Joseph Corcoran.[17] He spoke of the dual course of an otherwise peaceful country – landlordism and coercion. This fight and the killing of a policeman inflamed the feelings on both sides. Young men in the League began to procure arms and the members of the force, committed by law to protect the agents and bailiffs, began to show more animosity against local League leaders everywhere.

At Keadue, a drive of eleven miles skirting Lough Key, on Lord Kingston's place at Kilronan dreadful evictions took place. Tatlow was the agent. Lord Kingston was seen sitting on the wall near the gates pointing his gun in mockery at the evicted tenants who were wild with grief. Fr. Reddy, the local priest and Jasper Tully were trying to pacify them. A vivid description of some of these happenings can be found in a diary of an English M.P. Wilfred Scawen Blunt, who came to Ireland to see for himself what the situation was like. He became friends with Michael Davitt, John Dillon and the bishops who were on the side of the tenants; Dr. Duggan and Dr. McCormack. He took a train to Ballaghaderreen and on Michael Davitt's instructions called to Mrs. Deane. There he found Dr. McCormack and his chaplain Fr. O'Hara at dinner. Both strong Home Rulers and Land Leaguers, they immediately became friends with Mr. Blunt. Fr. O'Hara took him out to see the Edmondstown Estate which he (Fr. O'Hara) had helped the tenants to purchase and they called on several of them.

William Blunt kept a diary, a section of which I quote here:

April eight 1886: 'A great day at Ballaghaderreen, which we spent wondering how things would be in the House of Commons, for this is the day of Mr. Gladstone's speech on the Home Rule Bill. I did not go out but enjoyed the comfort of a well ordered house, writing letters and composing notes with Mrs. Deane. Mrs. Deane's mother was a sister of John Blake Dillon and so she is a first cousin of the John Dillon of today. She told me a good deal about his private history. He and Parnell and O'Brien were together after they were released in 1882, John Dillon went to America and was now in much better health, but he meant to retire from public life as soon as he had freed his country. If they failed, she thought they would all leave the old country in despair, for there would be terrible trouble. She talked a good deal too of Parnell, who had been once or twice to her house.' Coming only with a spare shirt and a comb folded up in a piece of newspaper'. He was an aristocrat at heart, but a true patriot. He had ruined his fortune for the cause and the £39,000 the Irish people had subscribed for him was to repair this. But they did not love him, except a few, as they loved Michael Davitt. Michael Davitt was the real hero of the Irish poor, for he had suffered so much and had funded the Land League, which transformed them and for the first time organised them. He had begun here in East Mayo, between Ballaghaderreen and Castlebar and had come with Dillon to hold a first meeting on the Dillon estate. John Dillon is no traceable relation of Lord Dillon. At first she had not fancied Davitt's coming, but John insisted and from the moment she saw him she was converted to a blind idolatry. Davitt's portrait hangs on the wall beside Dillon's. Mrs. Deane is a clever woman of about fifty-five. Her mother is still alive but partly paralysed – she is a thoroughly good, honest person, without pretence or nonsense. Indeed it is astonishing what excellent, well-bred people these Nationalists are. When the Land League was suppressed by Foster; she had been made president of the Ladies' League. She is not ambitious of honour, however, 'except for John'. Of the Fenians and dynamiters she said that the Coercian Act had had this merit, that it had frightened them out of Ireland, so made the road easier for the party of constitutional agitation. I have enjoyed my talks with Mrs. Deane more than anything yet and they have been most instructive'.

April Ninth –

To Castlerea by mail car, passing through the Dillon estate and Loughglynn, all wretched poor land, but bringing Lord Dillon a rental of £22,000. I got particulars of this estate from Fr. O'Hara. It was £5000 in Arthur Young's time in 1778. From Castlereagh by train to Athlone and Woodlawn, then on again by car to Loughrea. Woodlawn is the trimmest property I have yet seen, Lord Ashtown's Park being quite English in appearance, and there are several model cottages especially near the railway. The meadows too are enclosed in clipped hedges and there is an air of respectability about the whole place quite unusual in Ireland. It is impossible however, not to suspect that the fair appearance conceals a sepulchre. The whole of the road from Woodlawn to Loughrea lies through a nearly uninhabited grass country, and one recognised the traces of old evictions everywhere in the little potato plots, with their marked ridges and furrows, now under grass and here and there the site of a house long swept away. Dr. Duggan, the Bishop, confirmed all this in the evening, when I called on him, and says that every acre of that estate was peasants' ground and reclaimed by them long ago from the waste and then taken from them by their landlords. Dr. Duggan, the Bishop of Clonfert, is the most wonderful and enchanting old man I have seen for many years. A vulnerable and altogether simple personage, with white hair and cassock, much bed-abbled with snuff. When he knew that I had come from Davitt, a smile broke out on his face as if I had spoken of a saint.' William Blunt was arrested at Woodlawn and thrown into Galway jail; He was later transferred to Kilmainham. He saw the wrongs committed against the Irish and took their part. Local items noted in his diary give us a vivid picture of that time [18].

A proclamation had been issued by the Lord Lieutenant of Ireland in 1881 declaring that the Irish National Land League was an unlawful and criminal association and that all meetings of this group would be dispersed by force if necessary. An answering challenge was issued by the Land League;

> 'To the People of Ireland'. – 'Pay No Rent. Hold the Harvest'. The Government of England has declared war on the Irish people. The organisation that protected them against the ravages of landlordism have been declared unlawful and criminal. A reign of terror has commenced. Meet the action of the English Government with a determined passive resistance. The NO RENT banner has been raised'.

This was a period of acute tension and conflict between landlord and tenant. Although the Government from 1870 passed a number of acts reforming the laws governing land tenure, the number of tenants who had actually availed of these acts was small – because annual repayments on purchase loans were generally greater than the annual rents.

CHAPTER 10

1881-1903

LAND TRANSFER IN CO. MAYO

In the preceding chapter we have seen the state of turmoil in the area surrounding Ballaghaderreen towards the close of the nineteenth century. Anger, frustration and poverty together with meetings and agitation led to much unrest. Neighbours were turning against neighbours and strong language was used to waken the poor from their apathy. In 1881 a Land Act had been passed by the Westminster Government which appeared to be an answer to the problems besetting the Irish tenants. It provided for fair rent, free sale, fixity of tenure and the establishment of a Land Commission. But it did not meet the immediate needs of the tenants and was far from being a final solution to the land question. It was definitely inadequate for the over populated west. Many leaseholders and occupiers were already in arrears with their rent.

The bill was extremely complicated. John Dillon and Parnell opposed it in the House of Commons. They claimed that it was not economically viable or straightforward. Passing the Act was no doubt a political gain for the British Government but it did not mean an end to agrarian outrage and disturbance. Parnell and other land leaders were arrested and brought to Kilmainham.

When Parnell was arrested he is said to have remarked that 'Captain Moonlight would take his place' and this is what seemed to be happening[1]. Gladstone's reason for arresting Parnell was his opposition to the Land Act. In the course of his imprisonment, however, an understanding was reached – the so-called Kilmainham Treaty. The arrears question was to be dealt with and the leaseholders would be admitted to the benefits of the Land Act. Parnell and the Irish MPs were to co-operate with the Liberal Party in the future in measures of general reform. Parnell and his colleagues were set free.

This was a bitter blow to Michael Davitt whose ideas for nationalisation of the land were now dashed. John Dillon, Parnell and J.J.O'Kelly were released on 3rd May 1882. They made a brief appearance in the House

ROCKINGHAM

of Commons and then escorted Michael Davitt on 6th May from Portland prison to London. That very day in Dublin the new Chief Secretary, and T.H.Burke, the Under Secretary were murdered in the Phoenix Park by the Invincibles, a secret society. Both countries were horrified. Another coercion act was passed. Parnell's party now strove for constitutionalism although the land question was still, especially to the people in the west, a crucial one. The Land League was dominated by the Parliamentary Party. Preparing for county conventions, selection of candidates and raising of funds were important functions of the League now. A change of strategy had come about – the campaign for Home Rule was to be combined with agrarian reform. One could not progress without the other, or so it was thought. In 1885 the Conservative Government dropped coercion and passed a new act – the Ashbourne Act, providing five million pounds to enable tenants to borrow the whole of the purchase money for their holdings. This could be paid back by 4% annuities over a period of forty nine years. But by 1887 tenants were unable to pay the rent fixed by the 1881 Act, due to a combination of exhaustion of the soil, failure of crops, American competition and the restriction of credit. Parnell and his party still sought Home Rule in the House of Commons, and at the same time they tried to bring in a Tenants' Relief Bill. When this failed the situation in Ireland became explosive. John Dillon, William O'Brien and Timothy Harrington devised a scheme called the Plan of Campaign in 1886 – a plan of collective bargaining on individual estates. The tenants combined to offer the landlord reduced rents. If he refused they were to pay him no rents at all. Instead they were to pay the money into an estate fund, which was to be used to help tenants who were evicted. This Plan of Campaign caused the Government much trouble, as it was seized upon by farmers in the west especially and in the south. In 1889 Dillon went to Australia to collect money. A new organisation was formed to make an appeal for funds – the Tenants Defence Association. £61,000 was subscribed for the relief of tenants. The Government enlisted the aid of the Church. Pope Leo XIII issued a rescript in 1888 condemning the Plan and the boycotting as illegal and warning the Irish Church to stay clear. Irish feelings rose high. Most of the Irish bishops were non-committal. John Dillon in speech after speech laid down the basis for Church/State relationships opposing interference from Rome.[2] On estates from Rockingham in Co. Sligo to Woodlawn in Co.Galway and Mitchelstown in Co.Cork eviction followed eviction. The authorization of the RIC to use battering rams, saws, shields, and to obtain military support and ladders made evictions easy. These were tough bitter years for the evicted and the MPs who supported them. It seemed absurd to say that the landlord was without guilt in evicting one hundred families, as King-Harmon of Boyle did and that those who were evicted were murderers because they tried to hold on to their little homesteads. Small wonder the close of the nineteenth century saw the re-emergence of the secret societies of the early years of the century, *the Right Boys, the Threshers, Steelboys, Captain Right* and *Captain Moonlight.* All believed firmly, as their songs and legends helped to keep alive, that Cromwell's followers would lose again their lordships in Ireland and that the long downtrodden would claim the land as theirs. It was the spirit of the Irish in their songs, music and tradition that kept this feeling uppermost in their minds. Despite poverty and hardship they were never too despondent for long. The second phase of the Land War beginning in 1886 saw Dillon, O'Brien and Harrington more implicated than Parnell. They openly spoke against landlordism and advised tenants to organise themselves for the struggle. At Woodford, near Portumna on the Clanricard estate, little or no rent was paid after a fifty per cent reduction was refused. In 1887 Parnell spoke strongly against the opposition of the Church but was not in favour of the

Plan of Campaign. He had been ill while all this was afoot. Dillon and O'Brien were arrested several times and spent some periods in jail. Dillon was beset by ill health all his life as was Parnell. Despite this, he visited Australia and New Zealand, raising £33,000 for the Plan of Campaign. The Plan lasted from October 1886 until the Parnell split in 1890. A further Land Act was passed in 1886 extending the purchase facilities for tenants. Balfour decided that the Plan could be defeated by the arrest of its leaders, Dillon and O'Brien. They were put on trial at Tipperary but although under intensive police guard they escaped and made their way to France. From there they proceeded to New York. They immediately started to collect funds for Ireland. Less than a week after their arrival the news of Parnell's divorce case reached them. They sent a cable denouncing Parnell. History has recorded the sad details. Enough to say that the inevitable split took place. Parnell had built the Irish Party into a force to be reckoned with. He won to his side in the country not only all the constitutional forces making for nationalism but the revolutionary forces who sought an Irish Republic. He was the leader of a United Irish Nation. His untimely death in 1891 was a heavy blow for Ireland. Parnell's death left warring factions within the party. Tim Healy a leading anti-Parnellite was hooted at Parnell's funeral, as was John Dillon. In July 1889 at a general election Parnellite fought Parnellite.[3] The result was nine Parnellites elected against seventy one anti-Parnellites. Division in the anti-Parnellite camp was deep also. Tim Healy and John Dillon were bitter enemies. In 1892 Michael Davitt agreed to enter parliament and became a key figure in the party. Dillon, Davitt and William O'Brien were close friends who stood by each other in those years. William O'Brien for some time now was living in Co. Mayo near Clew Bay, after being declared a bankrupt. An enormous claim had been brought against him personally for law costs over the Paris funds[4] (monies collected for the evicted tenants and not released). As soon as the English Court of Bankruptcy learned the truth it put an end to the bankruptcy and the Hibernian Bank loyally disclaimed any intention of raising the question of personal liability in reference to the evicted tenants' overdraft of £4000, which was duly paid off on the release of the Paris funds. During this period Mayo was listless and the political struggle in Dublin was far away. The establishment of the Congested Districts Board in 1891 by the Chief Secretary of Ireland, Mr Arthur Balfour, was the beginning of a happy prospect for the west. The Board consisted of the Chief Secretary of Ireland Mr Balfour (who had visited Mayo to see conditions for himself), a member of the Land Commission and five other members to be appointed by the Queen. The Queen was also authorised to appoint three temporary members for business relating to fisheries, agriculture, and other special matters. Its first year was confined to making loans of £7,000 and £3,000 respectively to the factories established by the Sisters of Charity at Foxford and Ballaghaderreen.[5] All the loans were punctually paid back by the Superioress, the celebrated Mother Arsenius, with interest. O Brien had been pressing for many years for peasant ownership of land. To this end the Congested Districts' Board was to purchase the landlord's estate and all unoccupied farms and to divide them equally between his tenants. Clare Island was the first to be thus divided. It took six years to purchase 3,949 acres and make ninety-five families happy. Most of the funds of the Board now applied to land purchase. The French estate at Ballygar was bought and seventy five tenants became owners. The largest purchase was made when the estate of Viscount Dillon of Loughglynn, consisting of 87,669 acres was bought for £29,000. This was in 1899. Huge meetings were held throughout Connacht in those years, to try to paper over the Parnell split. One such was held at Ballaghaderreen in June 1896. It must have resembled the medieval inaugurations of the O'Conor Kings of Connacht. All the clergy from the parishes surrounding the area took their place on the platform erected on the square. It was one of the largest meetings since the early Land League days. Thousands moved in from Kilmovee, Ballyhaunis, Knock, Castlebar, Kiltimagh, Carracastle, Ballymote, Buninadden, Gurteen, Edmondstown, Tibohine, Frenchpark and Fairymount. The town presented a stirring appearance. Fife and drum bands led each group from outside towns. A large body of horsemen took their place in the square, each horse wearing garlands of flowers and rosettes. Tar barrels were set alight on the market square and young people in thousands sang national songs. The windows, with the exception of those of the Parnellites were illuminated and decorated. The distinguished visitors were met at the railway station and carried shoulder high to the platform in the square. John Dillon insisted first on visiting the convent at Friars Hill where small industries were thriving at the hands of the sisters. It is to be noted that the majority of the speakers were the clergy of the area: Fr Henry *(Kilmovee)*; Canon Stokes *Buninadden*; Rev Fr Stenson *(Buninadden)*; Canon O'Hara PP *(Kilmovee)*; Fr Doyle *(Carracastle)*; Fr McHugh, Fr Beaken *(Ballyhaunis)*; Fr M Keavney ADM *(Ballaghadereen);* Fr J Daly, J.O'Connor, Fr J. McDermott *(Killavil)*; Fr J. Madden CC *(Aghamore)*; Fr J. Moylan *(Knock)*; Fr J.Henry CC *(Gurteen)*; Fr J. Fr McDonnell CC *(Charlestown)*; Fr P.Morrisroe *(Ballaghaderreen)*; Fr J.Henry *(Kilmovee)*, just to mention a few. All these were on the platform as were many prominent lay men whose feelings ran high; *Dr McDermott, J.A.Flannery, J.Jordan, J.Cawley, L.Dillon, J.Irwin, G.Cawley, J.Kilmartin, D.Watters, J.Murphy,*

P.Gallagher, J.Flynn, M.Doyle, P.Doherty, E.Gilmore, J.Casey, P.Finan, and *M.O'Donnell.* A vote of thanks was proposed by Canon O'Hara to John Dillon for the priceless service he had given in the past, chiefly in securing the passage of the Home Rule Bill. The vote was extended to Michael Davitt MP and Mr Colleary MP. Canon O'Hara thanked the representatives of the Irish Parliamentary Party and Mr Justin McCarthy on behalf of the evicted tenants. Mr Gladstone and his Liberal Party were also thanked. Praise was given to the Congested Districts' Board for their help to the Sisters of Charity. Three counties were consolidated under the banner that day. But the leaders had whipped up enthusiasm which did not last. While John Dillon remained an ardent constitutionalist and Home Ruler the bread and butter issue in the west was growing.

William O'Brien, still at one with the men of Mayo, saw in the approach of 1898, the centenary of the Insurrection, an opportunity of organising a new party to reawaken the listless spirits of the people. So on 16th January at Westport the United Irish League was founded. John Dillon was there and saw once again the symptoms of vitality long missing from popular gatherings. Tim Healy attended also. Dillon however had misgivings – this may have been the beginning of the break between him and O'Brien. The League spread and was helped by Davitt who failed to see why Dillon had not given it his more active assistance. Fr Denis O'Hara in his own constituency told Dillon that the people of Ballaghaderreen and surrounding districts were beginning to remark that their area was the only one in Mayo in which no branch of the United Irish League was yet started, and unless he started one they would do it themselves.

Dillon feared that the League was abandoning the constitutional movement, and that O'Brien would eventually abandon Home Rule. Using his powers of conciliation Davitt convinced Dillon that the League was the one hope of breathing life into the whole country. This seemed to be borne out, at the Provincial Convention at Claremorris, when, despite a feud of ten bitter years Dillon and O Brien became full of hope for a national resurgence. But Davitt shortly afterwards threw up his seat in South Mayo and departed for South Africa. It was a heavy blow to Dillon and O'Brien.

Despite this, the organization continued to grow. It was a solid reality. The police had been watching it closely and they reckoned that the total number of branches had risen from one hundred and seventy five on 1st February 1898 to five hundred and seventy nine on 1st August. Mayo, Roscommon, Sligo and Galway had most of the branches but twelve other counties had branches and there was one in Belfast City. The movement was apparently constitutional in content and within the bounds of the law. Dillon realised its potential and made peace with O'Brien. In September 1902 the following letter appeared in the Irish newspapers:

> *Castle Taylor,*
> *Ardrahan,*
> *Co.Galway.*
> *September/2/1902.*
>
> Sir,
> *For the last two hundred years the land war in this country has raged fiercely and continuously, bearing in its train stagnation of trade, paralysis of commercial business and enterprise and producing hatred and bitterness between the various sections and classes of the community. Today the United Irish League is confronted by the Irish Land Trust and we see both combinations eager and ready to renew an unending conflict. I do not believe there is an Irishman, whatever his political feeling, creed or position who does not yearn to see a true settlement of the present chaotic, disastrous and ruinous struggle. In the best interests of Ireland and my countrymen I beg most earnestly to invite the Duke of Abercorn, Mr John Redmond MP, Lord Barrymore, Colonel Saunderson MP, the Lord Mayor of Dublin, the O'Conor Don, Mr William O'Brien MP and Mr TW Russell MP to a conference to be held in Dublin within one month from this date. An honest simple and practical suggestion will be submitted and I am confident that a settlement on terms alike satisfactory to landlords and tenants will be arrived at.*
>
> I have the honour to be your obedient servant,
> John Shawe Taylor, Captain.

Neither O'Brien nor most of the League ever heard of Shawe Taylor. He was a nephew of Lady Gregory and had served as an officer in the South African War. He had no land interest himself. The idea of solving the agrarian war had occurred to Archbishop Walsh fifteen years before this. Two days after this letter appeared it was followed by a public communication from Mr George Wyndham, Chief Secretary of Ireland, giving the project praise: 'No Government can settle the Irish land question. It must be settled by the parties interested. Those who come together will do so on their own initiative and responsibility. Any Conference is a step in the right direction if it brings the prospect of a settlement between the parties nearer and as far as it enlarges the probable scope of operations under such a settlement'.

Just a few months earlier in 1902, Mr Wyndham had appointed as his Under Secretary in Ireland Sir Anthony Mc Donnell (1844-1925). Sir Anthony had acquired a good reputation as an administrator in India. When John Dillon, John Redmond and William O'Brien were approached by Mc Donnell with the purpose of discussing certain points of the new

Land Bill about to be introduced, John Dillon refused to hold any discussion. Sir Antony's father Mark Garvey Mc Donnell was a Catholic landlord of Palmfield House, Carracastle, Ballaghaderreen who owned property at Calvagh, Hagfield, Doocastle, Srah and Palmfield during the nineteenth century. Sir Anthony entered the Indian Civil Service in 1865 and for thirty six years was one of their administrators. He returned to Ireland in 1901. He supported the *Wyndham Land Act* of 1903 and also *Devolution* which was a form of Home Rule for Ireland. In fact he played a major role in drafting the Land Bill. John Dillon remained opposed to Mc Donnell as long as the latter continued in office. The fact that both men had their origins in Ballaghaderreen seemingly did not help communication between them, even for the good of the tenantry. Sir Anthony resigned his position as Under Secretary in 1909 and was created a Liberal Peer in the House of Commons with the title of Lord Mc Donnell of Swinford.

We have seen that Mr Wyndham approved of Shawe Taylor's suggestions about a Land Conference.[6] The final decision was that the Earl of Dunraven and Major Colonel Nugent Everard, John Redmond, William O'Brien, Timothy Harrington, and T.W. Russell with Cardinal Logue in the chair, approved the Land Conference Project. They were supported by the majority of the landlord class, the tenants and the Catholic clergy. They assembled in the Mansion House in Dublin on 22nd, 24th and 31st December 1902 and 3rd January 1903. Never did the Irish Land Question seem so near a reasonable solution.

John Dillon, who was away in the United States while the Conference was taking place, strongly opposed it on his return. For weeks the debate continued. Michael Davitt was totally opposed to the Conference. Fr. O'Hara from Ballaghaderreen attended with some men from the area who were deeply committed – Dudley Costello, Joe Coleman, and Pat Higgins on 16th April when the Wyndham Land Act was dicussed. Those who attended were invited to pledge the faith of the nation to the acceptance of the broad principles of the bill, subject to the necessary amendments. The fundamental principle of the Land Conference Report had been adopted without reserve on 25th March despite slanderous letters and articles written in the *Freeman's Journal.* However a speech by Dillon in Swinford against the passing of the Act left the United Irish League in danger of a split.

The final outcome was that O'Brien resigned his parliamentary seat and his membership of the United Irish League to avoid a division in the country.[7] But the Wyndham Land Act was law and despite all the controversy it made headway even though Dillon and Davitt decried it from the beginning. They were adamant that the prices being paid were exorbitant.

A gradual extinction of the landlord system followed the Land Acts. In

1898 powers of local government and local taxation were transferred from the grand juries, which mainly represented the landlord class, to elective county councils. It was a truly momentous era in Irish history, when slowly but surely changes were coming about that neither John Dillon nor the rest of the Irish parliamentarians had foreseen.

It was interesting to find in the course of my study that Luke Dillon who was evicted from the De Freyne estate of Frenchpark was a descendent of that far-flung family of Viscount Dillon of the barony of Costello Gallen. To go back to Theobald Dillon, mentioned in previous chapters:–he was knighted by Queen Elizabeth I in 1559.[8] In 1582 she appointed him Collector and Receiver of Composition monies in Connacht. In 1662 King James gave him a grant of lands of Costello Gallen and title of Viscount Dillon. Many marriages brought wealth and property to Dillons. The family intermarried with O'Conor Don, Costello and Fitzgerald –to mention but a few. Before 1641 the lands at Lisheane (Lissian) consisting of one hundred and twenty eight unprofitable acres and one hundred and twenty six profitable acres belonged to Thomas Dillon who was Lord Viscount Dillon of Costello Gallen.[9] He also owned the lands of Lung, Banada and Keelbanada. After the land settlements John Dillon owned the land at Lissian. Later on, the lands became the property of De Freyne, Landlord of Frenchpark. Dillon became a tenant.

It was Luke Dillon, the grandfather of John Dillon MP, who was evicted from Lissian for non payment of rent. This Luke it was who moved into Ballaghaderreen and set up a small business which grew and flourished for one hundred and fifty years. The Dillons of Ballaghaderren never claimed relationship to the Dillons of Loughglynn, but history has proved that they were indeed related. The barony of Costello contained 26 proprietors in 1641 in the parishes of Castlemore, Kilmovee, Kilbeagh, Ahamore, Knock, Annagh and Beaken.[10] By 1663 there were 35 proprietors in that barony the largest of them being Viscount Lord Dillon with 53,301 acres. So the larger part of the lordship of MacCostello was held by the Dillons at the end of the 17th century.[11] In fact MacCostello ownership of land in the barony named after them, dwindled by 1685 to 558 acres of profitable and 1317 unprofitable acres.

While Home Rulers were concentrating on Home Rule, the younger generation were aiming for a republic. Even the transfer of ownership of land was not to deflect them. There were many who regarded the Land War, though initially necessary, as a prelude to the true realisation of the aspirations of our people – nationhood, breaking the connection with British tyranny, reviving our language, culture, music, games and traditions.

1881-1903 LAND TRANSFER IN CO. MAYO

BENADA ABBEY

CHAPTER 11

DIVISION OF THE ESTATES

The End of the Line of Dillon and Costello

In previous chapters we saw how Viscount Dillon acquired the castle of Gallagh on the shores of Loughglynn. The tradition of the common descent of Dillon and De Angulo is found in O'Clerys *Book of Pedigrees*. Not many associate the name Dillon with Loughglynn today, yet for more than three centuries Viscount Dillon was the owner of one the largest tracts of land in Connacht – 93,321 acres. Castle Gallagh, the ruin on the south side of the lake, was the family seat. It was said to have been built by a Norman Fitzgerald who was supposed to have married the daughter of O'Conor, the titular king in Connacht.[1] The village of Loughglynn is situated four and a half miles south west of Frenchpark and six miles from Ballagaderreen. Castle Gallagh was once a structure of considerable strength and extent but what was left of the ruins was carried to the north side of the lake for the construction of the mansion, Loughglynn House, now the home of the Franciscan Missionaries of Mary. The castle was defended at each angle by a tower. The western tower in the latter part of the eighteenth century was quite well preserved and was used for the safe custody of prisoners until they were transferred to the County jail. From a description written by Isaac Weld in 1832, one sees the former glory.[2]

> 'The village separated from the demesne by a thick screen of plantations formerly stood nearer the lake. The pastures are of great fertility, and were stocked with very large cattle. The village contains about forty-four cabins and four houses of two stories, a dispensary and a catholic chapel near the demesne. Some good houses had been latterly built and one or two shops were in a state of progress but complaints were general of want of employment and dullness of trade. To the westward, at the distance of less than two miles are to be seen the Turlough and also the sinking and subsequent reappearance of the Lung river; The general character of the district is that of insulated hills and ridges bounded by bogs. Altogether it is a wild country'.

A thickly wooded island rises from the centre of the lake at Loughglynn. Smooth green banks dotted with trees slope to the water's edge. The roof of the Dillon mansion was in old French style. The main entrance was on

DIVISION OF THE THE ESTATES

the north side but a door opened on the south side to a long flight of steps leading down to the lake. Angular bay windows on the ground floor and on the upper storey gave an elegant appearance. An inscription on the gable can be read today *'The Right Honourable Richard Lord Dillon (IVLY) 1/7/1715'*. The upper storey was burned before the turn of the century.

In the early eighteenth century the mansion of Loughglynn stood in the midst of an extensive and richly wooded demesne.[3] The demesne has been compared to 'an oasis in the desert, as the country around, as far as the eye can reach, though somewhat relieved on the south by the hilly ridge of Slievealvyn, is naked and boggy'. The lake is nearly an Irish mile in length and has a surface elevation of two hundred and eighty four feet above sea level.

For more than a century before the passage of the Purchase of Land Ireland Act 1891 the Dillons were absentee landlords. Life was miserable for the tenants at this period. From 1817 to 1822 typhus prevailed to an alarming extent. Potatoes were bad. People received aid both food and clothing, from the estate of Viscount Dillon. Consumption of spirits was on the increase. There was much illicit distillation as grain was cheap. The people were generally in great want and misery. Their food and clothing could not be worse. The houses and the cabins were dirty; beds were of straw. There was never meat to eat and seldom milk or butter; potatoes and salt were the main diet. Edward Kelly was the medical attendant in Loughglynn dispensary at this time.

The population of Loughglynn village in 1831 was two hundred and eighty four. In 1841 it was three hundred and two. The area of the village was fourteen acres. It had fifty five houses. It contained only one or two shops. The Loughglynn dispensary was within the Poor Law Union of Castlerea and served a district of 24,064 acres with a population of 9,230.[4] From 1839 to 1840 £121.12s 0d. was spent and two thousand nine hundred and ninety eight dispensations of medicine were made. The Protestant Church was built in 1815 by means of a gift from the late Board of First Fruits. Thirty people attended. The Catholic church had an attendance of one thousand two hundred. The village is in the diocese of Elphin. In 1834 there was one hundred and nineteen Protestants and ten thousand Catholics. There was no school. What a dismal account of an otherwise beautiful area.

Delay in tenants agreements in 1904 on the Dillon estate was due to the extreme difficulty of apportioning the turbary, so as to make the best possible provision for the 2,500 tenants. By the 31st of March £20,689 had been spent by the Congested Districts Board [5] on drainage of the estate. Demesne lands were divided among the tenants. One hundred acres of plantation were held around Loughglynn House. Fourteen acres close to the village of Loughglynn were held in common grazing for poorer inhabitants of the village. Dr. Clancy, Bishop of Elphin, bought Loughglynn House from the Congested Districts Board. The priest attached to the Catholic church at Loughglynn lived there alone for some time. Dr.Clancy, on a visit to Belgium met the foundress of the Franciscan Missionaries of Mary who had set up that foundation in France. [6] These nuns were fullfilling a need on the continent at that time, teaching the art of nursing and housekeeping to a rising generation who had not the financial wherewithal themselves. On Dr. Clancy's invitation these sisters came to Ireland in 1903. Their order is still at Loughglynn House.

The poverty around Loughglynn before the turn of the century was very great: The arrival of the sisters brought a large measure of relief. Large families, no work, poor land, and no hope for the future — all these drained the spirits of the people. But the Franciscan Missionaries changed things for the better. They started classes, teaching the local girls how to cook, clean, wash, iron and sew. They began to buy the milk from the local farmers. One sister was adept at cheese making and butter making. Eventually the butter and cheese of Loughglynn found its way into every corner of Ireland. They set up sewing classes and lace making — an industry in itself. The fame of Loughglynn lace spread. A knitting centre was started and girls were trained to turn out garments of superior quality. The sisters were to be seen driving in their horse and trap through Ballaghaderreen in the early forties selling their beautiful knitted suits.

As theirs was a foreign order, the sisters spoke English with a foreign accent loved by all. Some of them taught in the local school for a while. Irish postulants began to join the order and spent the first three months of their novitiate there. Then they had to go abroad to be professed — and many went as missionaries to foreign lands. The convent flourished. In the early forties the bishop blessed a new novitiate in Loughglynn and the new sisters were professed in the little chapel where the Strickland family (agents for Dillon) had attended Mass. These wonderful nuns spread their wings as far as Japan, China, Pakistan — the world over.

Times changed. In the late 1960s, with the decrease in vocations, the novitiate closed. The population had decreased in the demesne; the young had emigrated while the old were left. To help alleviate the problem many girls had gone to America and England. No need now to buy the farmers milk for making cheese. So the sisters had to make a decision about change. Another need had arisen throughout the country. There were many old people with no one to care for them. To help alleviate this new problem the sisters, about twenty years ago, changed the place into a nursing home for old folk. And what a lovely, brightly coloured, well lit spacious home it is today! Many of the trees are gone but the lake with its little wooded island continues to give pleasure to inhabitants and visitors. The beauty of the area and its wilderness has not changed, only its people – from Norman Fitzgeralds to Elizabethan Dillons, to the Belgian Franciscans sisters and now to the older people of the area and surrounding districts. God surely had a hand in all of this. Knox in his *History of Mayo* said: 'The MacCostellos lost their place among the great landowning families of Connacht; they were not turned out of their Castle lands but held on to English tenures paying a fixed rent'.[8] The Costellos owned the Edmondstown Demesne and it was this land Arthur George Costello sold to the tenants after the Land Act of 1881. It is noted in a deed of Conveyence dated the 20th of August 1857 that the Costellos paid a fixed yearly rent long ago to Viscount Dillon, of £31/6/10. It was it appears, a Composition rent under an ancient deed, made payable to Viscount Dillon when he was President of Connacht.

According to the Land Commission Records of Advances, Arthur Robert George Costello was J.P. in the Counties Mayo, Roscommon and Sligo and late Captain of the Seventh Dragoon Guards, living at Edmondstown, Ballaghaderreen.[9] His acreage in Mayo was seven thousand five hundred and thirteen acres, and one thousand and thirty eight in Roscommon. Total value of the eight thousand five hundred and eleven acres was £1,779. In the Land Commission office there is a record for advances for the purchase by the tenants made on the the first day of May 1884 in relation to the estate of Arthur R.G.Costello. (All these records are now lodged in the National Archives in Bishop St. Dublin). They include the townlands of Cloonlumney, Dernacartha, Upper Ballyoughter, Derrnaslieve, Derreen, Redridge, Derrycrumma, Parkroe, Largan, Islandmore, Attiantaggart, Boleysillagh, Cloomen, Frasnaduffa, Fallsolus and Creggane, Coolena, Tullaghanmore, Toobracken, Magheraboy and Keelbanada.

No returns of advances under Land Law (Ireland Act 1881) were printed, so that the only detailed record of these advances available was the manuscript entries in the Book of the Accounts and Purchase Branch.[10] When section 58 of the Land Act 1932 came into operation it became necessary, with a view to the registration of Possessory Titles, for the land registry to obtain a list of registered and unregistered holdings situate in Saorstat Eireann in respect of which advances had been made under the Acts of 1881-82. Possessory Titles were held by some tenants who were not legally registered for their land. Many to this day have not registered their holdings for thirteen years and not paying rent to anyone they are entitled to register the land with a Possessory Titles. Accordingly in September 1926 a book of such holdings in each of the twenty six counties was compiled with the assistance of the Land Registry. Six copies have been typed on a schedules printer for this purpose and bound for reference, together with a summary showing the total advances made under section 24-27 of the Act of 1881 in each estate of the twenty six counties of Saorstat Eireann. The powers of the Board of Works in reference to land purchase were by the *Land Act of 1881* (section 35) transferred to the Irish Land Commission constituted by that Act, and the amount which might be advanced was increased to any sum not exceeding tree-fourths of the purchase-money (section 24). The Purchase of Land Act, 1885, 48 and 49 Vict., c. 73, enabled the Land Commission to advance to a tenant the entire purchase money, provided the repayments were 'guaranteed'. When researching this some years ago this information was not filed but I presume that the National Archive in Bishop St. has all the information as all the material from the Land Commission was transferred to that archive.There were two hundred and sixty-nine tenants on the Costello estate who got advances to purchase their holdings.

As we saw in an earlier chapter Charles Costello's son, of Edmondstown married Maria daughter of James Creagh, of County Clare. When she died he married Dorcas Maria Daniel and he and Dorcas Maria had three children – Charles Edmund who died an infant, Arthur Robert George Costello, born 1832, and Isobella Mary who married Fitzmaurice Pratt. Dorcas Maria married secondly – Lawrence Langley in 1834. Arthur R.G. Costello built what is now the home of The Bishop of Achonry in 1865. Part of the Costello house with its orchards and coach house still stands as a reminder of those days.

The *Land Act of 1881* did not satisfy all demands but it gave a glimmer of hope. Only for the zeal of Fr. Denis O'Hara, the purchase of the Costello estate and its division after this Act was passed, might never have been accomplished. He proved that his work with the Land League was not confined to speechmaking and being treasurer of the local organisation. The Costello estate was one of the first in the west of Ireland to be purchased under this Act. This happened in 1883. There were two hundred and sixty nine tenants on the property. There was considerable trouble in apportioning the purchase money which came to £25,000, But eventually agreement was reached. Before this the landlord had given over 3,000 acres of mountain bog free to his tenants. As the estate was being purchased under the 1881 Act the tenants had to make up a quarter of the purchase money. This amounted to £6,250. All the tenants could make in cash was £1,500 –about £6 each.The balance, £4750, had

DIVISION OF THE THE ESTATES

to be raised in the local branch of the Hibernian Bank on the joint security of every six of the tenant purchasers, and guaranteed by the two principal traders in Ballaghaderreen. It was a major responsibility but Fr. Denis had confidence it would succeed. They got seven years to repay the £4750 to the bank in seven equal installments. Every shilling was paid punctually. Neither the bank nor the guarantors lost one shilling. Fr. Denis had to walk each section of the land with the purchaser and fix what each man would pay. His involvement with the scheme shows the trust his people had in him. We have seen in an earlier chapter when Wilfrid Scawen Blunt visited Mrs. Deane in Ballaghaderreen, Fr. Denis brought him out to Edmondstown to view the work that was being done. The land now belonged to the tenants and the feeling of ownership stimulated them to improve their standard of living. Fr. Denis O'Hara was highly thought of because of his tremendous effort in this project.

A.G.R. Costello held on to the residence and home farm of 315 acres for some time longer. The estate of eight hundred and fifty one acres had been mortgaged many years before this by Dorcas Maria Costello Arthur's mother and her second husband Lawrence Langley and Arthur George himself. They redeemed the estate in 1857 by a payment to Francis Moore of Bath in Somerset of £5,000. The estate included Tullaghanmore, Tullaghanrock, Larga Fallsolus, Frasnaduff, Creggane, the Float, Tobracken. Tonroe(called at the time Greyfort or Grayfort), the Mill at tonroe, Ardvarna, John French's fourteen acre park, Curry, Coolena, Magheraboy, Atteentaggart, Cloonamore, Cloonlumney, Derrinasleeve, Ballyoughter, Derrnacartha, Redridge, Parkroe and Islansmore, Bolisillagh, Little Cahir, Derrygea, Keelbanada, Banademore, (called Morris's Keelbanada). All these were at that time in County Mayo. Lands in Creggane were described as Creggane Pound, and Giblan Creggane, Middle Creggane, Henry and Creggane Float, Monument Field, Creggane Sharkett, and Esker Creggane, Barnadoona, Derrycrumma, and Conor's Ford Keelbanada. The point was made that the lands at Keelbanada were once in the barony of Costello, County Mayo and in 1859 were by an Act of Parliament transferred to the barony of Frenchpark, County Roscommon.

On the 20th August 1885 one of the Land Judges of the Chancery Division of the High Court of Justice in Ireland drew up a memorial of a Deed of Conveyence. It was the beginning of the ownership of the tenants– the end of the Costellos. About 1885 or thereabouts the home farm was mortgaged as Arthur George Costello was unable to to keep his finances in order, after building the 'Palace' as the local people called it. So, after negotiating with the Ballaghaderreen Church authorities, Dr.

URLARE ABBEY

Lyster, Bishop of Achonry, Fr. Kearney, and Fr. Daly, the three hundred and fifteen acres and the Costello residence were purchased. They were helped by a loan from the Congested Districts Board.[11] Every penny was paid back, as can be verified from the parish archives 1913 at St. Nathy's, as the 'Palace' came to be called. At first the clergy thought it would be a good idea to rent the cottages on the home farm but it was impossible, in view if the poverty of the people, to collect the rent. The clergy then felt it was not their place to become landlords. So, Dr. Lyster took over the residence and twenty five acres to use as a Diocesan College and they sold the remaining acres to the Land Commission who in turn sold it to the occupiers and some new people who had not lived on the estate before. These occupiers continued to purchase the land of the Costello home farm through the Land Commission in the same way as the two hundred and sixty nine tenants had already purchased 7,300 acres with the help of Fr. Denis O'Hara.

The name Costello has scant relevance for the people of today in the area. Landlords owned all the land in the nineteenth century and the people working on that land were as slaves. Many of the older people talked of Captain Costello and his agent Mr. Forbes. Forbes collected rent on horseback and was known to cut down and trample on freshly washed clothes as he made his way to the doors. A garden in Tallaghanmore is still known today as Forbes's garden. Little is now remembered of the man. The pomp and glory of those days have passed away. Many landlords ruled with a rod of iron. Tradition has it that a woman from Creggane (my great grandmother) got two months in Boyle jail for picking a 'besom' on Costello bog. A besom was the heather in bloom cut to the root and used to sweep the cabin floors.The stalks were tied tightly with twine and gave a clean sweep.

Two other agents for Captain Costello at the end of the nineteenth century were Mr.Lougheed and Mr. Higgins. So the land of the MacCostellos came into the hands of the tenants who became property owners for the first time. The days of the overlords were gone. On the Sligo road the monument called the Four Altars, facing north, south, east and west stands on a small hill. A circular stone wall surrounds it with little more than walking space inside. Tradition has it that it was built during the Penal Days. It belongs to the church authorities and the Deeds are in St. Nathys, Edmondstown House[12] An extract from a letter published in the *Roscommon Herald* in October 1967, draws attention to the Four Altars. It was written to Bishop McCormack in 1878.

'My Lord,

As your Lordship made some remarks about the old monument here, in your sermon last Sunday and as there is some ambiguity as to its founder, I beg leave to inform you that it was built by the Costellos of Creggane na gCrann during the Penal Days and not by the Costellos of Tullaghan Mór as is commonly supposed. The good priest who read Mass at Atteentaggart in Bockagh also read Mass here when circumstances permitted and usually resided with that truly hospitable family in Creggane. Like many another noble Irish family it ended in Holy Church as the last of that family was Dr. Costello. The bishop at the time was Bishop Flynn of Achonry, from 1809- 1817. One gable of the old house is still standing within a couple of hundred yards from the monument. I had all these particulars from my poor father who was a sincere Catholic, a true Irishman and a great seanachie, and he had them from his grandfather who lived to be an old man. When he was a boy he saw over two hundred men at Mass at the monument each armed with rude weapons of the day, fearing an attack from Lord Dillon's troupers, but I think they never put in an appearance.The good and much remembered Fr. Michael Farrell was the last who read Mass at the monument[13].

I most humbly ask your blessing
P.Costello.

(The original letter is in the archives at the home of the Bishop Of Achonry, Dr. Thomas Flynn).

A few hundred yards from the monument are the remains of a wooded avenue leading to Creggane na gCrann. The knarled old trees, pine, palm, oak, chestnut, sycamore and mountain ash stand stately with branches leaning over as if trying to tell a tale as the wind rustles their leaves. A well known tale of that area is sad to hear. A few hundreds yards from where the big house stood is a circular area of fine tall trees where babies who died without baptism were buried. This had to do with the church not with the Costellos.In 1897 Fr. J O'Conor curate in Ballaghaderreen, gathered the neighbours together to recite the Rosary one October evening. The monument belongs to the Church; the last of the Costellos of Creggane bequeathed it to them.

In the lonely Abbey of Urlare on the shores of the lake of that name, once the home of the Dominican Friars founded by the Costello dynasty long ago, there is a headstone bearing the name Arthur Robert George Costello, last dynast and Baron De Angulo, who died on the 31st January 1891, the end of the line which first conquered Sliabh Lugha more than six centuries earlier.

You may wonder why I called my History Sliabh Lugha? Lugh, the Sun God or Lugh the God of Light was a pagan God of prehistoric times. The range of mountain land from Kilkelly in Mayo to Drumacoo in Co. Sligo is called after him. Ancient manuscripts such as *The Book of Invasions, The Book of Ballymote, The Book of the Dun Cow* and *The Annals of the Four Masters* all mention Lugh.

Our children should be told these tales which are full of bravery and great deeds – of the Mythological Cycle, the coming of the Partholonians, the Nemedians, the Fir Bolgs, The Tuatha De Danann, the Milesians and the Celts. We are told the Celts held elaborate religious rituals in honour of Lugh. Lugh, Son of Cian was the chief Sun God of all Celtica. He was recognised as the supreme solar force throughout Celtic Europe. Some tales say Lugh was the father, by the Milesian maiden Dectera, of Ireland's Heroic figure Cuchulainn. The feast of Lughnasa took place on 1st August and was first and foremost a harvest festival. Lugh is said to have created this feast in honour of his foster mother Tailtu. In my days in the west of Ireland the harvest, when gathered in from the fields, was always celebrated by gathering into each others houses and partaking of food, drink, music and dancing. It was a continuation of the Festival of Lugh.

Here I conclude my research. The physical features remain as in ancient times although new roads are changing this. Sadly the populations has declined but the beautiful landscape is there for our children to behold. A visit to this area brings alive the shadowy figures of the past and the mystery of this past, which I longed to solve when only eleven, has now become a little more clear. For me the *'Draoícht'* will always be there.

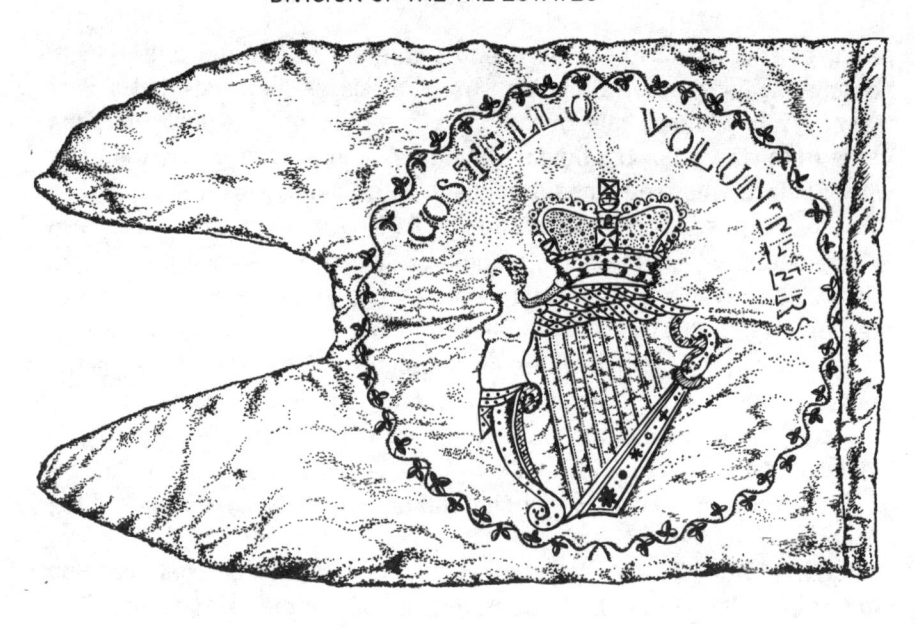

The Costello flag was a highly important colour of the Costello volunteers, one side of crimson silk embroidered with the crowned harp and within a wreath of green and gold shamrocks. The other side was of black silk applied within a white and brown silk circle and embroidered with a cavalryman on a charger before Hibernia and below an inscription *Mo Righ agus Mo Thír* (My King and my Country) the whole fringed in white, yellow and silver 23' x 36'. Charles Costello wears a scarlet coat with black facings.

Appendix One

LEASEHOLDERS ON THE DILLON ESTATE c.1805

(ACRES, ROODS, PERCHES)

1. ADROGOOL (pt.) [Addergoole, p. Aghamore]
   1788: John & Willm. Lan (25-6-10). Thos. Fitzmaurice & co.(37-14-6); Thos. Beasty & co. (20-18-6); James McDonnell & Co.(20-18-6).
2. AGHATARNA [Aghataharn, p. Aghamore]
   1789: Peter Rutlidge (102-17-4).
3. ARDCULL (pt. BRUSNAGS) [Ardkill, P. Castlemore. BRUSTNAGS - ?]
   1790: Francis McCarthy (93-12-10).
4. AGHALOOR (pt.) [Aghalour, P. Tibohine].
5. AGHEDRISTIN (pt.) 7 pt. AGHADERRY {Aghadrestan, Aghaderry, P. Tibohine] 1794: Phineas Coayne(43-8-6) 1799: James Hughes (41-0-0)
6. AGHADUFFIN [Aghadiffin, p. Kilmovee]
   1794: Terence Cafferky & co.(23-8-2); Patrick Cox & co.(16-4-6); Michael Grady (16-4-6); Patrick Higgins & co.39-2-2).
7. AGHADERRY [Aghaderry, p. Tibohine]1796: John Moran & co. (26-3-0); Thomas Casey & co. (26-17-0); Edmond Flanagan & co. (28-13-9). ((782-13-0))
8. BALLYGLAS & c.[Ballyglas,p.Aghamore or Kilmovee]
   1713: Sir Robert Gunning (25-15-4).
9. BALLYHAVNIS (pt.) [t.Ballyhaunis, pp. Annagh & Bekan] 1788: Joseph Boyd (65-11-6) 1800: Revd. Luke Knight & ors. (0-1-0).
10. BALLAGHADERREEN:(pt.)[t.Ballaghaderreen, p.Kilcolman] 1788 John Bellingham (0-0-1); Edward Brooker (0-0-1)
11. BALLYKILLEEN [Ballykilleen p. Annagh]1788: Andrew Palles (206-0-0).
12. BOHALIS [Bohalis,p, Castlemore] 1790: Charles Dillon (56 14 10)
13. BOHANE & CURRAGHTIMORE [Bohaun, Curraghteenmore, p. Knock] 1791: Connell O'Donnell (56-14-10).
14. BECAN [Bekan,p.Bekan]1791: Mary Rogier (206-12-6)
15. BALLYHINE [Ballyhine, p. Aghamore] 1790: Theobald Nolan (41-7-4).
16. BARCOIL [Barcull, p. Kilmovee] 1794: James Coyel & co. (26-16-8
17. BRACKLON (pt.) [Brackloon East, p. Bekan] 1794: Edmond Dyer & co. (21-0-0)
18. BRACKLOW (pt.) [Brackloon West, p. Bekan] 1794: Thomas Sloyan & co. (35-16-8); John Sloyan & co. (17-6-8)
19. BALLINAKILL (sold) [?] 1794: Thomas Geoghegan (14-17-0).
20. BALLYGLAS (pt.) EAST [Ballyglass ?] 1796: John Madden & co. (24-12-0); James Gilligan & co. (24-12-0)
21. BALLYGLASS (pt.) WEST [Ballyglass ?] 1796: Andw. Gara & ors. (42-0-6).

LEASEHOLDERS ON THE DILLON ESTATE C.1805

22. BALLYMULLAVILL (sold) [Ballymullavil, p. Mayo] 1796: Patrick Staunton (41-0-0).
23. BALLYMAGING &c. [Ballymaging or Castlemore, p. Mayo] 1798: Walter Plunket (278-4-4)
24a. BRACKLOW (parish of Bekan) [Brackloon West,p.Bekan] 1798: Walter Kelly (103-10-8).
24b. CLOONTYGARVY [?]1798: Michl. Grady & co. (25-14-7).
25a. BAGHTIDUFF (pt. BRUSNAGHS) [Boghtaduff,p.Castlemore. BRUSNAGHS ?] 1799: Anthony Regan & co. (77-4-10).
25b. MILL 1799: Daniel Dodd (4-13-3)
26. BALLINFULL [Ballinphuill, p. Bekan] 1799: Thomas Kerrane & co. (96-14-4).
27. BARNIBOY [Barnaboy,p. Castlemore] 1799: Martin Towey & co. (96-14-4)
28. BOOLYROE [Ballyroe, p. Knock] 1799: James Beirne & co. (31-16-7)
29. BOLLYDORIS ['Ballinderris', Carownamallaght,p.Knock] 1799: Dominick Flatley & co. (35-5-0)
30a. BALLYNACLOGH (pt. called Carrowbaun) [Ballynacloy, Carrowbawn, p. Aghamore] 1801: John Taffe (131-19-8), Garret Dillon & co.(15-13-3)
30b. (pt. called Carrowbeg) [? Carnbeg, p.Aghamore]1801: George Stenson & co. (48-17-9)
30c. (pt. called Carrowscully) [Carrowscoltia, p. Aghamore] 1803: John Burke (63-11-1).
32a. BARNALYRA (pt. otherwise CARNE) [Barnalyra, Carn, p.Kilbeagh]. 1803: Patrick Carroll & co. (68-13-8),Patrick Quin & co. (86-0-8) 1801: Patrick Gurrin & cc. (16-12-4).
   b. (pt.called Poulbane) [?] 1802: Margaret McDonnell (48-17-9).
32. BECAN (pt.) [Bekan,p.Bekan] 1802: Edward Connelly (2-6-6).
33a. BARGARIFF (pt. called DERINTOGHER) [Bargarriff, Derrintogher, p. Annagh] 1802: Thomas Devanney & anor. (48-17-9).
   b. (pt. called GURTNAGEERA) [gortnageera p.Annagh] 1802: James Fitzgerald & co. (48-17-9) , James Cox & co.(108-1-3).
   c. (pt. called ADARRIG) [Aderg, p, Annagh] 1802: Michael O'Gara & co. (39-2-2), Thomas Loftus & co. (37-1-0)
34a. BARNICOOGUE (North-east Div.) [Barnacahoge, p. Kilbeagh] 1802: Peter Cannon & co. (73-11-8).
   b. (South East do.)1802: Rd. Prendergast &c (41-0-1)
   c. (North West ditto.) 1802: Mich.Costello & co. (51-6-4).
   d. (South-west Div.)
35. BRUFF [Bruff p. Aghamore] 1802: Patrick Rafferty & co. (58-13-3).
36a. BALLINFULL (pt.) Ballinphuill, p. Tibohine]1805: Thomas O'Brien & co. (35-15-10).
   b. & pt. AGHADERRY [Aghaderry,p. Tibohine].1805: Patk. & edmd. Groarke (56-12-1).
37. BECAN [Bekan, p.Bekan] 1791: Lady Dillon's profit (Rent of 150-0-0). (2974-5-6)
38. CLAGNAGH [Clagnagh,p. Bekan] 1781: Edmond Dillon (165-2-0).

LEASEHOLDERS ON THE DILLON ESTATE C.1805

39. CLOGHVOOLEY [Cloghvoley, p.Aghamore]1788: Peter Rutlidge (77-12-2)
40. CLOONCARY (pt.) [Clooncarha, p. Kilmovee] 1789: Charles Carroll & co. (86-9-4), ThomasMcDonough (0-0-1).
41 a. COOGUE (East div of) & KILGARRIFF [Cooge, Middle, north & South; & Kilgarriff, p. Aghamore] 1789: John Dillon [d. 1832] (205-15-0).
   b. (East div.) 1794: Owen Muldoon & co. (72-9-5)
   c. (West div). 1794: Thomas Conway & co. (78-11-4)
42. CLOONARIGID 7 CLOONICHALLY [sold] [Cloonargid & Cloonacolly, p. Tibohine] 1789 Richard Grady Senr. (13-5-0).
43. CLOONCAGH [Clooncah, p.Aghamore]1789: Alexr. McDonnell (36-0-5).
44. CURRINA [Currinah, p. Kilbeagh] 1789: Patrick Taffe (66-19-10).
45. CLOONMULLIN [Cloonmullin,p. Tibohine]1789: Edmond Taffe (153-15-0).
46 a. COOLNEFARNA (north) [Coolnafarna, p. Annagh] 1790: Arthur Burnes & co. (25-3-8)
   b. (south) 1790: James Bowines & co. (27-3-8)
47. CASHILCOLANE [Cashelcolaun, p. Castlemore] 1790: Charles O'Connor (26-6-5)
48. CLOONIVULLANE [Cloonavullaun, p. Castlemore] 1790: James Dillon (24-3-11).
49. CARTOON 7 CARROFARRIFF [sold] [?Cartron, p. Kilbeagh]; Carrowgarve, p. Tibohine] 1790: James Dillon (151-1#4-0).
50. CASHILAHENNY (pt. BRUSNAGHS) [Cashellahenny, p.Kilmovee. BRUSNAGHS ?] 1790: Garrett Dalton (29-18-2)
51. CLOONERIN [Cloonierin, p. Kilmovee] 1790: Thomas Dalton (29-18-2).
52. COOLIGARRY (pt.) [Coolagarry, p. Tibohine] 1790: John Gibbons (32-7-1). 1793: Revd. John Daly (20-10-0), James Foley (15- 7-6).
53. CALVEAGH [Calveagh Lr. & up., p. Kilbeagh] 1790: Keadh McDonnell (59-16-4).
54. CARRONEGNOCKANE [Carrownaknockaun, p. Tibohine] 1790: Faragh McDonnell (71-15-0).
55. COLLNCRAFIELD [sold] [Clooncrafield, p. Kilkeevin] 1790: Bryan O'Connor (34-17-0).
56. CLOONLEE [cloonlee, p. Knock] 1790: Anne Prendergast. (63-18-4
57. CARROREAGH (pt.) [Carrowreagh, p. Bekan] 1791: James Fitzgerald (55-1-2). 1800: James McGarry & co. (16-19-8), Charles Gilligan & co. (80-4-4).
58. CARROBEG & WEST GLANVULLYNO [CARROWBEG ?. glenmullynaha West, p. Kilbeagh] 1782: Michael Grady (96-18-2)
59 a. COLLHENA [Collnaha N & S, p. Aghamore] 1792: Patrick Gleeson & co. (86-19-17).
   b. (north) [Coolnaha North, p. Aghamore.1792: Walter Waldrum (85-19-1).
60. CLOONFALIS [Cloonfaulus, p. Kilmovee] 1794: William Cox & co. (30-17-6)
61 a. CRUSSARD (north div.) [Crossard, P. Aghamore]1794: Augustine Neary & co. (67-16-1)
   b. (pt.) 1802: James Flynn & co. (52-11-9).John Boland & co. (39-12-5), Thomas Keane (5-8-half).

LEASEHOLDERS ON THE DILLON ESTATE C.1805

62. CLOONGOONAGH [Coongawnagh (Burke) & C (Cosgrave), p. Aghamore.] 1796: Thomas Burke & co. (76-4-4). 1798: John Cosgrave & co. (113-2-4).
63. CARONEMONISTER (pt.) [Abbeyquarter, p. Annagh] 1796: John Clarke (17-6-0) 1802: Samuel Daniel (3-1-6).
64. CARGINBEG & pt. CARINGMORE [?carrigan Beg & More p. St. John's, B. Athlone] 1796: Simon John Dowell (235-15-0).
65. CARNAGH EAST (pt.) & CALDRAGH [sold] [Carnagh e & w, p. St. John's Caldragh ?]
66. COOLEENA & CROSS [sold] [Colleena & Cross N & S p. Kilcolman] 1796: James & Christr. Hughes (144-3-0).
67. CURGARRIFF (pt.) [Corgarriff, p. Kilmovee] 1798: Edmond Connilan (27-2-2) 1799: Jamed Hemming & co. (41-6-0)
68. CLOONAVEEMA [Cloonaweena, p. Kilbeagh] 1798: Peter Duffy & co. (30-17-6).
69. CLOONFAGHTRIN [sold] [Cloonfeightrin, p. Kilturra] 1798
70 a. CLOOMEEN (W) [Cloomeen E & W, p. Kilbeagh] 1798: Anthony Jordan & co. (56-12-1).
   b. (N) 1798: THomas Phillips & co. (36-0-5).
71. CARROWMUNAGH & CARROWCARS [?] 1798: Edmond Kelly (168-11-3).
72. CLOONFANE [Cloonfane p. Kilbeagh] 1798: Edward Phillips (61-15-0)
73. CLOONCOUSE [Clooncous, p. Kilbeagh]1798: Dominick Tarpy co. (51-9-2
74. CARRONLACKAGH [Carrownlacka, p. Kilmovee] 1799: Andreas Horan & co. (73-1-6)
75. CULLINTRAGH [cullentragh, p. Bekan] 1799: John Egan & co. (44-5-6). 76. CALDRAGH (pt. Carronemallagh) [Caldragh, Carrownamallaght,p. Knock] 1799: Luke Doyle co. (31-4-0)
77. CLOONBROOKE (half) [expire 1814] [Cloonbookeighter, Cloonbookiughter, p. Bekan] 1799: David Flyn (44-5-2); Thomas Mulkeen &co. (44-5-2).
78. CULLAGH (pt.) [Culliagh, p. Kilmovee] 1799: Patrick Higgins & co.(42-7-1).
79. CLOONTURNANE [Cloonturnaun, p. Knock] 1799: Michael Phillips (45-3-1).
80. CLOONAMNA [Cloomnamna, p. Kilmovee] 1799: John Quin & co. (55-14-4).
81. CASHILARD [Cashelard,p. Castlemore] 1799: Owen Regan & co. (543-4-8).
82. CREEVY [Creevy,p. Tibohine] 1800: Michael Flyn & co. (143-10-0).
83. CLOONAGLERAGH [Cloonagleragh, p. Knock] 1800: Michael Doyle & co. (23-9-1).
84. CLASSAGHROE [Classaghroe, p. Annagh] 1800: Thomas Lyons & co. (48-17-5).
85. CARRAMORE (pt. called BULKANE) [? ,Bulcaun, p. Kilbeagh] 1800: Owen Mulligan & co.(47-6-10).
86 a. CURRANE (pt. called BRACKLAGH) [? , Bracklagh, p. Kilbeagh]1800: Martin Mulligan & Co. (55-11-6).
   b. (pt. called PONTOBEG) [? ,Puntabeg,Kilbeagh] 1800: John Jennings & co. (41-3-4).
   c. (pt. called TAWNAGHMORE) [? ,Mountain, p.Bekan] 1800: Patrick Flyn & Co. (44-9-7).
   d.(pt. called Gurteenmore [? ,Gorteen More, p. Bekan) 1800: Bartholomew Flatley & co.(33-7-0); Rd. Fitzmaurice & co. (16-12-10).

LEASEHOLDERS ON THE DILLON ESTATE C.1805

    e.(pt. called GRALLAGH GARDEN) [? ,Grallaghgarden, p.Bekan] 1800: Dominick Nowlan (6-1610).

    f. (pt. called LISBANE [? , Lisbaun East, p. Bekan] 1800: John Fitzmaurice & co.(14-13-2).

88. CARRAMORE (pt.) [Carrownmore, p. Knock] 1800: John Forde (64-7-5); John Timothy (59-14-10); Richd. McHugh & co.(10-1-6); John Flatley Senr.& co.(13-7-6); Myles McCarran & co. (29-6-7); Patrick Brady (18-10-6);1805: James Curry & co.(33- 19-3) John Horkan &co. (32-3-1); Edmond Morrally & co.(93-19-1); Patk. McLaughlin & co. (21-12-3).

89. CLOONLYON [Cloonlyon, p. Kilbeagh] 1801: James Murray & co.(35-3-10).

90. CLOONBOOKEIGHTER [Cloonbookeighter, p Bekan]
    1801: Patrick Lynch (35-1-5).

91. CLOONTARIFF [Cloontarriff, p. Aghamore ?; or Knock?] 1801:
    Bryan Lyons & co. (97-15-5).

92 a. CLOONFAGHNA [(pt.) [Cloonfaughna, p. Knock] 1801: Andrew & Henry French (69-16-1); Hugh Morally & co. (35-12-1).

  b. (pt.called CARROWCUR) [Cloonfaughna, Carrowcor,p.Knock] 1801: Patrick Waldrum 7 co. (23–16-11).

  c. (pt. called GRAGANERANAL) [Cloonfaughna, Crockaunrannell, P. Knock] 1801: Thomas Morrally (58-13-3).

  d. (pt. called DERRADDA0 [Cloonfaughna, Deradda, p.Knock]
    1802: Andrew Waldrum & co. (69-13-4).

  e. (pt. called CURRAGHLAHIN) [Cloonfaughna, Curraghlahan, p. Knock] 1801: James Royan & co.(51-9-2).

  f. (pt. called MAGHERAMORE) [Cloonfaughna, Magheramore, p. Knock] 1802: Jno., Thos. & Hy. Clifford (111-6-0); John Fitzgerald (40-7-9).

93 a CURRANE (pt) [Corraun, p. Annagh]1801:Michael Waldrum & co. (24-8-8); Martin Mulloy & Jas. Costello (7-11-11); Denis Moore & ors. (61-15-); Darby Finn & c0. (44-9-7)Edward Clifford & Waltr. Kelly (39-0-2); Thomas Beirne & co. (38-10-2). (pt called Derryleagh) [Derrylea, P. Annagh].

  b 1801: Thomas Sullivan & co.(35-3-10)

94 CASHILL (pt) [Cashel, P. Kilbeagh] 1801: Peter Higgins & co. (34-4-0); Thomas McLaughlin & c0. (12-14-0) Patrick Kelly & Co. (49-17-0).

95. CAPULCURRAGH {Cappulcorragh, p. Kilbeagh 1802 Dominick Battle & co. (102- `18-4)

96. CLOONFEIGHRY (pt.:EAST DIV) [Clooonfeaghra, p. Kilmovee]

97. DRIMNELASSON [Drumnalassan, p. Castlemore] 1790: The Honble Browne (175-3-4)

98. DRINEY pt.[Driney, p. Tibohin] 1790 James Derrick (41-0-0) 1794:James Moran (16-0-3) Thomas Giblin & Ch. Cafferky (23-3-9)
    1795 John Thomas (24-12-0)

99. DRIMBANE [Drumbaun, p. Annagh] 1795: Bryan Morris (41-7-4)

100. DRIM 7 CLOONDEASE Drum, Cloondace, p. Knock];
    1792: Patrick Nolan (185-2-10)

LEASEHOLDERS ON THE DILLON ESTATE C.1805

101　DEEEYNACONG [Derrynacong, p. Annagh] 1794: Thomas Boland & co.. (40-6-10)
102　DERRYLAHIN [Derrylahan, p. Bekan] 1794: Andreas Royan & c0. (20-12-0)
103　DROMACCOO (pt.) (sold) [drumacoo, P. Kilcolman]1796: William Coleman & co. (74-4-7);Thomas Goolrick & co. (77-4-10)
104　DERRYNABROCK (sold) [Derrynabrock, p. Kilbeagh]
　　　1798: Peter Carney & co. (56-12-1)
105　DERRYMORE [Derrymore, p. Bekan] 1799P Patrick Waldrum & co. (56-14-10)
106　a.　DOOGERRY (WEST DIV.) [Doogary, p. Aghamore]
　　　b　1802: Patk & Edmd Groarke (120-2-3)(MIDDLE DIV.)
　　　c　(EAST DIV) 1802: Thomas Cosgrave & co. (96-15-1)
107　DRIMMADERRY [Drumaderry, p. Annaghj] 1802: John Waldrum & co. (181-9-2)
108　DRIMENAGH (pt) [?Drimnagh, p. Ogulla, B. Roscommon]
　　　1805: Luke Dillon (143-0-10)
109　DUTY TURF (commutation of) (74-4-0) 1540-18-8)
110　EGOOL [Uggool, p. Kilmovee] 1800: Miles Phillips & co. (76-4-4)
111　FLUGHINY & CLOONIKILLINY (sold) [Flughany, Cloonakillina p. Kilturragh] (1798: Tim. McDermott ((195-10-10)
112　FAULEEN [Fauleens, p. Kilbeagh] 1798: ED. Phillips (71-17-11)
113　FAUGHIL [Faughil, p. Knock] 1799: John Doyle & co. (34-19-2) [301-19-2]
114　GRALLAGH & ATHYSHONIN (Johnstown) Grallagh, p. Annagh] 1788: Graallagh p,. Annagh.(84-14-8)
115　GLANVULLYNO EAST [Glenmullynaha East, p. Kilbeagh]
　　　1790: Patrick Taffe (35-0-8).
116　GURTANURE [gortanure,p. Kilbeagh.] 1790: Mark McDonnell (76-4-4)
117　GLASSON MILLS (sold) [Glassan, pp. Bunown, Kilkenny West B. Kilkenny West, Co. Westmeath] 1791: Josh Sproule & Arthur, Dun (10-5-0)
118　a.　GOWEL (pt.: DRINY) [Gowel, P. Kilbeagh; Driney, p. p. Tibohine]
　　　　　1796: Thomas Kelly & ors. (34-0-0)
　　　b. (CLOONTYGARVY) {?]1798: Edmond Fitzgerald & co. (72-0-10)
119　GORTASTEELANE (pt.CARRONMALLAGH) [Carrownamallaght,
　　　p. Knock　1799: Roger McDonnell & co (11-17-0) {322-2-6)
120　a.　HAWKESFORD (pt) & TONRIGEE [Hawksford, Tnregee, p.Kilcolman] 1796: Garret & Michael Dalton　(41-4-2); James Coleman & co .(52-8-8)
　　　b. (MILL OF)　1796: Francis Mcdonagh　(7-9-1)　[101-1-11)
121　ICELANE, CRUNNANE & RAHEROLIS {Ishlaun, Crunaun, p. Castlemore; Raherolus, p.Kilmovee.1791: James Taffe(277-10-4).
122　INCHMORE & NUNS ISLAND [Inchmore, Nuns Island, p. Bunown, B. Kilkenny West,　Co. Westmeath.] 1791: Robert Sandys　(42-2-6)
123　KNOCKMANE (pt) [Knockmeane, p. Kilmeane, B. Athlone Co.Roscommon. 1778: Eneas McGrath　(7-10-6) (sold) 1794: John Glover (61-10-0) (sold)
124　a.　KILLOVEENY WEST [killoveeny, p. Knock] 1790: Coll Dillon (87-9-10)
　　　b. KILOVEENY EAST {Killoveeny, p. Knock] 1791: Edmond Taffe (118-7-2)
125　Kiltobranks [Kiltybranks, p. Tibohune]1798: Charles O'Connor (164-0-10)
126　KEAME [=Churchfield, p. Knock] 1790: Anthony Madden (144-12-0)

LEASEHOLDERS ON THE DILLON ESTATE C.1805

127 KILMORE [Kilmore, p. Kilmovee] 1790: Anthony Madden (103-1-0)
128 KILKELLY OR WOODFIELD [Kilkelly, p. Kilmovee] Woodfield, p. Aghamore] (?) : Edmond Taffe (208-1-6).
129 KILCOLEMAN OR FRYARS HILL [KilcolemanP. Kilcoleman; Friars Hill, P. Castlemore; 1793: James Hughes (272-16-4)
130 KILLACLARE [Killaclare, p. Kilmovee];1794: Owen Filan & ors. (41-3-4)
131 KILLUNAGHER [Killunagher, p. Annagh]; 1794: Thomas Kelly & co. (62-17-10)
132 KILGARIFF [?Kilgarriff, p. Aghamore]; 1795: Faragh McDonnell (103-1-0) [1374-10-61)
133 KILLEENREWAGH (pt), CARNAGH WEST, Ballinure & (pt) CALDRAGH (sold) [?Killeenrewagh, p. Killinvoy: Carnagh West, p. St. Johns, B. Athlone; ?; ?;; 1796: Winifred O'Connor (378-18-1)
134 KILGARRIVE [?Kilgarriff, P. Kilbeagh]; 1798: Patrick Geever & co. (72-0-10)
135 KILTABOE& pt. DRINEY [Cuiltyboe, Driney, p. Tibohine] 1798: John Thomas (87-2-6)
136 KILLCASHEL [Kilcashel, p. Kilmovee]; 1799: Timothy Dudican & co. (50-12-6)
137 KINCUNN [Kincon, p. Knock]; 1799: Patrick Staunton & co. (35-10-11)
138 KILLEENLEA (Killylea, P. Bekan.]; 1799: Bryan Kerin & co. (23-10-9).
139 KILTOMAIN (sold) [Kiltymaine, p. Tibohine];1800: Michael "flyn (95-5-0)
140 KILLITURLY (pt) [Killaturly, p. Kilbeagh]; 1801: Martin Durken & c0. (39-2-2)]; James Hansboro & co. (68-8-9); James Lenegan & co. (34-4-2).
141 a. KILLEEN [Killeen, p. Kilbeagh] 1801: John Lee & ors. (88-2-4)
    b (pt. called STRIPE) [Stripe p. Kilbeagh];1803: Coll Dillon 80-3-6).
142 KILCASHILL (pt. called the WILD WOOD) [Kilcashel P. Kilmovee;?] 1805: Thos Cosgrave & co. (26-5-0)[2446-16-2)
143 LAVAGH [lavagh Beg, Lavy More, p. Kilbeagh 1789: Edmond Taffe (66-19-10)
144 LOUGHGLIN/LOUGHLIN TOWN [Loughglin, L. Demesne, L. Town P. Tibohine];1803: No. 1. Thomas Dillon & J. Derrick (2-0-1);2, 3, 4, 5, & 6. John Hunt: (5-17-9) . 7. Widow Smiley (3-0-0); 8. Chapel plot in hands (0-0-0). 1792. James Derrick (2-1-0); 10. Charles Carty (2-1-0),; Bridget Tipher (2-1-0-); 12. Patrick Gill (2-1-0-) 13. James Derrick (2-1-0); 14. James Reddin (2-1-0); {n.d.}: 15.Terence Mcguire (4-2-0). [94-6-7) 1793: 16. Andrew Walsh. (2-1-0); 1792: 17. Christopher Taffe (2-1-0) ; 18. John Dillon (2-1-0); 19. Anne Cosgrave (2-1-0); 20.Hugh Seery (2-1-0); 21. Anthony Burke (2-1-0); 22 & 23, James Dillon (4-2-0); 24. Revd. Henry Clifford (2-1-0); 1789: Alexander Mc Donnell (0-0-1); 1792: 26. Patrick Hort (2-1-0); 27. Patrick Gordon (2-1-0) 28 & 29. James Toley (4-2-0); 30. Anthony Donnellan (2-1-0); 32. Owen Carney (2-1-0); 1803 .33 Peter Rutledge (2-1-0); 1803; 33 & 34.: John Rogers (4-2-0)
145 LEVEELOCK [Leveelick, p. Kilmovee] 1790: Edmond Fitzgerald (39-19-8).
146 LURGA [lurgan, p. Bekan; or Lurga, Lower & Upper, p. Kilbeagh] 1790: James Jordan (72-2-4).
147 a. LISDRUMNEAL (pt.: 1st. DIV.) [Lisdrumneill, p. Tibohine] 1794: Edmond Gilligan & co. (27-12-9) [sold]

LEASEHOLDERS ON THE DILLON ESTATE C.1805

    b.(pt,: 2nd DIV.) 1794:   Martin McGarry & co.   (24-0-0) [sold]
    c.   (pt) 1794:   Cormick Callaghan & co. (9-16-0). [299-17-5)
148   LISANISKEY & CLOONBULBIN [Lissaniska, Cloonbulban, p. Bekan
    1796: James Jordan (359-17-0)
149   LISCAT [liscat, p. Aghjamore]; 1798: Christopher Tyrrell (92-19-8)
150   LECARROW (pt.:BRUSNAGH) [?lwcarrow, p. Kilbeagh, or p. Knock; ?
    1799: John Flatley & co. (56- 11- 2)
151   LISPATRICK [Lispatrick, p. Knock]; 1799:   Brian & Patrick Kerin (9-5-6).
152   LISBANE [lisbaun West, p. Bekan]; 1799: Danl. & Andreas Fyn (9-5-6).
153   LOUGHGLIN CUSTOMS [cf. Loughglinn, L Demesne, L. Town,]p.
    Tibohine1805: Michl Mc Nulty (20-10-0).
154 a LOWPARK ((pt., otherwise GORTALOUGHAUN called East Ballyglass)
    [Lowpark,? Ballyglass East, p. Kilbeagh] 1800: John Regan & ors. (43-
    0-8) (pt. called Ballyglass & Mill) [Ballyglass East, Ballyglass West, p.
    Kilbeagh].
    b 1805: John Brady (47-9-11)
    c (pt., & pt. SUNNAGH) [Sonnagh, p. Kilbeagh]; 1800 Thomas Taffe (12-4-8)
    d (pt., & pt., BALLYGLASS [Ballyglass) [Ballyglass East, Ballyglass
    West, p. Kilbeagh]; 1800: John Mulligan   944-5-1); Patrick Quinn, &
    co. (21-10-3) { (986-16-10)(pt)
    e 1800: John McGowan & co. (28-16-4)
    f (pt. called BALLYGLASS WEST) [Ballyglass West. p. Kilbeagh]
        1800 Owen McGuire & co.   (19-11-1); 1801: John Brady   (27-7-5)
155 a LEACARROW (pt.) [Lecarrow, p. Kilbeagh] 1800: Peter Gavaghan (29-6-9)
    b (pt.. called SPECK) [Speck, p. Kilbeagh]; 1800: Hugh Regan & ors. (12-14-0)
    c 1800: James Dogherty & co. (11-14-7)
156. LEOW [leo, p. Annagh]; 1802: Edmond Kilkenny & co. (133-15-10)
157 a LURGAN, (EAST DIV of) & LISNAGRUSS [Lurgan, Lisnagross p.
    Annaghmore] 1802: Michael Burke & co. (83-15-0)
    b. (MIDDLE DIVN. OF) & LISNAGRUSS)[Lisnagross, p. Aghamore]
        1802: Matthias Kelly & co. (89-0-5)
    c (WEST DIVN. of) & LISNAGRUSS [Lisnagross, p. Aghamore]
        1802: Thomas Prendergast & co. (81-6-1)
158 a LURGA (pt.: UPPER DIVN.) [Lurga Upper p. Kilbeagh]
        1803: Phelim Dogherty & c0. (80-3-4)
    b   (pt. : LOWER DIVN.) [Lurga lower, p. Kilbeagh]
        1803: Patrick Flatley & c0. (80- 3- 4) {1689-19-31)
159   MAGHERABOY [magherboy, p. Kilmovee]
    1792: Eneas McDonnell (99-0-10)
160   MULLIN (pt.) (sold) Mullen, p. Tibohine]; 1793 : Thomas Dillon (82-0-0)
    1794: John Thomas (38-19-0);1795: Peter Burnes Senr. & co. (18-9-0);
    John Casey Senr. & co. (3-1-6); John Casey Junr. & co. 99-4-6)
    James Dillon & co. (12-6-0); Thomas Gara & co. (9-4-6); Thomas
    Greene & co. (10- 5- 0); Laurence Greevy & co. (12-16-3); John & comy

LEASEHOLDERS ON THE DILLON ESTATE C.1805

(24- 12- 0); Mark Gara &comy. (12-16-3) [332-14-10);
Thady McGarry & co. (16-8-0); Patrick McGarry & co.(11-5-6);
Thomas Oates & co. (25-12-6); Bryan REILLY & co. (12-16-3).
1796: Hugh Callaghan & co. (10- 5-0); 1793: Patrick Duffy (30-15-0);
William Dolan (41-0-0); James Tighe (35-17-6); 1795: Christopher Taffe (82-0-0); 1796: Andrew Creaton & co. (25-12-6) ; Henry O'Brien & co. (57-8-0);   (681- 15-11)

161 MULLINMADOGE [Mullen madoge p, Kilbeagh]
     1797: John Thomas (102-17-4)
162 MONEYMORE [Moneymore, p. Annagh]
     1802: Thomas Cribben & ors. (25-0-10) [810- 13-3]
163 ORLAR [Urlaur, p. Kilmovee]; 1789: James Pales (205-14-8)
164 OGHTABOY & SHANVAGHERY [Aghtoboy, Shanvaghera, p. Knock
     1790: Anne Staunton, (175-0-0) [380-14-8)
165. PULBEE [Pullboy, p. Castlemore] 1799: Michael Regan & co. (25-5-11).
166 ROUSKEY [Roosky, p. Knock] 1783:   Patrick & Thomas Jordan (61-17-4)
167 RUANE (pt.,: CARRONEMALLACHT) [—: Carrowmallaght, p. Knock.]
     1791: Patrick Egan & comy. (35- 16-10).
168 RAHEELY (pt) [Raheely p. Tibohone];1795: John Dockery & comp. (14-1-0); Thady Finneran & comy. (13-16-9);Laughlin Gara & comp.   (20-10-0) Patrick Gara & ors. (15-7-6) John Golden (23-1-3); Ml.McGarry & comy. (15-7-6) Frans. Sharcott 7 comy. (21-10-6). [221-9-6)
169 SHAMMER [Shammerbaun, Shammerdoo p. Kilmovee]
     1795: Christopher Taffe (102-17-4).
170 SCRIG [Scregg, p. Annaghmore [1796 Ml. Freehilly (37-1-8)
171 SINVOLLANE (part of) [Sonvolaun, p. Lilmovee] 1796: Laurence Bones & co. (17-8-8); Darby Connor & Co. (26-13-9); Martin Forkin & co. (37-11-8); Ml. O' Beirne & co. (37-1-3)
172 SRAHEEN (part : BRUSNAGHS) [Sraheens p. Kilmovee; ? Patrick Duffy & co. (22-14-8)
173 SKEEHEEN [Skeheen, p. Kilmovee]; 1799: Edmond Rush & co. (42-3-6)
174 SPADAGH & ARDERRY [Spaddagh, Arderry, p. Annagh]
     1800: James Lyons & co. (52-15-9)
175 a. SUNNAGH: (pt. of) [Sonnagh, p. Kilbeagh]; 1800: Thomas Dillon (20-11-4); David Kelly (17-9-11); James Walsh & co. (13- 6-7) [427-16-11] 1801; Ml. McIntyre & co. (19-11-1); Anthony Garvey & co; (78-4-4)
     b. pt of called HARDERRA [?]; 1801: Daniel O' Connor; (24- 8-9)
176 a SHUNNAGHMEEL (pt of)[Shanaghmoyle, p. Knock]
     1802: Patrick Lee & co. & co. (108-1-3);
   b. (pt. called DERRAGH)· [Derragh) [Derragh, p. Knock]
     1802: William Flatley (17-9-11). [675-11-5]
177 a Tullaghan (pt. of Called GARRANE) [Tullaghan, Garraun, p. Annagh]
     1801: Bryan Mullarky & co. (76-5-2
     b (pt. 0f called BALLYBEG) [Ballybeg, p. Annagh]

LEASEHOLDERS ON THE DILLON ESTATE C.1805

      1801 Patrick Gunning & co. (37-0-3)
c   (pt of called MIDDLETOWN) [?]
      1801: Martin Gildea & co. (136-& co. (82-2-1).
178 TAMPLE [Temple, p. Kilbeagh]; 1801: John O'Donnell &, co. (82-2-1).
179 a. TAWNINA [(pt. of: UPPER DIVISION) [Tawnyinagh Upper, p. Tawyinagh Upper, P. Kilbeagh]; 1803: James Mc Donnell& co. (136-17-10).
     b (pt. of LOWER DIVISION) [Tawnyinagh Lower, p. Kilbeagh]
     1803: James Raftery & co. (42-0-10); Barth. Weever & co. (44-19-4) [1417-19-3].

COMPOSITION RENTS &c

AGHBOY (part: Tully)	Landen Newstead (1-7-1)
ANNAGH & LECARROW	Dillon & Skerrit (0-2-6)
BALLIVEEL	Richard Malone (2-11-4)
CLOONMORE	(Chief Rent) Thomas Phillips (1-5-0)
CORROHORE	William French (0-7-4)
EDEN	John Dillon (4-0-0)
GALLEN	Palmer & Knox (14-13-0)
ISLAND	Willian Knox (1-16-8)
LISCOLEMAN	Dominick Jordan (3-16-0)
LISAKILLEEN	John Dillon (4-0-0)
ORAN	Christopher Irwin (2-0-0)
TULRAHAN	Thomas Nolan (1-7-1)
TULLY	Richard Dillon (0-13-0) (34-4-10)

RENTAL OF IRISH ESTATES 1805, THE PROPERTY OF LORD VISCOUNT DILLON

A; 782-13-00   B; 2974-5-6;   C. 6464-17-6;   D:1540-18-8;
E: 76-4-4;   F : 301-19-2;   G: 322-2-6;   H: 101-1-11;
I: 323-12-10;   L: 1689-19-3;   M: 1810-13-3;   0:380-4-8;
P: 25-5-11;   R: 2211-9-6;   S: 675-11-5;   T: 1417-18-3.

In the 1666 it appears by the Patent Lord Dillon held in the Counties of Mayo, Roscommom and Westmeath:

Profitable Acres: 60,247   *Unprofitable:* 79,949.   *Total:* 136, 188

68,804 in the Barony of Costello of whichthere were 23,388 profitable; unprofitable 45, 416. Roscommon & Westmeath in the Barony of Gallen: 67,384.

                    [From Dillon Papers in Oxfordshire County Record Office, Oxford,
                                                 DIL. XII/b/7.]

LEASEHOLDERS ON THE DILLON ESTATE C.1805
LIST OF SURNAMES IN THE BARONIES

Battle 95; Beasty1; Beirne 28, 93; Bellingham 10; Beytagh 106; Boland 61, 101;Bones 171; Bowines 46; Boyd 9; Brady 88, 154; (2); Brooker 10; Brown 97; Burke30, 62, 144, 157; Burnes 46, 160.

Cafferky 6, 98; Callaghan 147;; Calligan160; Cannon 34; Carney 104,144; Carroll 31,40; Carty 144; Casey 7, 160 (2); Clarke; 63; Clifford 92, (3), 93., 144; Coayne5; Coleman 103, 120; Connelly 32; Connilan 67; connor47; Conway 41; Cosgrave 62, 106, 142, 144; Costello 34, 93; Cox 6, 33, 60; Coyel16; Creaton 160; Cribben 162; Crooley4; Curry 88;

Dalton 50, 51, 120 (2); Daly 52; Daniel 63; Derrick 98, 114 (3), Devanney33; Dillon 12, 37, 38, 41, 48, 49, 87, 108, 124, 141, (3) 160 (2), 175; Dockery 168; Dodd 25; Dogherty 155, 158; Dolan 160; Donnellan 144; Dowell 64,65; Doyle76, 83, 113; Dudican 136; Duffy 68, 160, 172. Dun 117; Durken 140; Dyer 17.

Egan 75, 167,

Ferral 4; Filan 130; Finn 93; Finneran 168; Fitzgerald 33, 57, 69, 92,118,145: Fitzmaurace 1, 87 (2); Flanagan 29, 87, 88, 150, 158, 176; Flyn 77, 82, 87, 139; Flynn 61; Foley 52; Forde 88, Forkan 171; Freenhilly 170; French 92 (2); Fly 152 (2).

Gara 21, 160, 168, (2); Garvey 175; Gavaghan 155; Geever 134; Geoghegan 19; Gibbons 52; Giblin 98; Gildea 177; Gill 144; Grady 6 (2), 24, 42, 58; Greene 160; Greevy 160; Groarke 36 (2), 106 (2); Gunning 8, 177; Gurrin 31.

Hall 160; Hanbro 140; Hemming 67; Higgins 6, 78, 94; Horan 74; Horkan 88; Hort 144; Hughes 5, 66 (2), 129; Hunt 144.

Jennings 86; Jordan 70, 148, 166 (2); Jordon 146.

Keane 61; Kelly 24, 34, 71, 93, 94, 118, 131, 157, 175; Kerin 138, 151 (2); Kerrane 26; Kilkenny 156; Knight 9.

Lan 1 (2); Lee 141, 176; Lenaghan 140; Lynch 90; Lyons 84, 91, 174.

McCarron 88; McCarty 3; McDermott 111; McDonnell 1, 31, 43, 53, 54, 116, 119, 132, 144, 159, 179; McDonough 40; McGara 160, 168; McGarry 57, 147, 160 (2); McGowan 154; McGrath 123; McGuire 144, 154; McHugh 88; McIntire 175; McLaughlin 88, 94; McNulty 153; Madden 20, 126, 127; Melvin 96; Moore 93; Morally 92; Moran 7, 98; Morrilly 96; Morriss 99; Muldoon 41; Mulkeen 77; Mullarky 177; Mulligan 85, 86, 154; Mulloy 93; Murray 89, 144.

Neary 61; Nolan 15, 100; Nowlan 87.

LEASEHOLDERS ON THE DILLON ESTATE C.1805

Oates 160; O'Beirne 171; O'Brien 36, 160; O'Connor 55, 125, 133, 175; O'Donnell 13, 155, 178; O'Gara 33.

Palles 11, 163; Phillips 70, 72, 72, 79, 110, 112; Plunket 23; Prendergast 34, 56, 157.

Quin 80, 154.

Rafferty 35; Raftery 179; Reddin 144; Regan 25, 81, 154, 155, 165; Reilly 160; Rodgers 144; Rogier 14; Royan 92, 102; Rush 173; Rutledge 2, 39, 144;

Sandys 122; Seery 144; Sharcott 168; Sloyan 18 (2), Smiley 144; Sproule 177; Staunton 22, 137, 164; Stenson 30; Sullivan 93.

Taaffe 30, 44, 45, 114, 115, 121, 124, 128, 143, 144, 154, 160, 169; Tarpy 73; Thomas 98, 135, 160, 161; Thighe 160; Timothy 88; Tipher 144; Toley 144; Towey 27; Tyrrell 149.

Waldrum 59, 92 (2), 93, 105, 107; Walsh 96, 144; Walshe 175; Weever 179.

INDEX OF PLACES
(by barony, parish, townland)

COUNTY MAYO

BARONY OF COSTELLO

1. PARISH OF AGHAMORE
Addergoole 1. Aghataharn 2. Ballyglass 8. Ballyhine 15. Ballynacloy 30. Bruff 35. Carn Beg 30. Carrowbaun 30. Carrowbeg 30. Cloghvoley 39. Clooncah 43. Cloongawnagh, (Burke) & (Cosgrave) 62. Cloontarriff 91. Coogue, East & West 41. Coolnaha, North & South 59. Crossard 61. Doogary 106. Kilgarriff 41, 132. Liscat 149. Lisnagross 157. Lurgan 157. Scregg 170. Woodfield 128.

2. PARISH OF ANNAGH
Abbeyquarter 63. Aderg 33. Arderry 174. Ballybeg 177. Ballyhaunis 9. Ballykilleen 11. Bargarriff 33. Classaghroe 84. Coolnafarna 46. Corraun 93. Derrintogher 33. Derrylea 93. Derrynacong 101. Drumaderry 107. Drumbaun 99. Garraun 177. Gortnageeragh 33. Grallagh 144. Killunagher 131. Leo 156. Moneymore 162. Scregg 170. Spaddagh 174. Tullaghaun 177.

3. PARISH OF BEKAN
Ballinphuill 26. Ballyhaunis 9. Bekan 14, 32, 37. Bracklagh 22. Brackloon East 17. Brackloon west 18. Carrowreagh 57. Clagnagh 38. Cloonbulban

LEASEHOLDERS ON THE DILLON ESTATE C.1805

148. Cullentragh 75. Cloonbookeighter & -oughter 77, 90. Derrylahan 102. Derrymore 105. Forthill 87. Gorteen More 87. Grallaghgarden 87. Killylea 138. Lisbaun East 87. Lisbaun West 152. Lissaniska 148. Lurgan 146. Mountain 87. Tawnaghmore 87.

4. PARISH OF CASTLEMORE
Ardkill 3. Ballymaging or Castlemore 23. Barnaboy 27. Boghtaduff 25. Bohalas 12. Cashelard 81. Cashelcolaun 47. Cloonavullaun 48. Crunaun 121. Drumnalassan 97. Friarshill 129. Ishlaun 121. Pollboy 165.

5. PARISH OF KILBEAGH
Ballyglass, East & West 154. Barnacahoge 34, Barnalyra 31. Bracklagh 86. Bulcaun 85. Calveagh, Lower & Upper 53. Cappulcorragh 95. Carn 31. Carrowgarve 49. Cartron 49. Cashel 94. Cloonaweema 68. Clooncous 73. Cloonfane 72. Cloonlyon 89. Cloonmeen, East & West 70. Currinah 44. Derrynabrock 104. Fauleens 112. Glenmullynaha East 115. Glenmullynaha West 58. Gortanure 116. Gowel 118. Kilgarriff 134. Killaturly 140. Killeen 141. Lavy, Beg & More 143. Lecarrow 150, 155. Loughglinn, Loughglinn Demesne 153. Lowpark 154. Lurga, Lower & Upper 179. Temple 178.

6. PARISH OF KILCOLMAN
Ballaghaderreen 10. Coollena 66. Cross, North and South 66. Drumacoo 103. Hawksford 120. Kilcolman 129. Tonregee 120.

7. PARISH OF KILMOVEE
Aghadiffin 6. Ballyglass 8. Barcull 16. Carrownlacka 74. Clooncarha 40. Cashellahenny 50. Cloonfaulus 60. Cloonfeaghra 96. Cloonierin 51. Cloonnamna 80. Corgarriff 67. Culliagh 78. Kilcashel 123, 142. Kilkelly 128. Killaclare 130. Kilmore 127. Leveelick 145. Magheraboy 159. Raherolus 121. Shammerbaun, Shammerdoo 169. Skeheen 173. Sonvolaun 171. Sraheens 172. Uggool 110. Urlaur 163.

8. PARISH OF KILTURRA
Cloonakillina 111. Cloonfeightrin 69. Flughany 111.

9. PARISH OF KNOCK
Aghtaboy 164. Ballyroe 28. Bohaun 13. Caldragh 76. Carrowcor 92. Carrowmore 88. Carrownamallaght (29), 76, 119, 167. Churchfield 126. Cloondace 100. Cloonfaughna 92. Cloonlee 56. Cloonnagleragh 83. Cloontarriff 91. Cloonturnaun 79. Crockaunrannell 92. Curraghlahan 92. Curraghteemore 13. Derradda 92. Derragh 176. Drum 100. Faughil 113. Killoveeny 124. Kincon 137. Lispatrick 151. Magheramore 92. Roosky 166. Shanaghmoyle 176. Shanvaghera 164.

LEASEHOLDERS ON THE DILLON ESTATE C.1805

BARONY OF CLANMORRIS
1 PARISH OF MAYO: Ballymullavil 22.

COUNTY ROSCOMMON

BARONY OF FRENCHPARK
1. PARISH OF TIBOHINE
Aghaderry 5, 7, 36. Aghadrestan 5. Aghalour 4. Ballinphuill 36. Carrowgarve 49. Carrownaknockaun 54. Cloonacolly 42. Cloonargid 42. Cloonmullin 45. Coolagarry 52. Creevy 82. Cuiltyboe 135. Driney 98, 118, 135. Kiltybranks 125. Kiltymaine 139. Lisdrumneill 147. Loughglinn, L. Demesne 144. Mullen 160. Raheely 168.

BARONY OF ATHLONE NORTH
1. PARISH OF KILLINVOY : Killeenrevagh 133.
2. PARISH OF KILMEANE: Knockmeane 123.

BARONY OF ATHLONE SOUTH
1. PARISH OF ST. JOHN'S:
Carnagh, East & West 65, 133, Carrigan, Beg & More 64.

BARONY OF CASTLEREAGH
1. PARISH OF KILKEEVIN: Clooncraffield 55.

BARONY OF ROSCOMMON
1. PARISH OF OGULLA: Drimnagh 108.

COUNTY OF WESTMEATH

BARONY OF KILKENNY EST
1. PARISH OF BUNOWN: Glassan 117. Inchmore 122. Nuns Island 122.
2. PARISH OF KILKENNY WEST: Glassan 117.

Appendix Two

TENANTS ON COSTELLO ESTATE

FOLIO NO. 2099. TENANTS ON THE HOME FARM OF ARTHUR GEORGE COSTELLO'S ESTATE. 1885.

Extracts from a Memorial of a Deed of Conveyance bearing the date the 20th of August 1885 which is in the words and figures following, that is to say:-
I the Right Honorable Henry Ormsby one of the Land Judges of the Chancery of Justice in Ireland under the authority of an Act passed in the twenty-second year of the reign of Queen Victoria, called 'An Act to facilitate the Sale and Transfer of land in Ireland', and of the Acts amending the same in consideration of the sum of £996/6/11 by the Irish Land Commission paid into the Bank of Ireland to the account of the Accountant-General of the Supreme Court of Judicature in Ireland and to the credit of the Estate of Arthur G.R. Costello, owner ex parte Richard Holmes, Petitioner, in part discharge of the purchase money of £25,087/15/- for which they have purchased the Hereditaments hereinafter granted and in consideration of the further sum of £24,091/8/1. ascertained by one of the said Land Judges to be due to the said Irish Land Commission on foot of Incumbrances effecting the said Estate and by one of the said Land Judges authorised to be retained by the said Irish Land Commission in discharge of the remainder of the said purchase money, of £25,087/ 15/- do grant unto the said Land Commission parts of the lands of...

Clonlumney -	2198 Acres, 20 Perches statute measure,	
Islandmore -	264 Acres 1 Rood & 35 Perches	"
Lorgan -	829 Acres 3 Roods 34 Perches	"
Boleysillagh -	516 Acres 25 Perches	"
Cloonmen -	183 Acres 19 Perches	"
Fallsolus -	149 Acres 1 Rood 21 Perches	"
Attiantaggart -	159 Acres 23 Perches	"
Frasnadeffa -	121 Acres 2 Roods 8 Perches	"
Tullaghanmore or Edmondstown Demesne -		
	124 Acres 2 Roods 39 Perches	"
Toobracken -	743 Acres 10 Perches	"
Tullaghanrock -	665 Acres 1 Rood, 6 Perches	"
Coollena -	104 Acres 1 Rood 1 Perch	"
Magheraboy -	175 Acres 23 Perches	"
Creggan -	674 Acres 3 Roods 25 Perches	"
Cross South -	263 Acres 3 Roods 15 Perches	"
Cross North -	16 Acres 2 Roods 10 Perches	"

All are in the Barony of Costello, Co. Mayo.

Keelbanada -	1044 Acres 3 Roods 33 Perches	"

COSTELLO ESTATE

These lands are in the Barony of Frenchpark Co. Roscommon.
All lands hereby conveyed are described in the annexed maps (now in National Library) with appurtenances together with a right of way for the said Irish Land Commission, their successors and Assigns and their tenants for the time being of the lands adjoining the same over the level crossings of the Sligo and Ballaghaderreen Junction Railway... TO HOLD the same unto the Irish Land Commission, their successors and Assigns FOR EVER, subject in conjunction with other parts of the said lands of Tullaghanmore or Edmondstown Demesne containing 315 Acres 3 Roods 13 Perches, statute measure, ...to the perpetual yearly chief Rent – composition Rent, Rentcharge or annual sum of £31/ 6/ 10 now payable to Lord Viscount Dillon created by some ancient Deed or other assurance not now forthcoming ... and all costs and expenses occasioned by the non-payment thereof by the said other parts of Tullaghanmore or Edmondstown Demesne which have ordered to be sold by the said Land Judges subject to the whole of said perpetual sum of £35/6/10. in full indemnification of all other lands liable thereto and also subject in conjunction with the said other part of ...Tullaghanmore or Edmondstown Demesne ... to an annual or yearly rentcharge of £600 for the life of Dorcas Maria Langley Created by Indenture dated 26 February 1827 and made between Charles Costello of the first part George Robert Daniel and Dorcas Maria Daniel of the second part and Thomas Orde Lees and John Clarke of the fourth part, so far as same may be necessary to secure the payment of two annual sums of £100 & £134/ 15/ 10. For the life of the said Dorcas M. Langley ...IN WITNESS whereof I the said HENRY ORMSBY have hereunto set my Hand and the Seal of the said Land Judges this twentieth day of August in the year of Our Lord 1885.

    Signed and Sealed by;

          Henry Ormsby.

FIRST SCHEDULE REFERRED TO IN THE FOREGOING CONVEYANCE DENOMINATIONS

PART OF THE LANDS OF CLOONLUMNEY, IN THE BARONY OF COSTELLO, CO. MAYO.

Tenants names	Yearly Rent	Quantity of Land,	Statute Measure
John Breheny	£8/19/10.	23 Acres	2 Roods 38 Perches.
James Roddy.	£6/13/.	15 "	3 " 14 ".
Patrick Breheny	£5/16/2.	8 "	2 " 11 "
John Breheny	£5/11/4.	12 "	0 " 6 "
Edward Duffy	£5/11/4.	11 "	1 " 28 "
John Roddy	£4/7/2.	15 "	1 " 0 "
Thomas Breheny	£10/3/10.	25 "	3 " 14 "
Patrick Breheny	£5/16/2.	11 "	2 " 1 "
James Flannery	£6/13/0.	15 "	2 " 14 "
James Gannon	£3/3/3.	7 "	2 " 2 "

COSTELLO ESTATE

Tenants names	Yearly Rent	Quantity of Land,		Statute Measure	
Charles Gannon	£3/3/3.	9	Acres	2 Roods	27 Perches
Martin Rogers	£3/19/8.	14	"	3 "	13 "
John Roddy(Ml.)	£8/15/6.	21	"	0 "	33 "
Patrick Dooney	£8/13/4.	19	"	3 "	7 "
Dominick Mauriceroe	£7/19/2.	23	"	1 "	25 "
Anthony Mauriceroe	£7/19/2.	24	"	1 "	25 "
John Flannery	£8/17/4.	23	"	1 "	24 "
Thomas Breheny	£7/19/2.	20	"	2 "	3 "
Thomas Duffy	£7/12/4.	12	"	1 "	26 "
Luke Duffy	£6/13/4.	14	"	3 "	27 "
Catherine Carney (now the wife of James Morley in her right)					
	£5/16/10.	13	"	1 "	4 "
Thomas Duffy	£4/11/2.	35	"	1 "	27 "
Patrick Morley	£8/15/4.	35	"	0 "	14 "
Francis Roddy	£3/0/0.	15	"	2 "	23 "
Patrick Casey	£4/19/4.	19	"	3 "	21 "
Bridget Roddy	£3/4/10.	13	"	2 "	33 "
Patrick Cullen	£3/4/10.	13	"	2 "	3 "
Margaret Roddy	£3/1/7.	14	"	0 "	34 "
Patrick Roddy	£3/3/7.	14	"	11 "	13 "
Michael Reid	£6/2/6.	27	"	1 "	34 "
Thomas Dooney	£4/1/4.	11	"	0 "	34 "
Dominick Reid	£3/0/0.	14	"	2 "	35 "
Thomas Reid	£3/2/6.	10	"	0 "	20 "
Anthony Roddy	£13/1/4.	35	"	0 "	33 "
Martin Durcan	£6/6/0.	19	"	1 "	9 "
Bridget Cullen (Widow)	£9/17/6.	21	"	1 "	8 "
Patrick Cullen	£7/8/6.	20	"	3 "	7 "
Michael Cullen	£7/6/4.	26	"	1 "	24 "
Ml.Towey (Jun)	£8/15/5.	32	"	3 "	4 "
James Dooney (Junior)	£8/2/2.	20	"	3 "	28 "
John Dooney	£8/5/4.	19	"	1 "	12 "
James Towey	£8/9/10.	18	"	3 "	7 "
Ml.Towey(Laskir)	£8/4/10.	19	"	0 "	3 "
Thomas Grady(Tom)	£8/5/6.	17	"	3 "	1 "
Andrew Dooney (Tom)	£5/9/0.	11	"	3 "	35 "
Michael Towey(James)	£8/10/	19	"	0 "	30 "
James Dooney (Pat)	£5/10/	17	"	2 "	0 "
Thomas Grady(Martin)	£4/5/	17	"	1 "	12 "
Edward Kilgariff	£4/5/0.	15	"	2 "	5 "
Michael Moran	£4/5/0.	15	"	2 "	22 "
Edmond Dooney(Ned)	£4/18/6.	20	"	0 "	32 "
Martin Towey (Martin)	£4/15/6.	23	"	1 "	10 "

COSTELLO ESTATE

Tenants names	Yearly Rent	Quantity of Land,		Statute Measure			
Martin Towey(Owen)	£6/8/8.	13	Acres	3	roods	8	perches
Thomas Towey	£3/2/4.	9	"	3	"	23	"
Hugh Towey(James)	£5/3/0.	18	"	1	"	11	"
Bridget Hannon(Widow)	£3/32/2.	15	"	1	"	35	"
Ml. Hannon (John)	£2/7/0.	9	"	3	"	18	"
Patrick Cassidy	£0/15/0.	1	"	2	"	24	"
Mary Dooney	£3/15/2.	16	"	2	"	28	"
Patrick Vesey(ML.)	£4/14/4.	16	"	0	"	0	"
Michael Vesey(Mich)	£4/14/4.	13	"	3	"	37	"
James Dooney (Sen.)	£5/0/0.	23	"	3	"	3	"
Martin Towey & John Towey	£4/0/0.	25	"	0	"	20	"
John Vesey	£4/0/0.	21	"	2	"	29	"
Thomas Towey (John)	£2/19/8.	20	"	0	"	11	"
Anthony Vesey (Anthony)	£2/0/0.	13	"	0	"	8	"
Michael Towey(Dominic)	£4/0/0.	22	"	1	"	4	"
Patrick Vesey	£2/0/0.	14	"	0	"	27	"
John Freyne	£5/2/0.	17	"	0	"	2	"
John Towey	£4/8/2.	16	"	0	"	0	"
Patrick Towey	£4/15/6.	13	"	3	"	16	"
Peter Regan	£3/4/4.	13	"	2	"	30	"
John Towey(Martin)	£5/3/0.	15	"	2	"	36	"
John Towey (Owen)	£3/4/4.	10	"	2	"	12	
Martin Towey (John)	£3/16/10.	13	"	1	"	4	"
John Kelly	£3/13/4.	19	"	3	"	11	"
Michael Towey(sen.)	£3/4/4.	9	"	2	"	0	"
Andrew Towey and Martin Towey(Andy)	£3/14/4.	16	"	2	"	25	"
Thomas Regan(Andrew)	£5/9/6.	20	"	0	"	1	"
James Towey	£5/6/6.	18	"	0	"	3	"
Thomas Regan (John)	£4/18/6.	20	"	2	"	12	"
Andrew Regan	£4/15/6.	23	"	3	"	20	"
Patrick Freyne	£4/3/8.	21	"	3	"	16	"
Thomas Doherty	£1/15/0.	6	"	2	"	24	"
Michael Doherty (Pat)	£1/15/0.	7	"	2	"	29	"
John Doherty	£3/10/0.	9	"	1	"	23	"
James Roddy(rep.of)	£2/17/11.	11	"	0	"	38	"
		1	"	2	"	19	"
John Towey (John)	£2/16/8'	9	"	3	"	39	"
Patr. Roddy (John)	£6/1/0.	17	"	3	"	27	"
Ml. Doherty (rep.of)	£2/14/2'	5	"	3	"	17	"
Bridget Gallagher	£2/4/0.	3	"	2	"	11	"
John Mulloy	£2/3/5.	10	"	3	"	17	"
John Towey (Pat)	£2/4/0.	12	"	1	"	7	"

COSTELLO ESTATE

Tenants names	Yearly Rent	Quantity of Land,	Statute Measure	
Michael Doherty (Henry) rep.of.	£3/7/6.	10 acres	3 roods	14 perches
Martin Freeny (John)	£3/7/6.	10 "	3 "	26 "
Patrick Freeny (John)	£1/3/9.	7 "	1 "	26 "

ISLANDMORE, BARONY OF COSTELLO AND CO. MAYO.

Tenants names	Yearly Rent	Quantity of Land	Statute Measure	
Thady Carney & Thomas Towey	£4/3/2.	22 acres	3 roods	4 perches.
Thomas Duignan(sen) & James Forkin	£3/18/2.	21 "	3 "	7 "
Thomas Forkin	£1/17/0.	12 "	2 "	2 "
Thomas Duignan(jun)	£1/17/10.	14 "	1 "	8 "

The several tenants on this townland have a right of turbary for their own use on the bog situate on this townland.

LARGAN, SITUATE IN THE BARONY OF COSTELLO, AND CO. OF MAYO.

The rent for the following six tenants is included in their holding in Islandmore.

Tenants names	Yearly Rent	Quantity of Land	Statute Measure	
Thady Carney & Thomas Towey	-	7 acres	1 rood	1 perches
Thomas Duignan, senr. & James Forkin.	-	5 "	3 "	15 "
James Forkin	-	2 "	2 "	14 "
Thomas Forkin	-	5 "	1 "	1 "
Thos. Duignan,(jun)	-	5 "	1 "	0 "

The remainder tenants on this townland have a right of turbary for their own use on the bog situate on this townland.

John Freyne	£3/11/2.	15 acres	3 roods	31 perches
Thaddeus Freyne	£3/0/0.	10 "	0 "	7 "
John Mearan	£5/10/0.	19 "	0 "	3 "
Richard Grady(rep.of.)	£5/7/4/	18 "	3 "	0 "
Dominick Freyne	£2/18/0.	16 "	0 "	22 "
Hugh King rep.of.)	£3/12/6.	11 "	0 "	3 "
Patrick Freyne	£3/11/2.	12 "	0 "	38 "
Thomas Drury	£2/9/2.	12 "	0 "	29 "
Mary Sharkett	£2/8/5.	6 "	0 "	2 "
Patrick Higgins	£6/0/6.	12 "	3 "	21 "
Michael Flannery	£8/18/0.	18 "	2 "	0 "
Daniel King	£4/0/0.	14 "	2 "	34 "
Michael Smyth	£3/11/2.	9 "	0 "	7 "
Bartley Hannon	£3/15/4.	7 "	2 "	11 "

COSTELLO ESTATE

Tenants names	Yearly Rent	Quantity of Land,	Statute Measure		
Patrick Cassidy	£3/0/5.	6 acres	3 roods	19 perches	
Mary King	£3/17/10.	9 "	2 "	25 "	
Thomas Grady	£3/1/6.	7 "	0 "	28 "	
John Phillips	£2/14/0.	8 "	0 "	2 "	
Patrick O'Grady	£3/18/6.	8 "	1 "	21 "	
Michael Dowd	£8/0/8.	14 "	2 "	5 "	
Patrick Flannery	£6/6/6.	10 "	1 "	28 "	
Patrick Grady	£6/0/8.	11 "	2 "	3 "	
John Regan	£2/4/8.	0 "	1 "	0 "	

This rent incules the rent of John Regan's holdings in Boleysillagh and Cloomeen.

BOLEYSILLAGH, SITUATE IN THE BARONY OF COSTELLO AND CO. MAYO

The several tenants on the townland have a right of turbaty for their own use on bog situate on this townland.

Tenants names	Yearly Rent	Quantity of Land	Statute Measure		
Patrick Casey	£3/3/0.	19 acres	1 roods	27 perches	
Thomas Casey (rep.of.)	£2/2/1.	13 "	1 "	6 "	
James Casey	£2/2/1.	9 "	0 "	37 "	
John Casey	£2/2/1.	7 "	3 "	10 "	
John Regan	£ --	0 "	1 "	0 "	

The rent of this holding is included in the rent of £2/4/8. paid by this tenant for his holding on Cloonmeen.

CLOONMEEN.

Tenants names	Yearly Rent	Quantity of Land	Statute Measure	
John Regan	£ -	7 "	3 "	12 "
Michael Quinlan	£2/5/7.	5 "	0 "	13 "
James Mulhern	£6/17/4.	16 "	3 "	18 "
Edward O'Donnell	£3/2/4.	14 "	4 "	38 "
Michael Sherlock	£7/0/10.	18 "	0 "	28 "
John Duffy	£1/10/0.	6 "	2 "	£5 "

The several tenants on this townland have a right of turbary for their own use on the bog situate on this townland, and also on the adjoining townland of Attiantaggart.

FALLSOLLUS

Situate in the Barony of Costello and Co of Mayo. These tenants have the same turbary rights as the foregoing.

Tenants names	Yearly Rent	Quantity of Land	Statute Measure		
Margaret Coleman	£8/3/0.	11 acres	3 roods	38 perches	
Patrick Coleman	£8/3/0.	11 "	1 "	3 "	
James Coleman	£7/10/6.	12 "	2 "	27 "	
Michael Mulligan	£7/8/4.	16 "	2 "	9 "	
Thomas Towey	£12/6/2.	18 "	23 "	23 "	

COSTELLO ESTATE

Tenants names	Yearly Rent	Quantity of Land,		Statute Measure	

ATTIANTAGGART

Tenants names	Yearly Rent	Quantity of Land		Statute Measure	
Peter Grady	£3/18/6.	19	acres	0 rood	11 perches
Michael Towey	£3/16/8.	26	"	3 "	13 "
Richard Grady	£4/0/7.	18	"	1 "	31 "
John Grady	£4/0/7.	20	"	1 "	22 "
James Grady (darby)	£0/10/0.	1	"	2 "	39 "
James Grady	£4/0/7.	15	"	0 "	21 "
Patrick Towey	£2/1/6.	13	"	3 "	16 "
Martin Grady	£3/13/4.	18	"	3 "	13 "
John Feeney	£ -	2	"	0 "	1 "

The rent of this holding is included in the sum of £2 paid by this tenant out of his holding in Toobracken.

FRASNADUFFA

Tenants names	Yearly Rent	Quantity of Land	Statute Measure	
James Coleman	£15/0/4.	43 "	0 "	33 "
Patrick Coleman	£20/14/6.	39 "	0 "	0 "
Patrick Rogers	£20/8/10.	39 "	1 "	5 "

PART OF THE TULLUGHANMORE OR EDMONDSTOWN DEMESNE

Tenants with the same turbary rights as the foregoing

Tenants names	Yearly Rent	Quantity of Land	Statute Measure	
Patrick Grady	£3/7/10.	18 "	3 "	9 "
Thomas Golden	£5/3/0.	14 "	2 "	14 "
Thomas Grady	£3/3/6.	13 "	2 "	16 "
John Vesey	£10/17/0.	28 "	3 "	39 "
Patrick Spelman	£13/8/0.	41 "	1 "	39 "

PART OF TOOBRACKEN IN THE BARONY OF COSTELLO AND CO. MAYO

The rent of £2 paid by this tenant includes the rent of his holding at Attiantaggart.

Tenants names	Yearly Rent	Quantity of Land	Statute Measure	
John Feeney	£2/0/0.	0 "	1 "	25 "
Patrick Davey	-	9 "	2 "	23 "

The rent of this holding is included in the rent of his holding on Tullaghanrock.

Tenants names	Yearly Rent	Quantity of Land	Statute Measure	
Patrick Grady	£1/0/o.	2 "	0 "	0 "
Patrick Farrell (John)	£3/18/10.	23 "	1 "	37 "
Patrick Farrell (Patrick)	£2/14/10.	28 "	0 "	3 "
William Golden	£4/0/6.	12 "	2 "	38 "
John Rush	£4/0/6.	13 "	3 "	7 "
Thomas Dooney	£5/1/2.	12 "	1 "	1 "
Michael Flannery	£15/11/2.	21 "	3 "	37 "
John McDonagh	£5/18/6.	13 "	0 "	34 "
Patrick Mauriceroe	£15/19/8.	21 . "	1 "	39 "

COSTELLO ESTATE

Tenants names	Yearly Rent	Quantity of Land,	Statute Measure		
John Grady	£7/13/8.	15 acres	0 rood	22	perches
Dominick Mauriceroe	£4/15/0.	8 "	1 "	7	"
John Grady (Mich.)	£4/19/6.	8 "	3 "	21	"
William Grady	£5/0/0.	11 "	0 "	2	"
Michael Higgins	£7/15/6.	11 "	3 "	31	"
John Davy	£4/5/6.	8 "	2 "	36	"
Thomas Duffy	£3/4/0.	6 "	2 "	1	"
Catherine Maguire (widow)	£1/1/6.	2 "	0 "	22	"
James Flannery	£4/14/4.	9 "	0 "	10	"
Bridget Freyne	£2/14/2.	3 "	1 "	31	"
Thomas Coleman	£3/8/2.	5 "	2 "	38	"
Michael Higgins(Thomas)	£79/9/8.	103 "	0 "	30	"
Patrick Mauriceroe one-half & Michl.Flannery	-	2 "	2 "	2	"

This land is held in common in equal shares. Rent paid by tenants for their holdings above include this holding which they hold jointly.

Robert Loughheed	£18/0/0.	19 "	1 "	31	"
Widow McCann	£13/6/2.	14 "	1 "	7	"
Roger McDonnell	£5/0/8.	3 "	0 "	24	"
John Callally	£12/2/0.	10 "	2 "	10	"

PART OF TULLAGHANROCK IN THE BARONY OF COSTELLO

The following tenants have the same turbary rights as the foregoing.

PART OF TULLAGHANROCK IN THE BARONY OF COSTELLO AND CO.MAYO

John Flannery	£25/17/10.	25 Acres	0 roods	22	perches
Bartholomew Grady	£4/12/2.	15 "	3 "	25	"
John Doherty	£2/17/6.	11 "	0 "	27	"
John Grady (Michael)	£4/12/2.	19 "	0 "	20	"
James Coleman	£4/0/10.	11 "	1 "	36	"
Roger McDonnell	£1/5/0.	3 "	3 "	23	"
Robert Lougheed	£4/0/2.	9 "	0 "	26	"
Patrick Davy	£3/0/0.	7 "	3 "	27	"
Patrick Towy	£5/3.8.	13 "	0 "	10	"
John McDonnell	£23/19/10.	22 "	3 "	25	"
John Grady	£1/5/0.	5 "	3 "	7	"
Thomas Dowd	£7/11/10.	17 "	1 "	7	"
James Grady	£7/11/10.	17 "	3 "	20	"
Michael Spelman	£7/17/6.	18 "	0 "	15	"
Patrick Grady	£3/18/8.	8 "	3 "	4	"
Thomas Coleman	£8/2/4.	18 "	1 "	37	"
John Towy	£8/5/0.	17 "	3 "	13	"

COSTELLO ESTATE

Tenants names	Yearly Rent	Quantity of Land,	Statute Measure	
Patrick Keenan	£5/8/2.	17 acres	2 rood	32 perches
Thomas Coleman one half & John Towey, one -half.				
	-	2 "	1 "	29 "
Widow McDonnell	£11/0/0.	19 "	0 "	38 "
Thomas Costello	£0/0/1.	1 "	1 "	9 "
James Coleman	£8/14/0.	9 "	1 "	27 "
John Callally	£9/8/0.	15 "	2 "	30 "
Rep. of Dominick Maguire	£5/15/6.	10 "	2 "	16 "
Bridget Callally, the wife of Peter Rogers and the said Peter Rogers as her husband				
	£ 5/9/0.	10 "	2 "	16 "
Thomas Towey	£7/1/2.	13 "	3 "	31 "
Michael Connor	£6/6/8.	11 "	2 "	31´ "
John Regan	£10/0/2.	14 "	2 "	6´ "
Thomas Conroy	£19/4/0.	17 "	3 "	9 "
Patrick McCann	£9/13/6.	22 "	2 "	27 "
John Cooney	£4/3/1.	8 "	0 "	0 "
Thomas Mauriceroe	£10/19/6	16 "	1 "	27´ "
Margaret Gara	£20/0/0.	32 "	3 "	26 "
Patrick Gill	£7/13/6.	23 "	1 "	33 "

PART OF COOLLENA IN THE BARONY OF COSTELLO AND CO MAYO

Tenants names	Yearly Rent	Quantity of Land,	Statute Measure	
John Gill	£13/1/0.	23 "	1 "	33 "
Bridget Towey	£8/7/6.	17 "	1 "	8 "
John McCann	£6/6/0.	11 "	0 "	5 "
John Towey	£6/11/2.	11 "	3 "	18 "
Stephen Gill	£1/10/0.	1 "	3 "	34 "
Bridget Casey	£6/11/0.	12 "	3 "	38 "

PART OF MAGHERABOY IN THE BARONY OF COSTELLO

Tenants names	Yearly Rent	Quantity of Land,	Statute Measure	
Charles Costello	£1/2/6.	3 "	0 "	21 "
Widow Mary Costello	£1/2/6.	2 "	2 "	33 "
Reps. H. Caldwell	£7/19/2.	10 "	3 "	15 "
John Cunnane	£3/13/4.	7 "	1 "	36 "
Patrick Freyne	£3/0/4.	6 "	0 "	17 "
James Fitzpatrick	£4/7/0.	5 "	0 "	26 "
Thomas Higgins	£59/6/11.	69 "	1 "	14 "
Henry Stuart	£58/2/8.	70 "	1 "	30 "

PART OF CREGGAN IN THE BARONY OF COSTELLO

Tenants names	Yearly Rent	Quantity of Land,	Statute Measure	
Patrick Rush	£7/0/0.	11 "	1 "	37 "
John Rush	£6/8/0.	12 "	1 "	17 "
John O'Donnell	£13/12/0	20 "	3 "	37 "

COSTELLO ESTATE

Tenants names	Yearly Rent	Quantity of Land,	Statute Measure	
Patrick Harrington	£27/8/2.	38 acres	2 roods	18 perches
Patrick White	£16/2/0/	20 "	2 "	10 "
Patrick Costello	£16/9/2.	27 "	0 "	3 "
Martin Brennan	£15/5/3.	28 "	3 "	26 "
Patrick Durcan	£7/12/6.	13 "	0 "	37 "
Roger McDonnell	£1/0/0,	1 "	2 "	9 "
James Coleman	£7/1/10.	6 "	3 "	4 "
Michael Higgins	£8/2/0.	10 "	0 "	20 "
John Drury	£11/19/2.	23 "	0 "	15 "
Mary Gara	£1/19/6	3 "	1 "	8 "
Bridget H. White	£10/8/1.	20 "	1 "	"
John Durcan	£7/12/7.	17 "	2 "	34 "
Henry Stuart	£77/6/8.	82 "	1 "	9 "
James Brennan (junr.)	£15/2/5.	17 "	2 "	25 "
James Brennan (senr.)	£7/8/0.	18 "	1 "	11 "
Dominick Sherlock	£18/14/0,	29 "	3 "	36 "
Michael Coleman (reps. of).	£9/12/6.	31 "	1 "	5 "
Thomas Costello	£11/0/0.	25 "	0 "	4 "
John McCann	£ -	1 "	1 "	3 "

The rent of this holding is included in the rent of £6/6/paid by this tenant for his holding in Coollena.

PART OF CROSS SOUTH, IN THE BARONY OF COSTELLO IN CO MAYO

Patrick Duffy	£10/3/4.	20 "	0 "	4 "
John Brierty	£2/0/0.	10 "	0 "	4 "
Hugh King	£11/11/6.	17 "	2 "	3 "
James Grady	£1/11/8.	2 "	2 "	27 "
Patrick Grady	£1/11/8.	3 "	0 "	32 "
Elizabeth Casey	£12/12/0.	18 "	0 "	3 "
John Doohan	£17/12/0.	33 "	3 "	32 "
Patrick Duffy(senr.)	£37/0/6.	69 "	1 "	25 "
Catherine Rogers	£27/4/4.	42 "	0 "	27 "
James Coleman(junr.)	£11/1/6.	14 "	2 "	19 "
Thomas Rogers	£13/0/0.	19 "	3 "	31 "
James Coleman(senr.)	£8/15/0.	11 "	3 "	2 "

CROSS NORTH, IN THE BARONY OF COSTELLO

Catherine Rogers	£ -	16 "	2 "	10 "

COSTELLO ESTATE

Tenants names	Yearly Rent	Quantity of Land, Statute Measure		

PART OF KEELBANADA FORMERLY SITUATE IN THE BARONY OF COSTELLO, CO OF MAYO NOW UNDER AN ACT OF PARLIAMENT IN THE BARONY OF FRENCHPARK

Tenants names	Yearly Rent	Acres	Rood	Perches
Charles Morahan	£18/14/8.	44 acres	0	17
Roger Sweeney	£8/7/2.	6 "	2 "	22 "
John Sweeney	£8/7/2.	5 "	3 "	17 "
Bridget Morahan (widow)	£5/9/2.	12 "	2 "	39 "
Michael Hanley	£6/11/8.	7 "	0 "	20 "
Andrew Hanley	£6/11/8.	7 "	2 "	12 "
Mich. & Andrew Hanley	£ -	14 "	3 "	19 "
Roger Sweeney & reps. of John Sweeney	-	17 "	3 "	26 "

These dual ownerships are held in common in equal shares.

Dominick Sherlock	-	2 "	2 "	33 "

The rent of this tenant's on this townland is included in his rent of £18/14/ for his holding on the townland of Creggan.

Roger Morahan	£0/10/0.	8 "	2 "	36 "
		1 "	0 "	18 "
Edward Morahan (Wm)	£5/9/2.	11 "	1 "	19 "
Ed. Morahan (senr.)	£5/9/2.	15 "	1 "	39 "
Maria Rochford (widow)	£2/4/8.	5 "	1 "	34 "
Bridget Dowd (widow)	£9/3/3.	8 "	3 "	5 "
Maria Rochford & Bridget Dowd (widows)		13 "	2 "	27 "

This land held in common in the respective shares of three fourths of the holding by Bridget Dowd and the remaining one fourth of the holding by Maria Rochford.

John Byrne (Martin)	£8/19/0.	5 "	8 "	25 "
John Beirne (Pat)	£3/3/0/	13 "	0 "	6 "
John Beirne (Pat) & John Beirne (Martin)	-	13 "	0 "	36 "
Martin Hanly	£12/0/6.	26 "	0 "	16 "
		0 "	2 "	10 "
Michael Morahan	£7/4/0.	15 "	0 "	3 "
Andrew Morrisroe	£6/12/0.	13 "	2 "	7 "
Thomas Hopkins	£13/6/8.	26 "	2 "	30 "
Patrick Cooney	£6/6/4.	6 "	3 "	37 "
James Cooney	£6/6/4.	7 "	0 "	20 "
Patrick Cooney & James Cooney	-	14 "	0 "	3 "

COSTELLO ESTATE

Held in common in equal shares.

Andrew Farrell	£5/8/10.	12 acres	1 rood	0 perches
Mathew Towey	£18/2/0.	32 "	3 "	6 "
Bridget Connor	£8/1/6.	12 "	3 "	18 "
Michael Connor	£14/13/4.	26 "	3 "	1 "
Stephen Coleman	£2/7/8.	6 "	2 "	24 "
John Regan	£27/12/10.	40 "	2 "	29 "
John Casserly	£32/0/0.	53 "	3 "	35 "
Michael Callaghan	£1/14/8.	5 "	0 "	23 "

Second schedule referred to in foregoing Conveyence:-
The right of the public to use the County roads intersecting or bounding the lands.The existing rights of all persons in respect of the waters of any streams or watercourses through or bounding the lands.A right of way on foot only, over the road marked on maps of Cloonlumney. A right of way for the public on foot, and with horses, Carts, cattle,etc., over the roads marked on maps of Islandmore, Largan, Boleysillagh, Cloonmeen, Fallsolus, and Attiantaggart.
(Maps in Land Registry)

Dated this 24 August 1885.
Registry of Deeds,
Dublin. A TRUE COPY.
J. Hanlon (Assistant Registrar of Deeds

Appendix Three

NAMES OF PARISHES COMPOUNDED FOR
UNDER THE TITHE COMPOSITION ACT BY PARLIAMENT

Names of Parishes	Amount Comp. For	No. of Parishes United	No. Comp. For	No. not Comp. For	Observations
Ballyinhaglish	£150	5	2	4	Half of these payable to Incumbent, half to lay Impropriator
Ardagh	£1111/15/4	5	2	4	
Kilcoran	£337	1	2	none	Half to Rector Half to Incumbent
Kilvarnet	£83	1	2	none	" "
Ballisodare	£461/10/9	not United	–	–	" "
Kilbeagh	£134/15/8	2	2	1	" "
Kilmore	£20/8/10	2	2	1	" "
Castlemore	£133/8/2	2	2	1	" "
Achonry	£646/3/-	1	1	–	" "
Ballisaheery	£368/11/8	1	1	None	" "
Kilmactigue Union	£332/11/6	not a –	–		Full tithes payable to Incumbent

NAMES OF PARISHES

Parish	Amount	Col1	Col2	Col3	Notes
Cloonoghill	£30	1	1	Half this parish not under Comp.	A moiety payable to a Layman not under Composition
Ratrea	£30	1	1	–	Half payable to Incumbent one third Impropriator Rector One third to appropriate Rectors
Dromard	£280	Not a Union	–	–	Full tithes payable to Incumbent
Kilcumne	£160	2	2	–	In no case in this diocese had the Comp. agreed upon been dissolved by the Bishop
Kilcolman	–	–	–	–	In progress of Composition

Taken from ths State Paper Office. Outrage Papers 18/17/1831 No. 687.
The Bishop was Frederick Samuel Stock, Bishop of Killala & Achonry.

The returns of Constabulary Stations within a radius of 12 miles of the town of Ballaghaderreen (1830-1834) as follows:-

Stations	Distance from Ballaghaderreen	County	No. of Men at each Stn.	No Available for immediate Duty.
Ballaghaderreen	–	Mayo	10	9
Carracastle	6	"	5	4
Bellaghy	11	Mayo & Sligo	5	2
Mullaghroe	8	" "	4	2
Frenchpark	8	Roscommon	6	4
Loughglynn	6	"	5	3
Clogher	4	Sligo	4	2
				26

S.P.O. Mayo Outrage 21/7003

Appendix Four

POEMS OF P.J. COLEMAN

by P.J. Coleman, editor of Catholic Herald, Toronto, Canada.

CASTLEMORE

Green is the grass in the halls of de Nangle,
  Moss on the smouldering masonry grows;
Violets sprinkle and buttercups spangle,
  Fields where the fortress in majesty rose,
Hushed are the chambers where Chiefs sat in council
  Filled the bright goblets and feasted in state;
Purple topped thistle and gold hearted grounsel
Bloom in the courts and the bowers of the great.

Quenched is the light of MacCostello's glory
  Lulled is the laughter once heard in their halls;
Levelled with earth are the battlements hoary
  Crumbling to dust are the desolate walls..
Never again in the vanguard of the battle
  High can the falcon exultingly soar,
Strangers it's hearth stone usurp, and the cattle
  Browse oe'r the ruins of grey Castlemore.

Proudly and bravely it challenged the Tudor,
  Battled the rage of the ravaging foe,
Flung out defiance to thief and intruder
  Keeping it's watch oe'r the Plains of Mayo.
Malby besieged it and Clifford assaulted
  Thief and robber it baulked of their prey
Dillon took over and Chichester halted,
  They did their best to keep the spoilers at bay.

Due was the day when with rapine and plunder
   Up from Roscommon rode Bingham the Black;
Castlemore shook to his cannon and thunder;
   Fell, a rich spoil, to his furious attack,
Fell, but anon, with the swiftness of leven
   Flashed to it's rescue Tirconnell's Red Hugh,
Blasting it's ramparts in ruin to heaven,
   So Never Saxon might seize it anew.

Little it matters, the blood of our fathers,
   Celtic or Saxon or Norman or Dane,
All to her bosom the kind mother gathers,
   Pours her bright spirit in various ways.
Blesses their souls with her Love's consecration,
   Nurtures them kindly and makes them her own.
Moulding the many at last to one nation
   Sinew of sinew and bone of her bone.

Praise to the race of de Nangle the knightly;
   Praise to the chiefs of MacCostello's blood,
Ever for Erin their Banner shone brightly,
   Ever for freedom and honour they stood.
Changed by the spell of her draoícht and magic
   Pledging their lives to the land they had gained
Won by her beauty, bewitching and warming
   Norman they came, but as Irish remained.

Now lies their home beneath meadow and flower,
   Sunk are the walls that once sheltered the bold,
Hushed is the sound of the Harpers and revel,
   Linnets are singing where the Bards sang of old.
Drop me a tear where the grass in a tangle
   Mantles with verdure the place of their pride,
Breath me a prayer for the Lords of de Nangle,
   True men who lived for this country and died.

POEMS OF P.J. COLEMAN

LOUGH GLYNN

There is a blue lake far away
  Set around with honeyed meads,
Where little breezes laugh and play
  Among the lisping reeds.
The lake: like a turquoise jewel
  Blue as a pigeon's wing,
Where little waves in music break
  And shadowy waters sing.

And in the midst a flowery isle,
  Enchantment's faery home
Where wood blossoms sweetly smile
  And shy wood creatures roam.
A place to sooth a poet's heart
  With balm of leaf and sod,
From tumult of the crowded world
  A place to dream of God.

The iris lifts a purple plume
  In oozy marsh and pool;
The flame-bright marigolds illume
  The Birchen shadows cool
The darting dragon fly
  In brilliant mail of burnished blue
with shivery wings flits by.

The water hen has there her home
  Mid lily-pads and reeds,
The heron wades the creamy foam
  that laps the fragrant meads.
The skylark hangs on flickering wing
  And pours from heaven his lay,
And finch and linnet flute and sing
  For joy the live-long day.

POEMS OF P.J. COLEMAN

The hazel whispers to the moon,
   The birches to the sun;
The flaggers shiver as they croon
   Where vagrant breezes run.
The blossom of the sloe is white
   And pink the wild-rose bloom;
The azure day and purple night
   are filled with mild perfume.

There to the fortress of the wave
   For peace of soul divine
Fled ancient prince and warrior brave
   Of Connacht's kingly line
From royal court and castle rude
   Brehon and bard and chief
Beneath the wood's beatitude
   Found refuge and relief.

All the poems by P.J. Coleman were given to me by the late Bishop of Achonry: Dr. James Fergus. These were part of letters and notes on the History of Achonry sent to the late Dr. Morrisroe who was bishop of Achonry and who corresponded with P.J. Coleman then living in Toronto .

Appendix Five

SERMON GIVEN IN CASTLEREA DURING THE FAMINE

BY THE REV. STONEY

To all those who are above want in this time of Famine - fellow countrymen.

'A grevious calamity is at our doors. God has visited our land with one of His sorest judgements; A wide spread devastating famine. The destroying angel knocks at the poor man's door. The father is paralised with terror, the mother sinking in despair, the children are famishing.

Shall we too give way to despair? Shall we, with folded arms, look on the miseries of the poor? Oh! no – a thousand times no; Avaunt pale demon of despair – come thou celestial hope and animate our hearts. With the Lords's help much may be done; and here is the way. Let everyone who is above want himself do something to supply the wants of others. Let no one wait for others to begin. Let everyone commence for himself – to prevent the markets from rising more than they should. When the report goes abroad that Mr such-a-body is selling at cost price, and Mr so-and-so, at a little lower than cost price, the holders up for famine prices must come down. Just like opening many sluices, the water soon finds its level.

Just see what happened in a market town lately. The demand for food was fearful to behold. The supply was large: then the dealer chuckled with delight: he expected that oatenmeal would go up to 25s a hundred weight – a famine price. But presently it became rumoured that meal was selling to poor people at a food store near hand, at the rate of about 17s a hundred. Multitudes thronged to the food store, bought and reported it about. The result was the market kept steady at 18 or 19s a hundred. And what the cost of this beneficial operation? A mere trifle in money, and a few hours trouble. Twenty pound's worth sold at a small loss, relieved a large number of poor families, kept the market in check, and gave confidence to the despondent. How much better would be the result if several persons thus procured each supply and sold it out at cost price in small quantities?

What is to hinder this good work? Nothing but want of energy to make a beginning. Let everyone do something. Procure ten tons – five tons – three tons – half, or even a quarter of a ton and like Joseph in Egypt, sell it out to your brethren. You will lose nothing if you sell at cost price, or very little; but if you chose to lower it a small sum beneath what it cost you, a little of your money may go but it will leave a blessing after it.

God will help you if you help others. Don't exclaim, there is a lion in the way, there are obstacles or difficulties. Come along then – let everybody do something: shake off dull sloth and manfully face the danger. The poor – oh! let us love the poor. The poor are God's diamonds. He sees the pearls rolling down from the mother's eyes, as her famishing little ones cry for food around her. God help the poor!...The poor man is hungry, weak and weary: his wife and children are hungry. Bring food to him.

Here is a method by which all may be useful who are above want themselves. Open food stores, large or small, in a great many places. No matter how little you can do – do something. Let food shops or stores for selling in small quantities to poor persons be set up by a great many individuals. The effects will be surprising. The neighbouring markets will feel them; they will fall or remain stationary. This is a great benefit to the poor; better than if you were speaking for a week about the famine. A quarter of a ton sold at a reduced price to poor hungry fellow creatures is better than an oration as long as the cable of a man o' war. ...I know a gentleman in a neighbouring county who has set up several food depositaries in different places on his estates where the poor are supplied at cost and at reduced prices, and his pleasure is to visit them and see that all is carries out well...Let me tell you that if you sat down to an empty table in your tapestried hall... maybe the gastric juice in your stomach would be a little turbulent...Let everyone do something. Go on then – Procure a ton – or half – or a quarter of oat or Indian meal. Get an honest scale, with a baker's bucket: sell in small quantities, once, twice, or three times a week. Be sure always to keep within the cost price, never over it. If you cannot get food to purchase today, try tomorrow – if not to be had in one market send to another. Avoid as much as possible doing an evil by raising the price in a market, by making a large purchase, except it be in the evening; your purchase can do little harm. But the mill or the seaport town is the best place to buy....

A word about soup kitchens or porridge for the poor. They are very good; the trouble is only in making a beginning. When the famine in any place becomes very intense – when the poor widow goes forth to gather two sticks to dress the last morsel in her barrel of meal and die! then there is nothing for it but the soup kitchen. ...Porridge for the poor is easily made: some oat or Indian meal, a little salt, a large pot or boiler. Don't wait for Committees to be formed – or for others who you think ought to commence – begin yourself. It is better in several places – in towns, or villages, or country houses, than with large cumbrous slow moving machinery. Let us thus carry on as if it were a guerrilla warfare against hunger – money goes farther in feeding the starving thus than in any other way... There is now a great deal of very inferior food which the poor are forced to buy. Forestallers and traffickers adulterate the food and sell it out at enormous profits; preying on the poor man's misery.

Every time you sell at cost or reduced price you help to defeat this. Begin then, you will find the work will go on better than you anticipated. Do a little – do something – do a great deal. It is not expected that this plan of having thousands of food stores selling throughout the country would cure the fearful evils of the times, but I have no hesitation in saying a great mitigation may be afforded if persons above want will exert themselves thus in a great many places at once to introduce the system recommended above.

And now, God grant success to this address. God bless those who feed the hungry. God bless the poor'.

Fellow countrymen, your faithful servant,
    William Baker Stoney, Rector of Castlerea,
    Co. Mayo, Ireland.

Appendix Six

LAND CONFERENCE

REPORT OF A CONFERENCE
THE MANSION HOUSE, DUBLIN, 1902

Whereas it is expedient that the Land Question in Ireland be settled so far as is practicable, and without delay;

And whereas the existing position of the Land Question is adverse to the improvement of the soil of Ireland, leads to unending controversies and lawsuits between owners and occupiers, retards progress in the country, and constitutes a grave danger to the State;

And whereas such settlement can only be effected upon a basis mutually satisfactory to the owners and occupiers of the land;

And whereas certain representatives of owners and occupiers have been desirous of endeavouring to find such a basis, and for that purpose have met in conference together;

And whereas certain particulars of agreement have been formulated, discussed, and passed at the Conference and it is desirable that the same should be put into writing and submitted to His Majesty's Government.

After consideration and discussion of various schemes submitted to the Conference, we are agreed:-

I. That the only satisfactory settlement to the land question is to be effected by the substitution of an occupying proprietary in lieu of the existing system dual ownership...

III. That it is desirable in the interests of Ireland that the present owners of land should not, as a result of any settlement, be expatriated, or,

IV. That for the purpose of obtaining such a result, an equitable price ought to be paid to the owners, which should be based upon income.

XII. That the amount of the purchase money payable by the tenants should be extended over a series of years...

We wish to place on record our belief that an unexampled opportunity is at the present moment afforded His Majesty's Government of effecting a reconciliation of classes in Ireland upon terms which as we believe, involve no permanent increase of Imperial expenditure in Ireland; and that there would be found on all sides an earnest desire to co-operate with the Government in securing the success of a Land Purchase Bill which, by effectively and rapidly carrying out the principles above indicated, would bring peace and prosperity to the country.

Signed at the Mansion House, Dublin, this 3 January 1903.

Dunraven (Chairman)
John Redmond, Mayo.   William O'Brien.
W. H. Hutcheson Poe.   T.W. Russell.
Nugent T. Everard.   T.C. Harrington.

Abbreviations

A.F.M. Annála Ríoghachta Éireann: Annals of the Kingdom of Ireland by the Four Masters from earliest times to the year 1616, ed. and translated by John O'Donovan (7 vols. Dublin 1851).

Ann. Conn. Annála Connacht: the Annals of Connacht (A.D. 1224-1544). ed. A.M. Freeman (Dublin 1944).

A.L.C. The Annals of Loch Cé: a chronicle of Irish Affairs, 1014-1590, ed, by W.M. Hennessy (2 vols, London 1871).

A,U, Annála Uladh, Annals of Ulster: Chronicle of Irish Affairs, 431- 1131, 1155-1541, ed. W.M Hennessy and Bartholomew McCarthy (4 vols. Dublin, 1887 -1901).

Calender of Pat. Roll Ire. Jas I
    Irish patent rolls of James I (Irish Manuscripts Commission, Dublin 1966).
N.L.I. National Library of Ireland.
P.P.I. Parliamentary Papers Ireland (National Library, Dublin).
S.P.O. State Paper Office (now in Kildare St., Dublin).
P.R.O.I. Public Record Office, (now contained in the National Archives, Bishop St, Dublin).
D.D.A. Dublin Diocesan Archives, Clonliffe College.
U.C.D. University College, Dublin.
T.C.D. Trinity College, Dublin.
R.I.A. Royal Irish Academy.
I.M.C. Irish Manuscript Commission.
H.M.S.O. His Majesty's Stationery Office, London.
O.S.O. Ordnance Survey Office, Phoenix Park, Dublin.
C.D.C. Congested Districts Board.

REFERENCES

REFERENCES CHAPTER 1

1. (a) *Annals of the Kingdom of Ireland* 1206, 1207, 1275. Vol. 7 ed. by John O' Donovan LLD. M.R.I.A.
   (b) *Leabhar na gCeart - Sliabh Lugha* 5, 19, 103, ed. by John O' Donovan.
   (c) Index to *Annals of Ulster* 1880 ed. by B. McCarthy 1901.
2. *Annals Senait* Index to Annals of Ulster 1880 ed. by B.McCarthy M.R.I.A. 1901.
3. MacNeill, Eoin - *Phases of Irish History*.(1968) second ed.
4. *Leabhar na gCeart Book of Rights* ed. by O'Donovan and published by the Celtic Society 1847 (Document on distribution and political relations of the State of Ireland in the early historical period).
5. *Tripartite Life of St. Patrick*, ed. by Whitley Stokes, D.C.L.,LLD, Part 1 1887. Printed by H.M.Stationery Office London.
6. *Leabhar na gCeart* (The Old Book of Rights and Privileges) ed. by John O'Donovan 1847.
7. *Annals of the Kingdom of Ireland*, A.D. 965
8. *Annals of Lough Cé*
9. Robin Dudley Edwards, *Anglo Norman Relations with Connaught*.
10. (a) *Annals of Connaught* 1235. A.D.
    (b) Orpen, Goddard, Henry - *Ireland Under the Normans 1216- 1233 (Vol II.)*
11. *Annals of Connaught*, 19 1235 A.D. p.57.
12. Ware, James, *Antiquities of Ireland Vol II* from MS. written at the beginning of the reign of Edward I and preserved in T.C.D.
13. Orpen, Goddard Henry, - *Ireland Under the Normans 1216-1233 Vol. III*
14. *Annals of Connaught*, 5. 1262 p139.
15. Ibid.
16. Orpen, Goddard Henry, - *Ireland under the Normans 1233-33*
17. *Annals of Connaught*, 1285 p11.
18. *Annals of Connaught*, 1330 p269 ed. A. Martin Freeman.
19. *Annals of Connaught* 1333 A.D. P277.
20. *Annals of Connaught* 1340 A.D. p285.
21. *Annals of Connaught* 1336. A.D. P299.
22. *Annals of Connaught* 1346. A.D. p299
23. *Annals of Connaught* 1366. A.D. p329
24. *Annals of Connaught* 1416. A.D. P427.
25. *Annals of Connaught* 1461, A.D. P501.
26. *Annals of Connaught*, 1468, A.D. p545,
27. Ibid.
28. *Annals of Connaught*, 1536. A.D.p691.
29. *Composicion Booke of Connaught*, Transcribed by A. Martin Freeman.
    Index to *Composicion Booke of Connaught*,- Hayes McCoy,G.A.
30. *Patent Roll of James 1* p56 XC11 - 50.
31. Registry of Deeds, Henrietta St. Folio No. 2099. *A memorial of a Deed of Conveyance of George A. Costello*, 20 August 1885.
32. Patent Roll 19 James 1 P532-1V-14.

REFERENCES CHAPTER 2

1. Bagwell, Richard ,*Ireland Under the Tudors*.
   Corish, Patrick J. T*he Catholic Community in Seventeenth and Eighteenth Centuries*. (Helicon

REFERENCES

History of Ireland1981)
2. Butler, W.F.T., *Confiscation in Irish History*.(C.S.P.I., 1631 p606 - Sir J. Jephson to Lord Dorchester.
3. O'Conors in Connaught from a Ms. of John O'Donovan for Rt. Hon. Charles Owen O'Conor Don1891.
4. Patent Roll 14 1617 James 1 XXU - 47.
5. Patent Roll 14 James 1 LVIII - 25 P321.
6. (a) *Burke's Landed Gentry*
   (b) O'Callaghan, J. Cornelius - *History of Irish Brigades in the Service of France* (1870)
   (c) Hayes,Richard - *Biographical Dictionary of Irishmen in France* (1949)
7. O'Callaghan, J. Cornelius - *History of Irish Brigades in the Service of France* (1870)
8. Simms, J.G. - *Williamite Confiscation in Ireland 1690-1703* (Studies in Irish History 1966 Vol.7)
9. Ibid.
10. D'Alton, John B.L.- M R.I.A. - Compiled from Ms. Genealogical Collection, *Pedigree of the family of French of Frenchpark*. (Printed by William Holde 1847)
11. Douglas Hyde LLD- M.R.I.A. *Love Songs of Connaught* 'An Craoibhinn Aoibhinn' being the 4th Chapter of the Love Songs of Connaught. (Introduction by Michael O'hAodha)
12. O'Callaghan, J. Cornelius - *History of Irish Brigades in the Service of France.* (1870)
14. D'Alton, John B.L. M.R.I.A. *Memoir of the family of French of Frenchpark.* (printed by William Holde , Dublin 1847). D'Alton mentions the castle at Tallaughan Rock as one of the Costello Castles.
15. Hyde, Dr. Douglas, LLD. M.R.I.A. ; An Craoibhin Aoibhinn' being the fourth chapter of the '*Love Songs of Connacht*' P59-61. (Introduction by Michael O' hAodha, Irish University Press,Shannon , Ireland)
16. O'Muraile, Nollaig - *Mayo Places, their names and origins*, F N T Mayo News Westport 1985.
17. Taken orally from Mrs. M Hussey, Nazareth Home Wrexham, North Wales. 1986.
18. *Composicion Booke of Connaught,* Transcribed by Martin A. Freeman.
19. Ibid.
20. O'Conor Archives, Clonalis , Castlerea ,County Roscommon.
21. *O'Conors of Connacht* from the MS. By John O Donovan for the Right Honorable Charles Owen O'Conor Don 1891.
22. O'Sullivan, Donal, *Carolan*, (Routledge and Keegan Paul Limited, London)

REFERENCES CHAPTER 3

1. Wall, Maureen, *Penal Laws, 1691-1760* - (Irish History series No. 1 Dublin Historical Association 1967).
2. Burke, William P.- *Irish Priests in Penal Times 1660- 1670.*
3. McDowell R. B. - *Irish Public Opinion 1750-1800*
4. Powicke, Sir F. and Fryde E.B. in *Handbook of British Chronology* (2nd. ed. 1961 (Royal Historical Society)
5. Taken from list of Bishops enshrined on wall of Protestant Cathedral of Achonry 1976.
6. McDowell R.B. - *Irish Public Opinion 1750 -1800.*
7. Young, Arthur - *Tour of Ireland 1775.*
8. National Library, Dublin. Ms. 52.
9. McDowell, R.B. - *Irish Political Opinion 1750 -1800*
10. O'Conors of Connaught from Ms. by John O Donovan for Rt. Hon. Charles O'Conor Don 1891.
11. S.P.O. - Westmoreland Correspondence No. 55, 1792
12. O'Conors of Connaught from Ms. by John O Donovan for Rt.Hon. Charles Owen O'Conor Don.
13. S.P.O. Westmoreland Correspondence No. 88. (Committee Report of Secret)
14. S.P.O. Westmoreland Correspondence 622/25/81.

REFERENCES

15 S.P.O. Rebellion Papers 1796-1808 620/25/33.
16 S.P.O. Rebellion Papers 620/24/81
17 S.P.O. Rebellion Papers 620/30/225.
18 S.P.O. Rebellion Papers.620/ 33/ 109.
19 Hayes, McCoy - *The Last Invasion of Ireland when Connaught rose, 1939.*
20 Ibid.

REFERENCES CHAPTER 4.

1 McParlan - *Statistical Survey of 1801* by kind permission of Mayo Co. Library
2 Weld, Isaac - *Survey of Co. Roscommon and Co. Mayo.*
3 Parliamentary Gazzatteer 1834.
4 *The Tripartite Life of St. Patrick* ed by Whitley Stokes 5D.C.L.,LLD.,1887 (Published by Her Majesty's Stationery Office London)
5 P.P. Supplement to First Report of Commissioners on the Poor in Connaught, Barony of Costello 1835.
6 Lewis Samuel - *Topographical Dictionary of Ireland 1837.*
7 Knox, Hubert T. *Notes on Achonry, Tuam and Killala.*

REFERENCES CHAPTER 5

1 Maxwell - *Irish Land Law and Land Purchase 1909* p. 125-126 Published by John Falconer, 53 Upper Sackville St, Dublin. 1909.
2 S.P.O. State of Country Papers 1019/9.
3 S.P.O. State of Country Papers 1031/50.
4 Brocker, Galen, - *Rural Disorder and Police Reform in Ireland 1812-36* p28.
5 S.P.O. State of Country Papers 1120/50-1
6 S.P.O. State of Country Papers 1120/61 - 4
7 S.P.O. State of Country Papers 1192/7.
8 Brocker, Galen - *Rural Disorder and Police Reform in Ireland* 1812-36. p45.
9 S.P.O. State of Country Papers 1338/15.
10 S.P.O. State of Country Papers 1338/20.
11 Rebellion Papers 1796-1838 620/11/130/43.
12 S.P.O. State of Country Papers 1338/20.
13 S.P.O. State of Country Papers 1408/24/.
14 S.P.O. State of Country Papers 1408/37/40 - 10.
15 Clonalis Papers Vol 111 - 4.
16 S.P.O. State of Country Papers 2073/3.
17 Strickland,Walter George - From Ms. Volume of Biographical notes.
18 S.P.O. State of Country Papers 2072/7.
19 S.P.O. State of Country Papers 2074/23.
20 S.P.O. State of Country Papers 1820 2175/9.
21 S.P.O. State of Country Papers 2175/20.
22 S.P.O. State of Country Papers 2176/ 14.
23 Brocker, Galen - *Rural Disorder and Police Reform in Ireland 1812-36* (1970)
24 S.P.O.Outrage Papers 1817/18311 No.677.
25 P.R.O. Parliamentary Papers 1831-1832, 177/355.

REFERENCES CHAPTER 6

1 O'Ferrall, Fergus - *Daniel O'Connell.*
2 P.R.O. Outrage Papers and State of the Country Papers 1799-1852.

REFERENCES

3 Dublin Diocesan Archives, Cullen Papers (Letters to Dr. Cullen)
4 P.R.O. Census of Ireland 1841.
5 P.R.O. Relief Commission Papers.
6 Quaker Relief Applications March 1847.
7 P.R.O. Abstract Report of Outrage 1843 Costello Co. Mayo. 21/5475 (An Unusual Happening).
8 Outrage Papers Mayo 1843 21/75 - 21/25637.
9 S.P.O. Outrage Papers Mayo 1843 21/17001.
10 S.P.O. Outrage Papers Mayo 1843 21/1901.
11   Ibid.
12 S.P.O. Outrage Papers 1844 21/6875.
13 Healy, John - *Death of an Irish Town.*
14 Strickland, Walter George - *Life Study of Strickland Family* 1928. (Published Malta).
15 S.P.O. Distress Papers 1846/D/900.
16 S.P.O. Distress Papers 1846/D/1331.
17 S.P.O. Distress Papers 1846/D/1367.
18 S.P.O. Mayo Distress 1847 15th February 11155.
19 S.P.O. Distress Mayo 1847 11785.
20 S.P.O. Distress ,Mayo 1847 6686.
21 P.R.O. Relief Barony of Costello, Co. Mayo RLF 3634.
22   Ibid. 5823.
23 P.R.O. Relief Commission Papers 1846 Barony of Costello Co. Mayo.
24 P.R.O. Dublin Society of Friends. Relief of Distress Vol. 72/1A/ 42/20.
25 S.P.O. Outrage Mayo Papers 1848.

REFERENCES CHAPTER 7
1 Akensen, Donal H. - *The Irish Educational experience 1970*
2 Corcoran,T., *Selected Texts on Education Systems in Ireland 1928.* and 'The Kildare Place Schools - their defined purposes. Irish monthly 1932.
3 P.P. Commissioners of Education Enquiry 1835.
4 Archivium Hibernicum 1731 p177. Report on the State of Property.
5 Powis Commission Report, National Library Dublin.
6 Lyons, F.S. - *Ireland since the Famine* P83.
7 S.P.O. 590. 1810-1831.
8 P.P. Second Report of Commissioners of Irish Education Enquiry. Vol. 12 1826-1827.
9 Daly, Mary - *Development of National School System.* 1931-1940. (Studies in Irish History 1979).
10 Irish Catholic Directory 1838.
11 P.P. Education in Ireland 1835.
12 P.P. Second Report of Commissioners of Irish Education Inquiry. 1826.
13 P.P. Education in Ireland 1836, 1837, 1839, 1843, 1844.
14 P.P. Commissioners of Education 14th Report 1846, 1847.
15 Dudley Edwards, Ruth - *An Atlas of Irish History 1973.*
16 P.R.O.Census of Ireland 1851.
17 P.P. Report by Commissioners of National Education in Ireland Vol.28 Part 5. 1870.
18 Irish Builder Vol. XV111 No.405 1st November 1876.
19 Archives of Sisters of Charity, Milltown, Dublin.1979.
20 Gildea, Denis Father - *Life of Mother Arsenius.*
21 P.P. Report of Congested Districts Board Vol. 1-8 1892-98.
22 De La Salle Christian Brothers' Records, Ballaghaderreen 1979.
23 O'Brien, R. Barry - *Fifty years of Concessions to Ireland 1821-1881.*

REFERENCES

24 Report on Endowed Schools Commission 1854-1855 and 1880.
25 Sligo Champion 1884.
26 O'Sullivan, Donal - *Life and Times of Turlough O'Carolan*, Vol.1 and 11.
27 McCartha, Fionan - *Amhráin ó Dheireadh an Domhain 1953*, Oifig an tSolathair, Baile Atha Cliath.

REFERENCES CHAPTER 10
1 Lyons, F.S. - *Ireland Since the Famine*.
2 Lyons F.S. - *John Dillon (A biography)*
3 O'Brien, William - *An Olive Branch in Ireland and it's History*.
4 Ibid.
5 Hicks, William L. - *An Account of the Constitution Administration and Dissolution of the Congested Districts Boards for Ireland 1891-1923*.
6 See Appendix for Official Report on the Land Conference.
7 Sheehan, Captain D.D. - *Ireland Since Parnell*
8 *Book of Survey & Distribution Co. Mayo* by R.C. Simington 1949.
9 *Composicion Booke of Connaught* - Transcribed by A. Martin Freeman.
10 *Book of Survey & Distribution Co. Mayo* by R.C. Simmington 1949.
11 *Composicion Booke of Connaught* - Transcribed by A. Martin Freeman.

REFERENCES CHAPTER 11.
1. N.L.I. Parliamentary Gazzatteer of Ireland 1846.
2. Isaac Weld, *Statistical Survey of Roscommon and Mayo* p578-603, (for R.D.S., printed by R. Graisberry).
3. I.M.C. *The Composicion Booke of Connacht*, (ed. A.M. Freeman Dublin 1936).
4. Parliamentary Gazzatteer of Ireland 1846.
5. Hicks, William, :*An Account of the Constitution , Administration & Dissolution of the Congested Districts Districts Boards for Ireland (1891-1903)*.
P.P. Report of Congested Districts Boards Vol. 1-8 1892-1898. (see end of Chapter on lease-holders on Dillon Estate 1805).
6. Taken orally from the Franciscan Missionaries of Mary , Loughglynn Convent 1980.
7. Knox, Hubert : *History of Mayo*, see chapter on Barony of Costello (p313-320) (Dublin Hodges Figgis 1904)
8. Registry of Deeds, Henrietta St, Dublin. Memorial 2099.
9. (i) Irish Land Commission Record of Advances under Land Law Ireland Act 1881 (July 1927) Now in the National Archives, Bishop St. Dublin. (ii)See the Statutes relating to the Law of Landlord and tenant in Ireland Part 1 pxi, containing Statutes from 1860 to 1880 (in order to see the changes from 1880 to 1927) by Francis Nolan & Robert Romney Kane. Dublin, E.Ponsonby, 116 Grafton St, Dublin, 1892. (iii) Irish Land Law and Land Purchase, Maxwell (see Chapt. on Land Purchase).
10. Irish Land Purchase Cases, 1904-1911compiled by T.Henry Maxwell, MA, LLD, at the request of the Land Commission to make advances under Ireland Land Act 1903, (3 Edw ., VII.,c 37, ss, 79,80, to tenants for the purchase of their holdings, provided such tenants are in occupation).
11. Hicks, William, *An Account of the Constitution, Administration*, Admin. & Dissolution of the C.D.B. p. 23. (noted in the Dr. Gilbert Library, Pearse St. Dublin, Pub. Eason & Son Ltd, 1925, 1891 - 1923)
12. Deeds of Four Altars in Diocesan Archives, St. Nathys, Edmondstown, Ballaghaderreen.
13. Roscommon Herald, Boyle, October 1967. Letter to Dr. McCormack Bishop Of Achonry.

INDEX

A Lament for Edward Duffy 118
Abbey of Urlare 159
Abstract of Parochial Returns 89
Achonry 9,50,52,54,88,90,92,98, et passim
Achadh Lóiste 86
Adams, C.J. 78
Adh Lethan (Ballylahan) 3,14
Ahascragh 20
Aghamore Aughmore (Achadh Mor) 9,12 et passim
Airteach 9,12,,16
Aileach Estrachta 12
Alderford 106
Allen, Larkin & O'Brien 115
Altamont, Lord 61
Amhrain Ghradha 34
Amhrain Dheiridh Domhain 108
Angulo, Baron De 14
Annagh 9,50,54
Armstrong, Sgt. Walter 133,134,135
Arsenius, Mother 95,96,98,100
Artuagh 30
Ashbourne Act 142
Association for the discountenancing of Vice Day schools 9
Assylin 22
Áth Cinn Deicet 14
Athlone 28,29,44
Attentaggart
Aughaherin 120
Aughalustia (Ara Coemhain) 54,90,108
Aughrim 27,29

Baildrin Mac Costello 15,16
Balla 15
Balfour, Arthur 144
Ballygar 145
Baslick 12
Ballyglass 73
Ballymote 78, 84,125,130,134
Ballaghaderreen (Bealach a' Doirin) 12,16 et passim
Ballina 46,49,50,51,52,53
Ballinlough 16,64
Ballinamuck 43,62
Ballynavness,46
Ballykileen 16
Ballyloughadalla 18
Ballyhaunis 9,12,16,21,29,42, et passim
Ballyshannon 26
Ballycastle 10
Barony of Frenchpark 156
Barony of Costello 29,30,31 et passim
Baron de Ginkle 29

Barroe 35,74
Barnalyra 30
Barrets of Tirawley 16
Baxter, John 25
Bellanagare 35
Beechmount House 102
Beirne, Patrick 131
Belgrade 28
Belan (Baeon)
Bekan (Becan) 45,51
Banada 14,65
Benada Abbey 35,36
Benson, James 120
Bermingham, Francis 34
Black and Tans 99
Blunt, Scawen William 138,139,140
Book of Lecan 54
Boyle Brenainn (Berchan) 48,49,50 et passim
Burrishrule (Burrsihrool) 50
Brannick 61
Brennan, Fr. William 105
Brennan, T 129
Browne, Bishop of Elphin 105
Browne, Denis 61,65,66
Br. Andrew Dowling 102
Br. Balwin Fitzpatrick 102
Br. Cassian 103
Br. Dominic O'Callaghan 102
Br. Eliseus Mac Nicholas 102
Br. Finbar Barry 102
Br. Francis Griffin 102
Br. Irilde 102
Br. Nathy 103
Br. Robert Egan 108
Brett, Constable 115
Broder, James 132,133,134,136,137,138
Brophy, Hugh Francis 113,114,115
Brusna 90,91,82,96
Bundrowse 26
Bunnyconlon 10
Bunnadden16
Burkes 15,18
Burke, Briget 27
Burke, T.H. 142
Butler, James 27
Brooklawn House 35,72,78
Byrne, Edward 115
Byrne, Paudeen 63

Calraige 10
Caislen Mór Mac Goisdealbh 15
Cairbre (Carbury) 11
Caislen Sliabh Lugha 15

INDEX

Callaghan, Michael (Mathew) 63
Campbell, Rev. Thos. 37
Campbell, Major Gen. Guy 74
Captain Moonlight 141,143
Captain Right 143
Carra 49,50
Carracastle 34
Carrack on Shannon 30
Cardinal Noailles 102
'Carding' 60
Carney, Owen 120,122,123
Carrigarriff 74
Casey, Canon 90
Casey, John 120
Castlebar 43,63,114,120, 124,125,139
Castle Gallagh 151
Castlemore 9,14,15,19,20,25,29 et passim
Castlerea 1,2, 9,12,78,79,80,83, 102, 122, *et passim*
Castletown 102
Castle Island (Trinity) 32,34
Cathal Crobhderg 13
Catholic Association 40
Catholic Committee 40,41
Cella Adrochtae 54
Celle Columbani 53
'Centre' 112,121
Charlestown 98,100,103,127
Charter Schools 88
Chatham, Lord 85
Chester Castle 115
Children of Mary 96,100
Ciarraighe Airdi 19,10,11,55,56
Cill Atracht 54
Cill Aodain 107
Cill Cholmáin 12
Clancy, Dr.153
Clann Costello 16,18,19,20
Clann Mhaol Runaidh 11
Clanmorris 48,90,125
Clann Philip 18
Clanricard Lord 143
Clare 45
Clare Island 145
Classical School 109
Clochan Athracht 109
Clogher 122,133,134,137,138
Clogher House 83
Cloonacool 126
Cloonacunny 79,54
Clooncrim 16
Cloonmore 45,49,59
Cluain Carthaig (Clooncartha) 17

Cody, John 116
Colman 53
Colman Finn 53
Colman Joe 148
Colonel Gore Ousley Higgins 93
Coneely, Michael 123
Congested Districts Board 152,153,157
Conlon, Charles 120
Conmaicne Cuile Talad 10
Conn Cetchathact 10
Connington, Fr.E. 126
Coolavin 11,14,17,21,22,37,41, et passim
Cootehall 32
Corcoran, Joseph 132,135,136,137,138
Corran 11,19
Corrib 51
Corydon 115, 116
Costello, A. G. 154,155,156
Costello, Captain 119
Costello, Charles 49,61,63,64,
Costello, Dorcas Maria 156
Costello, Dudley 30,105,148
Costello. Edmond 34
Costello Estate 154,155
Costello, Gallen 26,149
Costello, James 130
Costello, Jordan Boy 34
Costello, Mrs. 106
Costello, Thomas 31,32
Costello, William 34
Coughlan, Fr. 72,73,82
Craggaduff 52
Creagh 155
Creggane na gCrann 154,156,158,159
Crenane 57
Crennane 54
Cromwell 27,30,32
Crossfield, Joseph 73
Cruise, Andrew 120
Crocmolin a Cnoc Droma Calrai 10
Crow Island 53
Cuilmore 130
Curlieu 32
Cuppanagh Bridge 23
Curry 126,127
Curry, Dr. 40

D'Alton 68
Daly, Fr. 157
Daly, James 125,127,132
Daly, Dr 105
D'Arcy, Patrick 120
Davis, Thomas 109,111

203

INDEX

Davitt, Michael 125,126,127,131, 132, *et passim*
Davis, John 42
Deane, Mrs 93,97,98,138,139
Defenders 41
Devoy, John 125
De Angulo 14,15,80
De Burg 14
De Freyne, Lord 119,130
De Lacy 14
De la Salle 101,102,108
Derrymore 19,22,23
D'Exeter 14
Dillon 49
Dillon, Richard Lord Dillon 152
Dillon Viscount 41,51,89,90,93,95,144, 151,152,154
Dillon, Arthur 29
Dillon, Charles 27,37
Dillon, Edward 42
Dillon Estate 139
Dillon, Henry 29
Dillon, Jane 26
Dillon, John 49,60,125,127,128,138, 139
Dillon, John Blake 60,109,112
Dillon, Lord 27,50,52,60,64,68
Dillon, Luke 26,27,49,61,149
Dillon, Sir Christopher 26, 27
Dillon, Theobald, Viscount 25,26,27,30,149
Dillon, Thomas 27,149
Dillon, Tobias 31
Diocesan Classical School 103
Dominican Friars 159
Dominican Monastery 16
Donmasreery 45
Donnelly 133,134,137,138
Downes, Henry 42
Doyle, Bishop J 67
Drumad 12
Dublin Castle 40,42,60,61,62,63,et passim
Duff, Monica 85
Duffy, Edward 112,113,114,115,116,117, 118,119,121
Duffy, Charles Gavin 109
Duffy, Gavin 111
Duffy, John 120
Duffy, Joseph 120
Duffy, Patrick 75,76
Duggan, Dr. 126,138,140
Duke of Leinster 88
Dungar 56
Dunkirk 29
Dunmore 10
Durkan, Bishop Patrick 92,105
Durcan, (Durkin) Fr. Patrick 35
Durcan, Dr. Patrick 70,121
Dutch soldiers 63

Earl of Clonricard 27
Earl of Ormond 27
Earl of Antrim 27
Eamon an Mhachaire 16,17
East India Company 64
Edgeworth Mr. 78
Edgeworth Maria 78
Edmondstown 34,45,46,48,50,54
Edmondstown Estate 138
Edmondstown Park House. 105
Elec (daughter of Fergal O'Huiginn) 17
Elphin 90,105
Encumbered Estates Act 35
Established Church 59,65,68
Eugene of Savoy 35

Fay 121
Fenians 139
Fenian Movement 109,111,112, et passim
Ferdach(Feradach) 12
Fergal O'Taidg an Teglaig 13
Fergus, Dr. James 101,103
Fitzgerald 149
Flannery, Brian 132,133,135,136,137,138
Flannery, Owen 74
Flannery, Sarah 102
Flannery, Thomas 76
Flynn, Dr. 158
Flynn, BishopThomas 103
Fogarty 119,120
Forbes 157,158
Foxford 74,75,79,95,97,100,145
Franciscan Missionaries of Mary 151,153
French, Arthur 41,49,65
French, Dominic 56
Frenchpark Estate 149
French, George 62
Frenchpark 43,49,51,56,100,106,151,156
Friar's Hill 93
Furlong,Canon 105

Gailenga 9
Gallagher, D 105
Gallagher, Dan 74
Gallagher, Pat 76
Gallagher, John 83
Gallen 9,14,16,45

INDEX

Gallen Costello 50
Garnusch-Partenirchen (Garmisch) 10
Gilbert MacGoisdelbh 15,16
Gladstone 139,141,146
Glencalry 10
Goodsall, Lieutenant 63
Gorden 57
Goulbourn Act 59
Gregory, William 64
Gregraige 10,11
Gregory Clause 84
Grehan, Mrs 95,99
Grady, 120
Groarke, Fr. 72
Grogan, James 128,129
Gregory, Lady 147
Guisdhen-Shannon 51
Gunnis, Sergeant Thomas 133 134
Gurteen 89,98,100,125,126,127,131,132,136

Hanley, Thomas 74
Hanlon, Richard 62
Harbison, William 115
Hardiman, James 107
Harrington, Tim 143,148
Harris, Matt 125,128,129,132
Hart, Dr. John 106
Healy Dr. (Archbishop) 106
Healy, Tim 144,146
Hedge Schools 87,92
Hercait 12
Higgins 13
Higgins, Colonel 93
Higgins, Pat 148,158
Hollymount 43
Holmes, Elizabeth 84
Holmes, J.A. 76,82,83,84
Holmes, R. 52
Holywell 42
Home Rule 131,138,139 142-149
Hopper, George 113
Hughes, James 60
Humbert, General 43,60
Hyde, Dr. Douglas 107,108
Hyland, James 120

Iarnascus 13
Inch Island 21,23
Industrial Schools 96,100
Innsbruck 10
Insurrection Act 60,62
Irishtown 125
Irish Folklore Commission 32

Irish Lasallians 107
Irish National Land League 132,140
'Irish People' 113,120
Irish Poor Law 69
Irish Republican Brotherhood 111

James I 25
James II 27,101
Joceyln (Gocelin) 15
Jones, Daniel 35
Jordan Boy 18
Jordans 16,20

Kearney, Fr. 157
Kelly, Colonel 114
Kelly, Inspector J.J. 74
Kelly, Thomas 114,120
Kelly, John 74
Kelly, T 128
Kenmare, Lord 40
Keogh, Walter 35
Kilbeagh 9,22,51,78
Kilcolman 9,12,17,31, et passim
Kilfree 122,123
Kilkelly 9,12,46,159
Kilmaine 10
Killala 38,42,75
Killaraght Church 22
Killaser 103
Killeen 125,127,132
Killenfeagh 26
Kilmactighe 127
Kilmainham Treaty 141
Kilmovee 9,12,16,17,51 et passim
Kilronan 138
Kiltimagh 126,136
Kilturragh 9,51
King Charles 31
King John 14
King's Five Cantreds 14
Kingston, Lord 138
Knock 9,10,29,34,51,73,78
Knox, Hubert,T. 53,154
Knox, G. 84,85

Lake, General 43
Lambe, Peter 123
Land Conference 148
Land Commission 141,144,154,155,157
Land League Courts 131
Land Act 1881 141,142,155
Land War 125,131,143,147,149,154
Latin School 112

205

INDEX

Lavin, Patrick 131
Lawless, Emily 57
Leon 9
L'Estrange 20
Lewis, Samuel 52
Leyden 9
Leyney 9,16, 43
Liosargool 56
Lios Aedhain 55,56
Lessine (Lissian) 54
Liseane,(Lissian) 56,149
List of suscribers from Ballaghaderren 79,83
Loftus,Canon 104
Loch Cé 13,18,22
Loch Conn 42
Loch Gara (Loch Techet) 10,11,14,15,21, 22,23,53
Loch Gill 10
Loch Mannin 9
Loch Mask 10
Loch na nAirne 9,11
(Leitir Sliabh Lugha) 22
Loftus, Canon 104
Lougheed, William 158
Loughglynn 9,12,16,41,42,65,67,128,151,152,153
Luby, Thomas Clarke 112,113
Lucas, Lord 74
Lugh Lamhfhada 9
Luighne (Leyney) 9,16
Lyons 9
Lyster, Dr. (Bishop) 97,98,101,102,105,106,157

MacCostello 15,17,16,18,19,21,33
MacCostello, Baildrín 15,16,
MacCostello, Daibhidh 17
MacCostello, Gilbert 16
MacCostello, Giolla Dubh 19
MacCostello, Imag 15
MacCostello, Jordan Boy 18
MacCostello, Meiler Ruadh 20
MacCostello, Miles16
MacCostello, Sean Fionn 16
MacCostello, Sean Dubh 17,19
MacCostello, Siurtan 15
MacCostello, Walter Boy 16
MacCostello, William Caoch 17,19
MacCosdealbha, Dubhaltach 28
MacDermot 11,15,16,18,22,29
MacDermot,Canon 90
MacDermot, Cathal 13,15
MacDermot, C.J. 52
MacDermot, Gall, Magnus 16

MacDermot, Roe 18,106
MacDermot, Rúaidhrí 22,32
MacDermot, Sadbh Óg 22
MacDermot, Terence 63
Mac Dermot Úna 32
MacDiarmada, Cathal 11
MacDiarmada, Gall 17
MacDonagh 19, 20
MacDonnell, Alex Boy 34
MacDonnell, Anthony 34,147,148
MacDonnell, Cahir Mac Turlough 34
MacDonnell, James 34,35
MacDonnell, Coll 74
MacDonnell, Edward 80
MacDonnell, Joseph Mór 35,75
MacDonnell, Lady Mary 27
MacDonnell, Miles 35,49,50,60,73
MacDonnell, Mark Anthony 34,83
MacFeóirais (Birmingham) 15,17
Mac Finghin, Eoghan 15
MacGoisdelbh 15,16
MacJordan of Gallen 16
MacJordan 16
MacLoughlin Island 23
MacNicholas, Bishop 35
MacParlan, James 45
MacPhillips 35
MacPhilip Giolla Dubh 18,22
MacPiarais 19
MacWilliam, Walter 15
MacSweeney 17,22
Mc. Cormack Dr. 125,127,138
McDonagh 21,63
McGovern, James 74
McHale, Archbishop 70
McKeown 105
Mágh Aoí 9
Mahony, D. 114
Malby, Sr. Nicholas 22, 23
Mannin Castle 18
Manchester Martyers 115
Martin, T&C. 123
Marquis of Sligo 45
Matthew, Fr. 70
Maughan (O'Mochain) Cornelius 54
Maynooth 90,100,103,105
Mayo 27,45,49,50,52, et passim
Mayo Book of Survey 35
Midland & Great Western Railway 118
Milo de Angulo 14
Millbank 117
Mitchell, John 111
Monasteraden 132,133,134,135,137

INDEX

Moore, Francis 156
Mount Druid 83
Moy 51
Moygara 22,25,122
Moylurg 15,18
Muinchin Uachtair 18
Murrisk 50

Nathi 12
National Schools 32
National Board 51,57
Nealon, Ted 106
Newport 62
Newtownforbes 93
Neyll, General (Owen Roe O'Neill) 26
Nolan, J 60
Nugent, General 43
Nulty, Dr. 105

O'Brien, James F.X. 120
O'Brien, William 143,144,146,147,148
O'Cillín 16
O'Cleirigh, Br. Michael 25
O'Clery's Book of Pedigrees 151
O'Connell, Daniel 63,67,69,70,75
O'Conor 11,14,17
O'Conor, Aed 13,14,15
O'Conor, Charles 35,38,40
O'Conor, Denis 40
O'Conor Don 26,35,63,147,149
O'Conor, Kings in Connaught 14,15,145
O'Conor, Magnus 15
O'Conor, Owen 40,41
O'Conor, Rev. Thos 38
O'Conor Sligo 17,22,25
O'Conor, Turlough 14
O'Daly, Bishop Dominic 38
O'Donnell 122
O'Donnell, Con 22
O'Donnell, John 105
O'Donnell. Red Hugh 20
O'Donovan Rossa, Jeremiah 112,113,115, 117,119,120
O'Flynn 16,22
O'Gara, Cian 22,29
O'Gara, Charles Óg 29
O'Gara, Captain John 26
O'Gara, Cam 21
O'Gara, Colonel Oliver 29
O'Gara, Bernard 29
O'Gara, Donnshléibhe 13
O'Gara, Eoghan 22
O'Gara, Oilillín 22

O'Gara, (ÓGadhra) 25
O'Gara, Fergal (Ferrall) 13,17,25,26
O'Gara, Ruaidhri 13,15
O'Gara, Tomaltach Óg 17,21
O'Gara, Uriell 25
O'Grady, Henry 18
O'hEaghra 10
O'Hara 10,16
O'Hara, Brian 13
O'Hara Boy 17,22
O'Hara, Cormac 16
O'Hara, Colonel M.P. 43
O'Hara, Fr. Denis 105,125,126,127,135,155, 156,157
O'Huiginn, Ruaidhri 18,55,56
O'Kelly 20,
O'Leary, John 112,113,115,120
O'Láimhín, Dónal 18
O'Mahony, John 111,112,115
O'Malley 49
O'Maoilchonaire, 56
O'Mochain, Cathal 18
O'Rourke, Fr. Tadhg 35
O'Rourke of Breffní 35
Old English 26
Old Irish 25
Old Military Barracks 105
Orange Club 59
Orangemen 112
Owen Garrow 51
Ox Mountains 15,126

Palmfield 34,36,85
Paris 111,114,120
Parnell, Charles Stewart 121-25,139,141-145
Pay Schools 87.90
Peelers 67
Peels Amendment Bill 67
Penal Laws 87,89
Perrot, Sir John 20
Petty sessions 74,84
Plan of Campaign 143,144
Phillips, Thomas 35,62
Pioneer Abstinence 98
Poor Law Union 152
Pope Leo 143
Portumna 143
Presbyterian School 92
Prince Of Coolavin 106
Purchase of Land Act Ireland 152

Quakers 73,82
Rapparee 30,32

207

INDEX

Rathoath 34
Record of Advances 154
Reddy, Fr. 138
Redmond, John 147,148
Repeal Association 119,111
R.I.C 36
Ribbonmen 59,61,63,64,65,66,67, 122
Right Boys 143
Roscommon 49,50,56,154,156,158

Sanford, Joseph 68
Sayer, Alex 82
Seymour, C. 60,61,62
'Shambles' 112
Sharkey, Thomas 133
Shroove 132
Siggins, J. 75
Síol Maelrúin 16
Síol Muirdeadaigh 11
Sisters of Charity 93,95,96,97,99,100,145,146
Sliabh Lugha 9,10,11,12, et passim
Sliabh Muire St. Patrick 20
Sligo 45,49,50,52, et passim
Sligo Petty Sessions 132,136
Smith O' Brien 111
Society of Friends 80,82,84
Solan, Thomas 62,63
Spelman Fr. 89,90,92
Sr. Mary Oswald 95,99
Sr. Mary Martin 99,100
Stanley, Edward 88
Statistical Survey of Co. Mayo 45
Steelboys 143
Stephens, James 112,113,115
Stoney, Rev. William 80
Strickland, Charles 35,73,75-79,80,82,84,114
Strickland, Jarrard Edward 64,65,67,76
Strokestown 85
Strong, J.P. 114
St. Attracta 54
St. Colman 53
St. Francis Xavier 99
St. John's Monastery 102
St. Joseph's School 100
St. Martins (Hospital) 94,100
St. Nathy's College 100,109
St. Patrick 54
Swinford 66,125
Swinford Union 83

Taffe, William 25,60
Talbot,Head Constable 113
Talbot, Lady Mary 27

Tansy, Pat 130
Tasmania 111
Tatlow 138
Tawnamuckla 132
Tawnmuckleigh 53,55
Taylor, General 43
Taylor, J. Shawe 147,148
Tenants Defence Association 143
The 'Castillion' 30,31
Threshers 61,62,143
Tirawley 16,18
Tireragh 11
Tirerrill 11,14, 21
Tithes 59,60,64,65,67,68
Tithe Act 1838 67
Tulrohan 18
Tobar Athracht 54
Tobracken 32
Toby's Ford 31
Tolan 53
Townebrack 96
Towey, Thomas 130,131
tSléibhe, Tomás an 19
Trinity College 25
Trinity Island 32
Tripartite Life of St. Patrick 54
Tuam 29,43,54,70
Tubbercurry 43,75,84,127,132
Tullaghan 31
Tullaghanmore 154,156
Tully Jasper 34,130,138
Tulsk 41

Uachtar Tíre 32
Ua Conchobair 55,56
Uí Bhrúinn 11
Uí Fhiachrach 11
Ui Maelchonaire 55
Uí Néill 11
Úna Bhán 34
Urlar Loch 16

Waldron 16,20
Wentworth, Thomas 27
'White '47' 101
Whiteboys 61
Whiteboy Act 61,62
Wildgeese 27,34
William of Orange 35
WolfeTone 40
Wrexham 35
Wyatt 61,65
Young Irelanders 109,111